ASPHALT ASYLUM

ASPHALT ASYLUM

The Dark Roads to Light

Steve Theme

HALYARD PRESS
HALYARDPRESS.COM

 *Scan this QR Code for more information on this title.*

Asphalt Asylum
© 2016 by Steve Theme

Author photo by Tanya.
Cover and interior design by Masha Shubin / Inkwater Press
Images: Hitchhiker © Mr Korn Flakes, BigStockPhoto.com; Clouds © JupiterImage®; Hitchhiking gear © Steve Theme.

All rights reserved, which includes the right to reproduce this book or portions thereof in any form whatsoever except as provided by the U.S. Copyright Law. This book is available at quantity discounts with bulk purchase for educational, business, or fund raising use. For more information go to halyardpress.com.

Asphalt Asylum is available in the following formats:
Paperback   978-0-9863929-0-0
Kindle   978-0-9863929-1-7
ePub   978-0-9863929-2-4

2 3 4 5 6 7 8 9 10

To Mattson, Pierce, and Elana.
And to Sheila, for your unrelenting support.

Contents

Author's Note	ix
Prologue	xi
1. Anywhere but Here	1
2. Treetop Yodeling	10
3. Birthright Wrong	18
4. No Direction	26
5. Into the Desert	37
6. Mojave Morning	47
7. Body Language	54
8. Gentle Direction	60
9. Holes in the Sky	67
10. Integrated Discrimination	77
11. Hospitality and Hurricanes	88
12. Guide My Feet	101
13. Worlds Away	110
14. Bloodshed	125
15. While We Can	135
16. Tropical Claustrophobia	140
17. Shorty	147

18. Dead Man's Float	150
19. Mallory Square Bongo Boy	158
20. Attempting Normal	164
21. Fallout	174
22. Infected	187
23. Playing the Odds	197
24. Out of the Blue	204
25. Intersections	213
26. Windshield Reflections	223
27. Mojo Rising	234
28. Arabian Night	243
29. Connected	253
30. All She Has	260
31. Scars	265
32. Never What You Expect	270
33. Blind and Tired	281
34. Wide Nights	289
35. Temple Love	297
36. Eternally Yours	304
37. Hillbilly Heaven	309
38. Death and Porn	317
39. Yes	322
40. From Ashes	332
The Route	341
Epilogue	343
Acknowledgments	345
About the Author	347

Author's Note

All of the people in this story are real. In some instances they asked me to change their names. During this trek, I kept a journal and traced my evolving path on a map. For three decades I carted both of these around and they helped keep my memory in line as I wrote. Much of the dialog is verbatim; in other cases I've stayed as close as possible to the original events. Everything is true.

Prologue

I didn't squander my youth on responsibility.

That thought came to me in the summer of 1978 as I leaned over a pool table in a subterranean pub while lining up a shot. Several months before that shot, I'd returned from hitchhiking seven thousand miles alone. Desperate to shed my constant anger, disdain, and self-loathing, I left on that trek hoping that somewhere I might find a sense of peace. I had no idea what to expect, or even where I was going, but the journey changed me in ways I could never have imagined.

Hop in; let's go for a ride.

1
Anywhere but Here

	MARCH					
			1	2	3	4
5	6	7	8	9	10	11
12	13	14	15	16	17	18
19	20	21	22	23	24	25
26	27	28	29	30	31	

Kind of scared, kind of excited.
—Journal entry

MONDAY MORNING, MARCH 27, 1978

When I woke up I had no plans for the day. But once I stopped pacing in my basement bedroom, I dumped the books from my blue college backpack and filled it with clothes, a Buck knife, and two harmonicas. After I cinched a red flannel sleeping bag underneath the pack, I was ready to leave.

I took confident strides—until I reached the bedroom door. Its threshold became a one-way passage that, once crossed, would make my commitment final. Before taking that step I looked around: the pale walls and a faded blue rug, my semi-made bed below a poster from the movie *Easy Rider* with Peter Fonda cruising on his stars-and-stripes chopper, the dark Craftsman desk made during the Civil War, and books heaped on the floor next to the head of my bed. I stood in silence. My breath drew in deep and smooth, filling my nose with that basement smell of damp concrete and unwashed clothes. As I exhaled, I knew I'd never view this room the same again.

I walked upstairs and interrupted one of my mother's perpetual rounds of solitaire. "Can you drive me to the I-5 on-ramp?"

"Why do you need to go there?" she asked, drawing on a Pall Mall—longshoremen's cigarettes she liked to call them.

"I'm going to head out."

Her attention broke from the cards. "Head out?"

"I'm going on the road. You know," I hesitated, "to explore some more."

Her face dropped slack for a moment. "Where?" Smoke drifted from her mouth.

"I don't know."

A sheen crept over her eyes.

"But I'm going to start by heading south."

She took a deeper pull on her cigarette. "How're you going to do that?"

Now I needed to steel myself, like the moment before removing a deep splinter from a child's arm. "I'm going to hitchhike."

Her gaze dropped to the table.

There were no teary farewells or bon voyages. She and I simply loaded into the family station wagon without speaking.

Once we started driving, she asked, "What are you going to do for money?"

"I've got a couple hundred bucks, and when I need to work, I'll work."

Her words quickened. "Where on earth are you going to sleep?"

"Not sure, but I'll find places."

"What about food? That little pack doesn't hold anything."

"The pack's got to be light. Otherwise it's too clumsy getting in and out of cars."

She nodded, seeming to accept that this answer made some sense.

"There's a lot of weirdos out there." She turned to face me. "What if—"

"—I've got my knife."

She inhaled slowly, locking in words, and then sighed; years of regrets seemed to lace the air.

The drive to the on-ramp was mercifully short. Once we pulled to the shoulder, I swung open the door and stepped out. Closing the door, I stared south down the highway before giving a quick wave goodbye to the back of my mother's head as she drove off. The splinter now pried free.

Waiting at the 45th Street on-ramp in North Seattle, I wondered how long it would take to get my first ride. Holding my arm out with my thumb pointing to an empty sky felt awkward. Would anyone even want to pick up this baggage? I became acutely aware of my appearance: a curly scruff of long blond hair, worn denim overalls, a Led Zeppelin T-shirt, and brown leather boots covered with white paint splatters. I stood lean and muscular but felt I wasn't much to look at.

I couldn't shake the thought that I was running away from myself, my life, my emotions—a child taking his ball and leaving the game. That alternated with the feeling that I'd taken a bold move to clean out my attitude, with hopes of regaining the ability to respect myself—and others. Opposing emotions, but both very real. I could already tell any clarity waited a long way off.

Across the freeway I could see the campus of the University of Washington, my alma mater for the past two quarters. At school I felt surrounded by stale white bread. Too many classmates squealed about parties and cars. As they strolled through their rarefied lives, I couldn't stop viewing them as pampered pets. After classes I worked as a night janitor, mopping, filling dumpsters, scrubbing toilets, and emptying the special little containers for used tampons.

I'd started working forty hours a week every summer beginning when I was thirteen and now felt a self-righteous resentment. It didn't take long for me to develop an unhealthy justification to despise the other students—spoiled brat fucks.

I had taken to smoking pot all day: in campus bathrooms, behind trees, before/during/after work, when driving, while alone. Shoplifting malt liquor became a hobby. By the time I'd decided to leave I couldn't tell who I despised more, the fucks or myself.

My entire plan consisted of one promise to myself—no panhandling. I wouldn't spend time in the big cities as one of those sponging kids asking for money. I never respected people who had the ability to work but not the will.

As I stared across the freeway, I focused on the vaulted roof of the Suzzallo Library at the UW. The graduate reading room had been my refuge, where rows of dark oak desks each had a table lamp with a green glass shade. It was a soundless expanse except for the wisp of turning pages and the scratch of pencils. Benevolent oversight shone down from the impossibly large stained glass windows.

Around me nicotine-stained cigarette butts littered the pavement and all I could hear was the roar of I-5 traffic. Cars kicked up incessant grit.

"Are you sure this is what you want to do?" my younger sister Corrine had asked just before I left home. I was eight years older than she was and at times had been her hero. Behind her stood my other sister, Janelle. I was two years older than she was. They looked scared.

I didn't know how to answer Corrine's question, but my gut dropped and I felt like I was abandoning both of them. Many times I'd redirected my father's rage away from them, sometimes on purpose, sometimes because of how easily I pissed him off. But at least with me gone I figured a lot of the homebound volatility would cool.

"Are you going to come back?" Janelle asked.

"Yeah, I'll be back." I gave them both a weak smile, hoping I was right. "But not sure when."

Just before I turned to leave, Corrine reached out to hold my hand. "Sometimes you do things and we don't know why."

One of those things had happened the previous spring when I left high school before finishing my senior year. When the second quarter had ended in late March I'd already earned enough credits to graduate. Three days after that quarter I jumped on a ferry headed for Alaska. I didn't know anyone there but eventually found work as a salmon fisherman in Kodiak. One quiet afternoon while mending a net I realized that years of hiding my mother's alcoholism and my father's fists had scarred my psyche, but the wounds were too fresh to gauge how deep they ran. When I returned to Seattle that fall, my parents let me live at home while I paid for tuition and books. I wanted to be a writer—but I enrolled in the College of Engineering. There was no room in my father's house for artsy-fartsies. Even though they weren't charging rent, I couldn't pay the price any longer.

What the hell am I doing? Was I really standing on the roadside, hoping random strangers might stop, so I could get into their cars, when I had no idea of their destinations—or intentions? My emotional compass whirled among excitement, guilt, fear, and pride.

While I was still getting my bearings a memory surfaced from my senior year at Nathan Hale High School. Academics and sports offered a good escape from home life, and I'd earned the honor as the school's Scholar/Athlete of the Year as part of a district program for football players. At the awards banquet, honorees from other high schools looked spiffy in jackets and ties, all of us sitting with proud parents. I smiled recalling the table with its linen napkins, china, silver, and crystal—not a nostalgic smile, but the smile of an escaped prisoner.

Since starting college I'd felt that security bred complacency. I didn't want to know where I'd sleep, or if there'd be money, or even food. Anything that established a sense of place repelled me. My head pounded with *Anywhere but here! Anywhere but here!* That drum started beating before the first car passed me and didn't silence until the trip ended.

A CAR PULLED OVER AND I scrambled in the passenger door. A thin guy in his mid-twenties wearing a plaid shirt and thick black glasses sat with an open container of vanilla yogurt propped between his thighs. He must have noticed me staring at it.

"It's all I eat," he said. "I read in a magazine that if you eat only yogurt, it's good for your digestive tract."

"I see."

We started down the road and I took special notice while I inhaled my first breath of the adventure. It smelled like sour ammonia. "Mind if I roll down the window?"

"No problem." Mr. Yogurt held out his right arm, extending a drippy spoon of vanilla goo. He twirled his hand, as if motioning to crank down the window. "I took my dog on a drive a couple days ago," he said. "And while he stuck his head out the window he got so excited, he peed."

"In this seat?"

"Yeah...I guess so."

Delicious.

After several more rides, each only ten to twenty

minutes, I entered into the disjointed rhythm of hitchhiking.

Outside of Olympia, about sixty miles south of Seattle, a blue sedan pulled over. A middle-aged man smiled as I got in. He wore pressed clothes and his hair was cut in a businessman's close crop. I didn't think people who looked like him bothered with people who looked like me. We talked easily, and I confessed I was beginning a trip with no destination. The ride lasted maybe half an hour, but as we stopped at the end of an off-ramp, he said, "Can you wait just a minute?"

"Sure." I felt no rush to get anywhere.

He laid his hand on my knee. I didn't expect this. Not on the first day. My naïveté scared me. Would I be confronted with this every day? People picking me up just hoping to have sex with me? Should I slap away his hand? Jump out? (Then he'd drive away with my pack in the back seat.) Smack him in the face?

"I'd like to say a prayer for you."

That shattered my thoughts, especially as I realized this would be the first time to my knowledge that anyone had prayed for me, at least since my baptism.

The day of my baptism was my family's first, and last, visit to church. I was eight years old and my younger brother, Chris, was about five months old. I don't recall anyone else there, just our family and some man wearing a white robe. I stood stiff in a crisp white shirt as my brother, held in my father's arms, let out a resounding cherubic fart. My shoulders shook as I looked toward the floor and forced my lips together, suppressing a full laugh. Afterward in the parking lot, my dad smacked me to the gravel for not taking the rite seriously enough. Once home, I got the rest. My sacrament of baptism, my salvation, amounted to a fart and a beating.

On that day, I stopped believing any god could exist. As the years passed, I wanted religion to have its own section in libraries: Mumbo Jumbo for Morons. Physics and chemistry ruled the universe. In their stability I found comfort—they never got drunk or enraged, never told me I don't have the brains god gave an ant, never provided a haven for hypocrites or threatened people with eternal damnation.

"Gracious God." The well-pressed man closed his eyes and bowed his head. "Thank you for loving us so much and always being with us. Please look over this boy and rain your love down on him. Protect him as he travels and keep him safe."

What a load. But not knowing what else to do, I bowed my head.

"Guide his footsteps as he grows and help him reach out to you in his times of trial. Amen." He gave my knee a firm pat.

When I stepped out of the car, though, I felt somehow lighter and oddly glad he'd said the prayer. I'd need it.

2
Treetop Yodeling

		MARCH				
			1	2	3	4
5	6	7	8	9	10	11
12	13	14	15	16	17	18
19	20	21	22	23	24	25
26	**27**	28	29	30	31	

I'd made it only to Portland, Oregon, but had managed to get lost. Standing among a maze of freeway overpasses, I couldn't see any signs. A mystery on-ramp was on the other side of the freeway. Maybe I could see a sign from there, so I planned to reach it by dashing across six lanes of traffic. During a brief opening I crossed the first three lanes, but that left me stranded on a raised concrete median as rush hour engulfed me.

Luckily, the median was at the base of a pillar supporting an overpass, and it spread wide enough to make a somewhat safe space to wait. I was surrounded in a vortex of wind created by the traffic as I sat with my back against the pillar. Black tire dust covered the concrete but my view conjured a futuristic dreamscape—thousands of gleaming machines only feet away raced by with roaring engines as roads snaked above and below. I could see bridges crossing the Willamette River, each reflecting different stages of history, architecture, and technology: swooping suspension cables, arches patterned after Roman aqueducts, counter-weights and pulleys, dark iron girders. The bridges looked as if they spelled out the formulas that had created them. The structures represented millions of hours of work, lifetimes of achievement, laid down for the benefit of generations to come. How could people think that far ahead?

I hadn't packed a map, which left me feeling even more lost, so I decided when I reached the next gas station I'd buy one—for the entire United States.

When the traffic subsided, I trotted my way to the on-ramp I had headed for two hours earlier, found some signs, took another dash across several more lanes of another highway, clambered down an embankment to reach a southbound ramp, and stuck out my thumb.

A small purple truck with a homemade cedar camper slowed to the shoulder. I could see that the camper was a mixed breed of backwoods cabin and Swiss chalet. A black stovepipe extended from the front and elbowed to the peak of the roof. Two windows had shutters painted with red tulips over a white background, and a mini barn door was on the back. I couldn't wait to see the driver.

"Hey there! My name's Treetop." He extended a calloused hand with thick yellowed nails. Weather had worn his face, but I guessed him to be in his early thirties. He sat like Abraham Lincoln, disproportionately tall and thin. His straight gray hair blended with a long pointed gray beard. He wore a denim shirt rolled up to the elbows and the knees on his jeans were worn silver. His eyes shone with a young twinkle.

The cab smelled of cinnamon incense. The wood dashboard was stained crimson, making the pattern of the grain come alive like thin flames. Mounted on top of the dashboard stood a figurine of Jesus next to a bobbling hula girl. Glued above the door handle, there was a plastic prism picture that morphed from a guru wearing ornate blue robes to the purple Hindu god Vishnu floating on a lotus flower. Balanced above the radio was a medallion with the star and crescent of Islam, and Buddha was stuck to the glove box. A red-and-green Navajo blanket covered the bench seat. Was he going to try to convert me? But to what?

"See this?" he asked, gripping a red wooden apple on the end of the green shift lever. "My wife made it."

"This is quite a mobile you have here." I was relieved we were going to talk about his truck.

"Yep, designed it myself." Treetop pointed over his shoulder. "Heck, my second son was even born in back. We were in Utah and I decided to name him the way the Navajo do." He brought his hand back down and patted the wool blanket. "When a child is born, the father names it for the first things he sees after the birth." Then he said with a well-rehearsed flow, "I stepped out back of the camper, looked up, saw a butte in the distance with a pure white cloud floating over it, so I named him Butte Cloud."

"Cool" was all I could muster. But I envisioned Butte sitting in grade school dying to change his name.

Treetop enjoyed telling stories. But mostly, he liked

yodeling. "Two weeks ago I won the national yodeling contest. I'm the new U.S. champion."

Until then I didn't know such a champion existed. Yodeling struck me as something only a person with supreme confidence could pull off; sounding ridiculous isn't for everyone.

His voice brightened. "Yep, the competition was in Tennessee, and I won. Couldn't believe it!" He turned to me. "Want to hear me yodel?"

I blinked.

"I'm goin' to pull over," he said, "so we can step out."

Treetop was a vertical man. His long, thin frame pointed up, and his beard formed an arrow pointing down to his sapling legs. He cupped his right hand next to his mouth, making half a megaphone, tilted his head back, and let loose.

The pitch undulated from high to low and seemed to break through a musical sound barrier. He kept a quick rhythm and melody that reminded me of birds darting through trees. And although his pitch roamed wild, the hollow notes resounded with controlled ease. Once finished, he slapped his thigh and looked at me.

I stood motionless. Then, as if breaking from a trance, "Oh man! How'd you learn to do that?"

"Most people have never heard real yodeling," he said, clearly pleased. "Most folks think yodeling is all about Switzerland, but it's used in New Guinea, India, Brazil, all across the world. If you need to be heard over a long distance, you can't beat it."

His music jazzed me.

As we got back into the car and drove off, he settled

in. "There were these ol' boys at the county fair playing bluegrass—you know, banjos and mandolins, and one of them starts yodeling." He rocked his head back and forth and chuckled. "I was just eleven, but I was hooked. That was 1956." Treetop's arms hung loose on the wheel while we rode an open highway. "I went out and bought a record called *So, You Want to Yodel?*"

"You've got to be kidding." I laughed. "There's a record for that?"

"No, that's the truth, I swear," he said. "The first instructions told me to close the windows and doors."

I kept laughing, but now harder. Unfortunately, I could relate. "Yeah, I actually tried yodeling once when I was twelve. Don't know why. I figured no one could hear me since I was in my bedroom, but after about five seconds my mom shouted down asking if I was sick."

Now it was his turn to laugh. "Yep, a little embarrassment is good for the soul. Keeps us humble."

Why did he say that? Embarrassment isn't good for the soul. It made me feel small, less-than. One night at the family dinner table when I was ten years old I knocked over my milk, sending it spilling across the table and dripping onto the floor. I felt embarrassed.

My father shouted, "Why'd you do that, Dopus?"

I told him I didn't try to.

For some reason he seemed pleased, and I thought I was off the hook. "Well of course you didn't try to, Dopus, but it's what you did."

Now I knew why he was pleased. He'd invented a new nickname for me: Dopus. I was an A student, but from that point forward if I ever did something wrong he'd call me Dopus, especially when others were around. Whatever embarrassment I felt for making a mistake, my nickname kicked in some extra, making me more angry at myself.

"What do you mean?" I said to Treetop. "Embarrassment keeps us humble? Embarrassment is degrading."

"No, not really. It's just that when you get too big for your britches you're goin' to look the fool. Embarrassment lets us know where we need to work on ourselves. It reminds us we're just human."

"What if someone makes fun of you?"

"Then they're just a plain ol' asshole. It reflects worse on them than you."

He straightened up in his seat. "Here's how you yodel. You've got to use two voices and be able to switch between them without anyone noticing." He'd trained himself in vocal sleight of hand. "Singing from my chest gives the lower tones, and moving my voice into my noggin gives the higher notes." Now that I was armed with that knowledge, he prodded me into yodeling.

I sounded like crap, which is an insult to crap. That moment marked the end of any aspirations I may have had for becoming a famous yodeler. But I didn't feel uncomfortable, or even embarrassed. Treetop was a safe audience.

"Don't worry, it takes a lot of practice." He let out another quavering yowl, emptying the bellows of his chest. "Yodeling's not for everyone. Some people hate it, and they laugh at me, or tell me to shut-up. But you've got to do what you love, or at least something you like a lot. How else are you going to be happy? Otherwise, what's the point?" He sat quietly for a moment. "Too many people just aren't happy, but they're too afraid to change."

I nodded. I'd made a drastic change that morning, but it hadn't struck me to seek happiness. I just wanted to escape. I always figured accomplishments automatically brought happiness; money and being in charge brought happiness. Treetop didn't fit that mold, even though he'd accomplished a lot, but by doing something most people would think was nuts. Was happiness worth people's ridicule?

"I've seen a lot of people, and some radiate joy and some suck it right from you. Nobody can tell you what's going to make you happy, but deep down, we each know what it is. We've just got to be quiet enough to hear it come through. Have you heard it?"

"Me?" No one had ever asked me to listen from deep down before. "I don't know. What's it sound like?"

"It's not what it sounds like—it's more how many times you hear it. It might sound different every time."

"I thought plenty about leaving. So out of the blue I got on the road this morning. Is that something like hearing it?"

"Maybe. If you just started this morning it might be too soon to tell. But in time it'll let you know." He turned on the radio and out blared "A Hard Day's Night" by the Beatles. He tapped time with his fingers on the steering wheel. "Rock-n-roll doesn't have much yodeling, and that's a shame."

"No, it doesn't really seem to be a good fit." I looked up through the windshield, searching the sky. "That's probably why they didn't call themselves the Yodeling Beatles."

We laughed again.

I stopped talking and tried to listen, from inside. There were little voices, mostly arguing about what type of person I was and why I was doing this. Eventually they got tired.

Time drifted by, and in the back of my mind, I wondered what a man like this might do for a living—he probably couldn't make ends meet yodeling. I figured his job would be exotic, maybe spiritual, for sure kooky. But when I asked, he simply said, "Pick fruit."

I sat silent, realizing he, and probably his entire family, were migrant farmers, transients. He couldn't get much lower on the social ladder. Instead, I pictured Treetop higher, respected, a singular teacher.

3

Birthright Wrong

			MARCH			
			1	2	3	4
5	6	7	8	9	10	11
12	13	14	15	16	17	18
19	20	21	22	23	24	25
26	27	28	29	30	31	

The driver had obsidian hair and blank pale skin. With her smeared black lips, she looked wan even for a punk rocker. The passenger had white hair and pink eyes. Her face was splotched with red pimples. They were twins who had grown into negatives of each other.

We were headed to Roseburg, Oregon, and just after I got in, they started telling me how stoned they had gotten that morning: killer bud, body high—not really a mind high—thick and skunky, sticky purple hairs, big-ass bong, better than staring at walls, crappy concert the night before, half a hangover.

I watched the scenery, and after only a few minutes I think they forgot I was in the backseat.

"Jimmy's got some acid," the pimpled one said flatly.

"No!" The punk's hair flailed as she shook her head. "We've been doing acid all the time." She looked up. "Speed. We've got those cross tops, and I could use a boost."

"Yeah...you and the boosts."

"What?" snapped the punk. "Don't give me any shit."

The white one let her head slowly capsize forward until she stared into her lap. Then, in a whisper, "How'd we get so fucked up?"

"Huh?"

"Fucked up!" She stared hard at her sister. "How'd we get so fucked up?"

"Because I'm starved for attention," the punk said. Her answer seemed as if it had been a long time waiting.

"That's bullshit. We're always together. I'm the one starved for attention."

"Fuck you."

Sitting behind these two forced me to recognize the emptiness we shared.

We rode for the next hour in silence, giving me time for unwanted reflection. For the past year I'd felt almost constant bitterness and had convinced myself there wasn't much point in communicating. Before graduating I couldn't wait to get out of the house, get out of the sham. I resented my parents. We put on a great show, but I grew up behind curtains where I was getting thrown down stairs while my drunk mother screamed for my enraged father to stop. In Alaska I kept to myself. I didn't know anyone, and the fisherman I worked with didn't give two shits about me. I resented myself for returning to my parents' home. I resented the other students but couldn't tell if it was for assuming entitlement or because I wanted to steal their carefree attitudes. I wanted nearly everything I saw: laughter, friends making plans, self-confident people progressing, belonging. I wanted those things and I resented them. Resented my resentment; the rot had begun to feed off itself.

Maybe that's why I was leaving, to starve the hatred.

Not every part of my life was miserable. I knew people, had friends and family, and there were times I'd even been popular. In grade school my nickname was Babe Ruth, since I hit a lot of home runs in little league. One night, as my family sat eating dinner and I couldn't leave until I cleaned my plate, a group of kids stood outside our kitchen window chanting, "We want Steve! We want Steve! We want Steve!" During my senior year in high school I was chairman of the dance committee, and the committee consisted of ten girls who signed-up after I volunteered to chair.

I led my brother and sisters on adventures into woods and on uninhabited islands. We got along well and kept each other's spirits up. Our frictions were minor, like when I wrote with a black permanent marker on the cover of Janelle's *Girl Scouts Handbook*, "Janelle is dum." She happily brought the book to her next troop meeting.

People—good people—knew me. There was Mark, my closest friend. Shortly before I left, Mark and I had hiked along a river floodplain, gotten lost, and ended up walking across a farmer's muddy field. We were passing next to the barn when the farmer popped out from behind a corner. He leveled a shotgun at our eyes and said we were the ones who'd been vandalizing his property. Mark reached out and placed two fingers on the end of the barrel, slowly pushing the farmer's aim away from us. Then, like a schoolmarm providing direction to a wayward student, Mark said, "Now, now." His low voice flowed in an even cadence. "Let's not be hasty." I had his phone number memorized.

My close friends all played instruments. With his solid grounding Mark played bass. There was Scott, lead guitar and Hawaiian fisherman. Steve, rhythm guitar and recent U.S. Marine. Geoff, tambourine and, when we were in the mountains, lead Snow Pirate. There were others too: friends I'd ridden with on bicycle tours, teammates, hiking partners.

And Katie.

She was with me all the time, just not always front and center. Before I left for Alaska, Katie gave me a Buck 110—my knife: a four-inch stainless-steel blade with a handle of dark maple and polished brass. The blade folded so the knife fit into a small black leather sheath. Drivers couldn't see it because I clipped it to a button on my right hip, keeping it hidden as I sat in the passenger seat. In ornate script, she'd had my initials, *SWT*, engraved on the handle. Etched into the blade was the word *Live*.

I was out of touch with all these people now, and my decision to hitchhike had left me stuck with two stoners trying to decide how they wanted to get loaded. Is this what my days would amount to? Fucking great.

Finally reaching Roseburg, we crossed a bridge over

the Umpqua River, a fast slip flowing from the Cascade Mountains.

"A couple weeks ago, Jimmy and some of the boys threw a guy off this bridge," the punk said. "Look down there."

I peered over, seeing whitewater and car-sized boulders. *Are the girls accessories to murder?*

"But the guy lived." She turned back to me. "You hungry?"

I hadn't eaten since morning—no point in eating when it detracted from covering miles, and now it was early evening. "Yeah, I'm a little hungry."

"We've got some food at our place," she said. "You can have some."

I wasn't crazy about spending more time with them, but my hunger convinced me otherwise.

We parked at the base of a long, narrow staircase that climbed an ivy-covered hill to a faded-green Victorian house. Four columns on the front porch held up arched timbers with carved French curves. Above the porch, a wrought-iron handrail ran along a thin deck. Tall rectangular windows rose above the deck, and the roof formed a range of sharp mountain peaks flagged with weather vanes. The house was surprisingly grand for these two. Maybe it wasn't really where they lived. Maybe this was Jimmy's place.

I grabbed my pack and started trudging up the stairs. The iron handrail wavered with my grip. When we made it to the porch, I could see it was pocked with dry rot, the paint was peeling, and the windows were cracked. Had they lured me here so their drug-dealing friends could rob me? I gave my knife a quick pat.

We walked through the front door into a dim room.

"That's our mom," the white-haired one said, tipping her finger toward a wispy gray woman sitting in a wooden chair. "And that's my uncle, Whitey," she said, nodding at a middle-aged man lounging in a green vinyl recliner.

Whitey was a big albino with tangled strands of white hair that merged into a long white beard. Thick black glasses broke up the snowpack of his head. His chest glowed pink, with more white hair surrounding bright pink nipples. Pasty hands steadied a magazine resting upright on his lap. From under the magazine his chubby legs stuck out, with their own white fuzz, leading down to pink toes. He was—naked. I did a double take, not believing he'd just be sitting there nude as his nieces walked in. The magazine was a *Penthouse*.

Nervousness made me feel I had to fill the silence. "What's up?" Now I felt dumb, and was hoping he wasn't going to show me.

"Huh?" He glanced at me but focused back on his magazine.

"He's like that," the punk said with resignation.

I didn't have time to process the scene as we walked through the living room into the vast kitchen. I could see it had once been white, but now gray halos ringed the cupboard handles and the countertops were rough with countless scars, a lot like the floor. The girls offered me a small green apple that had been lying on the counter. I stood eating it while they opened cupboards rifling through the contents.

"This is one tart apple."

"We've got a tree," the punk mumbled while closing a cupboard. "But they're not ripe yet."

"Your house is huge." I heard my voice bounce off the hard walls.

"Yeah," the white one replied. "Our mom used to be a madam and needed to keep this house." She opened the fridge, bent down, and stuck her head in, then shouted from behind the door, "She grew up here. We grew up here."

The girl closed the door with a disappointed thud. Then she mimicked a game show hostess, swinging her arm in an accentuated arc to point out prizes. "This was quite the lively place. Yes, indeed. This was the house of ill repute. The House on the Hill. The jolly pump-a-rump." Her arm fell back to her side, and she dropped her hostess tone. "This was a hell of a place, at least until we had to come along."

Her sister filled in. "There'd be enough girls sometimes they'd have to sit in the kitchen and wait their turn until they'd get into the front room and meet the Johns." She tipped her head down, as if looking over glasses to scold a naughty boy. "No more girls here though, so don't be sproutin' a chubber." She slapped another cupboard shut.

My stomach clenched. "So were you two here then..." I didn't want to use the word, but couldn't think of any euphemism, "...when this was a whorehouse?"

Hard as concrete, the punk said, "That hookin' stopped when we were in third grade."

Raised in a whorehouse—these girls were raised in a whorehouse. My grasp of reality slipped. I'd never even thought about kids going into a whorehouse, let alone being raised in one.

Not feeling comfortable, or even safe—I thanked them for the ride and the apple. Passing back through the living room, I figured I'd get another dose of Whitey, but his chair was empty. I let myself out. The sour apple twisted in my stomach.

4

No Direction

	MARCH					
			1	2	3	4
5	6	7	8	9	10	11
12	13	14	15	16	17	18
19	20	21	22	23	24	25
26	27	28	29	30	31	

I'd spent my first night in a grove of alders near Grants Pass, Oregon, and on this second morning fields rich in spring-green grasses dotted with weathered cedar barns rolled by in postcard scenes as I passed Mount Shasta.

More rides kept me moving south into the Sacramento Valley. The vast corporate farms throughout the valley reminded me of a mechanized paradise: olives, oranges, rice, sugar beets, garbanzo beans, walnuts, wheat, tomatoes, cotton... The only thing missing was an apple tree with a serpent.

That night I reached Reno. Figuring I'd catch some local color, I tried my hand at gambling.

Assuming my best high-roller pose, which consisted of

taking off my pack, I slapped down three bucks to play Keno. At least I thought that's what I was playing. I sat with others, all of us watching TV monitors that showed numbers popping into a grid; it seemed like a cross between bingo and a lottery. I must not have been the only person without a clue since we all sat expressionless. When the game ended, I surveyed the folks around me—apparently no winners. They sat as if watching a commercial for used cars. This crew didn't reflect the ads I'd seen that showed people enchanted with gambling's thrill.

In the carpet, flecks and specks of vibrant reds and yellows directed people to the tables, dealers, and slots. Triangles, squares, starbursts, and bubbles all shouted from a background of dark sky under my feet. Even with machines covered in flashing neon lights, the carpet was the only captivating attraction.

Wandering away from Keno, I sidled up to a slot machine. Slots offer dumb luck at its best. I'll take luck any day, but sitting around waiting for it is too dumb. I'd already burned through my allotment of three bucks, so I gazed across the blinking landscape. Down from me an old woman hunched alone next to her drink and smoldering cigarette. She pulled on a machine's arm like she was groping a gigolo.

MY EMOTIONAL DISTANCE FROM HOME seemed infinite, even though I'd left only the day before. I hitched out of town and after midnight found a rural road where I played my harmonica to the infinite darkness.

About a mile down the road, I positioned myself

behind a tree on the edge of a one-acre lot with a house at the far end. There weren't many hidden places to bed down, so I gambled that the people in the house were asleep and I'd be up and gone before they woke. Plenty hungry, I prepared a dinner that would become my staple—a peanut butter and cheese sandwich: protein and carbs, tasty and simple. It was the perfect food on most nights, except when the bread was stale, when the cheese was greasy sour, or when the peanut butter jar was broken.

Full, I stood behind the tree with my feet spread shoulder-width apart like a gunslinger. I flinched my hand down to unsnap the knife sheath strapped on my hip, grabbed the brass butt of the knife, and yanked it out. But drawing it left me holding just the handle, leaving the blade still folded. I pinched the exposed back edge of the blade between my thumb and forefinger of the same hand and gave a quick flip of my wrist. The knife slipped and thunked to the ground. I picked it up and tried again. This time I held the back of the blade tighter, and the handle snapped down, opening the knife, but now I was holding it by just the back of the blade. Again, not too functional.

With an upward twitch of my hand, I jumped the handle into my palm. I stood with a solid grip on the handle and the blade pointed forward. Much better.

After a couple dozen more tries my consistency improved so that with every attempt the knife snapped into the ready position. Throughout the trip this quick-draw practice became a hobby, except twice, when it was live-fire.

Satisfied with my quick draw, I crawled into my bag as my thoughts drifted to Katie. With tumbling brunette hair and a soft smile, she could project kindness just standing still. In high school she'd started a club to help bring physically disabled kids into the mainstream, whether they used wheelchairs, crutches, or prosthetics. She walked next to them, helping make introductions and opening doors, literally and figuratively. She was the only one in the club without a disability.

We'd attended the same schools since our elementary years, but our interest in each other didn't start until we both ran as candidates for senior class president. As our paths crossed during the campaign, we started flirting, which quickly led to afternoons spent on a park bench making out.

I felt a tinge of heartache at the memory. Katie had left Seattle several months earlier to attend Washington State University in Pullman, about 300 miles away. We hadn't seen each other much since, so I didn't know if she was dating someone, thinking of me, or just glad to be on her own.

My searching hands found their way down my belly, down. I began fantasizing about times on that park bench, remembering how our tongues slid—a dog's bark hammered the night as he ran toward me.

I immediately propped an elbow under me to jump out of my bag but noticed the homeowner with a flashlight, headed my way.

"What's going on here?" he shouted, shining his light in my eyes.

"Nothing," I said, squinting. The dog lunged before

retreating to its master's side, still growling. I wanted to reach under the rolled-up leather jacket I used as a pillow and grab my knife. All I could make out was a tall silhouette. I quickly added, "I'm just hitchhiking through."

He came from a warm bed in a big farmhouse on acreage he owned; I came from a cloth sack hidden behind a tree after a day of riding in strangers' cars. I felt like a turd on his lawn. He towered over me and we remained silent as his dog barked. I wasn't sure if he wanted a confrontation—if he did, I'd lose. Finally, he told his dog to shut up, wished me good luck, and headed back to his house. I'd need to be more discerning about where I slept. Bedding down on the edge of someone's yard, even a big yard, wasn't going to cut it. Eventually, I would become a magician at disappearing into the night.

Momentum carried me toward Las Vegas, not for any gambling, not for any reason—just south. I spent most of the miles riding with Andrew, a traveling salesman who sold scales to laboratories.

"They help researchers develop medicines and engineers to invent new materials. They're used for all kinds of scientific processes." His crafted hair—trimmed half way over his ears—blue dress shirt, and neatly knotted tie all exuded success. "Some people might think scales are boring, but this job's a hell of a lot better than anything I've ever done, considering all I've ever done was drink." He sounded proud, like he'd slayed a dragon.

"I didn't lose my wife or home, nothing like that," he

said. "I didn't have a wife or home. I crashed in fleabag motels or vacant lots.

"It started out fun, drinking with buddies. No problems. We were just regular guys. At least they were." He pulled into the left lane to pass a car. "By the end of my drinking days I'd wake up with the shakes, take a drink and puke, mostly green stuff. I'd go through several shots like that until I could hold one down. Then I could drink enough to stop shaking. That was my main goal in life, to stop shaking."

I'd seen a progression like that, just not that far gone. Like Andrew, my mother had started as a social drinker.

One of my earliest memories of her was when I was about five years old. I lay warm under my bedcovers after she had just tucked me in. The room was dark, but some light came from the hallway and gave the room a gentle glow. She sat on the end of my bed and asked if I'd like her to sing me a song. Of course I said yes. In little more than a whisper, she began singing "Somewhere Over the Rainbow." I recognized it. Dorothy sang it in *The Wizard of Oz*. At first my mom's voice shocked me; it was so beautiful. I'd never heard her sing and she sounded better than Dorothy—softer, more loving. It wasn't lost on me that she was singing for only me. An angel had landed on my bed and the world became her voice, wrapping me in warmth and security. That remains the most special I've ever felt.

About the time I entered junior high school my mom's social drinking had grown to a daily habit and she hid bottles of gin around the house. She got good at hiding. Maybe that's all that kept her busy. When I'd come home she'd look up from her game of solitaire, ask how my day was, and attempt a normal conversation. But that would degenerate into her contorting her face to emphasize whatever she'd said repeatedly, and laughing when no one said anything. Then she'd ask, "Where's your sense of humor?"

Eventually an elephant lived in every room of our home. My father didn't want to acknowledge anything was wrong and immersed himself in work: logical, defined, separate, work. But he understood what was going on, and he was angry, condemned in his powerlessness to stop her. He knew taking his anger out by beating a woman would make him less of a man, so instead he used me as his punching bag, kicking me if I stayed down too long, and yelling how stupid I was.

As years passed I'd come to realize that my mother's ability to believe her own lies—that she was hurting only herself—fueled the rationalization that allowed her to keep drinking. She didn't *want* to hurt anyone.

Andrew laughed hard. "Can you believe it? I was in the gutter looking down on everyone. Five years ago a guy came up to me, completely out of the blue. I was sitting on the sidewalk outside a bar hoping to see someone I knew so I could tag him for a drink. I must have looked like hell, sitting there all watery eyed. Then, from above me this guy asks how I was doing. I thought he wanted to bum money so I told him to fuck off without bothering to look up." Andrew shook his head slowly. "But when he kept standing there I looked up and saw he was clean. Even had a shave." Andrew reached down and yanked a few times on the crease of his slacks. "He even wore nice clothes. Didn't look like he needed anything from me. But he definitely did.

"The guy asked me if I had ever wanted to stop drinking," Andrew laughed again. "I thought he was out of his fucking mind. Hell, I'd tried a thousand times to stop. I asked him if he had a merry fairy wand or something. That's exactly what I said, merry fairy wand. So this guy starts waving his arm over my head like he's holding some magic wand." Andrew took a hand off the wheel and swung his wrist back and forth as if casting a spell. "That really pissed me off. But hell, by then I felt pissed off at everything anyway."

His anger reminded me of my growing resentment toward everyone around me, especially toward my mother as she became sloppier. I'd immersed myself in school and sports: logical, defined, separate, school and sports. Eventually I won that Scholar/Athlete of the Year award.

Andrew reached for a pack of Marlboros on the dash. I looked at his face to see the landscape whizzing past, as if he were flying across the desert. I envisioned him progressing at that speed for the past five years, leaving his drinking behind. I probably romanticized his progress, but I envied it.

Andrew continued. "The guy could see his fairy wand imitation didn't sit so well with me, and he apologized. Then he actually sat down. Sat down with his nice pants on a dirty sidewalk. It didn't take much for him to convince me to try an AA meeting." He fumbled on the dashboard for his lighter. "Of course I figured it'd be a bunch of boring goody-goodies sipping tea. But it was a men's meeting, and when they spoke each one of them told parts of my life. I couldn't believe it. Until then I figured I was unique." He lit the cigarette, clamped it between his teeth and said out of the side of his mouth. "Been going to meetings ever since."

Andrew's story ignited a flicker of hope that someday my mother might follow the same path. But I suspected she wasn't going to get anywhere near AA. That would mean no more hiding. She'd have to admit her alcoholism—not just to others, but mostly to herself. Incomprehensible shame.

Andrew's story also scared me. I'd been drinking since I was thirteen, sporadically at first and then progressively more, and smoking pot every day, especially just before this trip. Once, when I was a sophomore in high school, a friend and I held a contest to see who could shoplift the most booze. I walked out carrying two bottles of wine and a forty-ounce malt liquor hidden under my coat. My buddy ran out carrying the manager on his back. As they wrestled I watched with disinterest, trying not to draw attention to myself—an assistant manager might appear next. My friend got dragged back into the store. I had a group of people I called night friends. That wrestling incident didn't stop us from stealing, and we generally stocked a good wet bar.

Even though I excelled at academics and sports, other elements of my life weren't so tidy.

The more my friends and I drank, the more I recognized my mother's traits in myself. From watching her, I knew my drinking held the potential to become malignant.

"So who was the guy?" I asked Andrew. "The one who

sat on the sidewalk with you?" I figured he'd now be one of his best friends.

"His name is Danny. I saw him only a few times after that. At first I thought he sat down that day to help me, which he did, but mostly he did it for himself. In AA, helping other alcoholics is pretty much the best way to stay sober ourselves. And of course we help others too."

Andrew gave me a long look, as if to say that's why he picked me up. His act was altruistic, yet also for himself.

"I didn't know it before," he said, "but AA is a simple program for complicated people. It's just spiritual, helps me stay in touch with God—my God, not some punishing SOB."

His personal god? Well, that must be nice, seeing as how everyone else has to share. Mumbo jumbo is crystal clear compared to this.

"The part that still blows me away is that God is doing for me what I couldn't do for myself. I just had to ask, and learn a little something about humility." Andrew paused and then quietly uttered, "I'm a miracle."

Miracle? He sounded more like he was delusional. I almost asked if a ray of light came from the clouds and knocked him over, or maybe doves dropped garlands on him. But I didn't want to appear flip about something that had radically bettered his life.

We talked about our drinking histories, which had far too many similarities, at least with his early days, and we pulled into Vegas as the sunset lost its color. I asked Andrew if he had plans for the evening, thinking we might eat dinner together.

"There's an AA meeting here I go to. It starts in about

a half hour and I'll need to show up early if I want to get a seat."

"Teetotalers in Sin City? Doesn't seem like they'd go together."

"Exact opposite. This town is AA fertilizer."

He then asked if I'd ever been to Vegas, which I hadn't, so he dropped me on the Strip, thrusting me into the neon fray: pink haze shone over barkers calling gamblers to easy money; the saturating sounds of pingbongbings from casinos reminded me of a lopsided calliope; and people skittered like kids between rides at a county fair.

Standing alone on that chaotic sidewalk, I imagined Andrew sitting on his sidewalk, head in his hands, with no direction, and wondered if that would be me someday.

5
Into the Desert

	MARCH					
			1	2	3	4
5	6	7	8	9	10	11
12	13	14	15	16	17	18
19	20	21	22	23	24	25
26	27	28	**29**	30	31	

The temperature had hit eighty degrees, but it was only noon and every truck that thundered by kicked up a dusty grit that clung to my sticky skin. I was now heading south out of Las Vegas when a brown sedan pulled over.

"Get in." The driver handed me his business card: Harvey Farrara, Sales Manager, Salvo's Portable Buildings, Las Vegas. Harvey was middle-aged, overweight, and wearing a brown dress shirt and brown slacks. He'd blend into any average crowd.

After some small talk about the heat, I wanted to get a better read on this guy. Listening had become my main defense and gave me a chance to gauge each driver's mental state. So I asked where he came from.

"I was born in Sicily," Harvey said. "You know, the old country."

I nodded.

"My mother died havin' me. How's that for a shithouse way to start?"

"Sorry to hear that."

"What the hell," he said. "We're all gonna die someday." He took his bloodshot eyes off the road and glared at me. "There's worse ways to go."

I nodded again but remained silent.

"When I was a kid my old man and me moved to the Bronx. That was okay, but a few years later he was driving truck and got shot. That killed him." Harvey sat up taller, raising his voice. "But I'm still here."

Harvey's wife had divorced him and he missed his young daughter. Her picture sat in a small gold frame on the dash, where she smiled out between apple cheeks. Glued to the dash next to her was a figurine of the Virgin Mary.

"We gotta pick up those!" Harvey blurted and pointed across the freeway.

I looked toward the north-bound lanes and saw two hitchhikers, teenage girls.

Harvey pulled a U-ey by slamming on the brakes, driving down the wide dirt median, and up the other side. The back tires sprayed gravel. By the time we emerged from our dust cloud, the girls were gone. We pulled another median duster and again headed south. I started to feel uneasy and wonder about his stability, let alone his morals.

Harvey pulled a half-empty bottle of vodka from under the seat and took a pull. As he tipped the bottle to his mouth, I couldn't help but picture my mother, who'd chug gin from the bottle when she thought no one was looking. The first time I saw her do this I'd come around a corner and she had her back to me. The bottom of the bottle was raised above her tipped-back head. I immediately retreated behind the corner so she wouldn't see me. From then on, each time I saw her I didn't say anything—let her think she was getting away with it. But I always felt a mix of disappointment and betrayal. After a while, that became my normal.

Harvey wasn't my mother, though, and aside from the abrupt U-turn, his driving was controlled and smooth, so I didn't worry that he'd suddenly become too dangerously drunk to drive. When he passed the vodka to me I easily accepted, figuring a swig or two might make the time pass more comfortably.

As I raised the bottle and tipped my head back, I wrestled with hypocrisy. *Am I any better than my mother? But this is different. At least I'm not hiding anything, and besides, this is social drinking*—even if I was sucking straight from the bottle in a car driving down the freeway. After several passes I ended up draining the last drops. "That's it."

"There'll be more."

As the miles passed, my uneasiness melted away.

Harvey mentioned how he'd been in prison at the Cummins Unit prison farm in Arkansas. "They laid me face-down on the ground and whipped me hard enough, it rolled me over." Harvey's jaw tightened. "The fuckin' guard wouldn't stop until I called him 'Father'."

I remembered hearing about the Cummins Unit

from a lot of news reports years before. Guards had been saying men were somehow escaping. When none of the escapees were caught, federal investigators came in. The investigators searched the prison grounds and ended up unearthing multiple sets of human remains; these were the so-called escaped men. The evidence showed they'd been tortured to death. That was around the time Harvey said he'd been an inmate.

I couldn't not ask. "What were you in for?"

"Nothin'. But I got a ninety-nine-year sentence for killing a guy while I was in the joint." His tone came across as if the killing were an aside. "But I got a good lawyer, and connections."

It became impossible to tell how much of what he said was the truth and how much was the vodka. He let out a wistful sigh. "My wife, she's a saint." He spoke as if they were still married. "But she couldn't take the family business."

I was willing to bet his family business wasn't Fletcher's Portable Buildings, but I wasn't ready to ask yet.

Harvey pulled over at a bar in the tiny town of Kingman, Arizona, where he bought me dinner. We had a couple more drinks—I wasn't legal drinking age, but nobody asked—and we shot some pool.

As we played he gave me a piece of advice. "When you set up in a new town and find yourself a hooker to get regular with, start eatin' pickled eggs." Leaning over the table, ready to take his next shot, he craned his head up and pointed with his eyes. "Like those. The ones in that jar behind the bar." He took his shot. "They make you harder. And when you blow it's more intense. So you get some extra bang for your buck."

Harvey was saw-blade rough, and I thought of parting ways, but I'd become half crocked and convinced myself he was okay company. *So he killed a guy in prison. That was a while ago.* My rationalization also included that he was driving to Phoenix, a good long ride. Even though I had no destination, speed and distance had become addictions as I raced away from my life. Harvey drove that night's race car.

The sun hung in early dusk and we got back on the road with a new bottle that Harvey shoved under the seat. The next town, Wikieup, lay over fifty miles away with nothing but empty road until then. This part of Highway 93 is called the Joshua Tree Forest Parkway of Arizona, although parkway isn't a word I'd use for this stretch of raw desert. I didn't see any trees, homes, barns, fields, or even derelict shacks, just deep canyons, rusty hills, and flats—massively expansive yet, at the same time, nothing. We drove past the sneeze that was Wikieup. To reach the next town, Wickenburg, meant driving through another seventy-five miles of desolate night. I'm not afraid of open spaces, but paranoia began creeping in, driven by empty distance and my stark exposure to the isolation.

The dash lights cast shadows across Harvey's mottled face, and his eyes blackened to empty holes. To him I probably appeared as nothing more than a silhouette.

"Ya know that card I gave ya? It's a phony." He smiled faintly, appearing satisfied he'd fooled another person.

I'd had enough to drink that I could now ask him. "So

then what do you do?" I didn't much care to know his real name.

His voice lowered. "I take care of problems."

The drone of the car sounded like we were riding on woozy tires. "What do you mean? Problems?"

In the brief silence, his head lolled. "Hits." He leaned my way with an exaggerated motion that left his face cocked sideways. "When the Family needs a hit they call me."

I swallowed hard, not because his answer was unexpected, but because I believed him. From nowhere my drunkenness leading the charge, I blurted, "It's a living."

"If you don't care how you live!"

Morbid curiosity compelled me. "So how do you do it?" I stammered on. "I mean...with a gun?"

"I'll get a call and get the mark's name and his town, maybe an address." Harvey paused and seemed to be considering if he should go on. He reached for a pack of cigarettes in his sports jacket. It took him awhile to get one lit. "Once I find him, I'll spend a few days scoping him out, you know, to figure a good time and place. Then I'll walk up, look him in the eyes, say 'Hi,' and shoot at least three times.

"Then I drop the gun. You know, right there." He flipped an open hand toward the floor. "It ain't like fuckin' stupid TV." He jerked his head, probably clearing double vision. "You gotta be up close—otherwise you might miss." His words trudged. "I keep it the same every time because it always works."

Now his drinking made sense.

Harvey fumbled under the seat, I thought to pull out the bottle, but he came up holding a black pistol. He swung his arm toward me, holding the barrel six inches from my temple. "I'll kill you with a smile on my face or without. It don't matter to me."

A jolt. I froze. I wanted to recoil, but there was nowhere to go. My thoughts raced, searching for a way to strike.

Then a clear-blue calm swept over me. The sensation brought a deep assurance that I shouldn't strike out. I became positive that if I didn't flinch, then I wouldn't die that day; the assurance felt vaguely familiar. I stopped thinking of batting away the gun, although I realized the calmness didn't make sense. Harvey was blazing drunk, and shooting me would have been easy—we were in the middle of nowhere, with no witnesses, and no one even knew we were together.

Time slowed, maybe stopped.

I thought of a hummingbird. It was one I'd caught using only my hands. I was eleven, standing alone on the deck of my cousin's beach house when I noticed the bird land on a low windowsill. As I stared at the tiny cluster of color, a thought sprang up for no reason—*I could walk over and catch it with my hands*. At first that struck me as ridiculous to even attempt, but a feeling of gentle assurance that I could hold the bird nudged aside my doubt. So I started slowly crossing the deck.

Moving toward the bird, I couldn't believe it stayed on the sill. Up to that point, I'd never seen hummingbirds do anything but hum. When I was within the last few feet, I extended my hands in smooth unison. Concentrating on the bird, I watched as my hands moved closer, seeing them as if they weren't mine. I knew hummingbirds didn't just sit while people approached them.

How is this happening? It's looking right at me. This definitely isn't going to work. But the assurance that I'd hold the bird kept me flowing forward at a gentle pace, no lunging, no snap-trap moves. My hands closed around it as if I were bringing them together to pray. The bird's metallic blue head turned to gaze at me, but it made no attempt to fly. *Why did I even try to do this? How did I know I could?*

It was that same distant assurance that filled me as Harvey held the gun to my head. Slowly inhaling through my nose, I turned my head to stare into Harvey's eyes. His voice rang in my memory, "Gotta be up close...." But I kept facing him. Looking down the barrel, I let my expression hang slack. His finger was already on the trigger, but I wanted to show Harvey I wasn't afraid. He might respect that. Earning respect was the only way out of this.

After several seconds, Harvey lowered the gun and stuck it next to the bottle. I exhaled as quietly as I could. He didn't say, "I'm just kidding," or "I wouldn't do that to you." His only reaction to what had just happened was a quick swerve to get us back on the right side of the road.

We sat in dark silence. I thought about asking him to stop, but we were in the middle of an empty universe and I told myself the worst had passed.

Ahead of us some lights came into view. As we got closer I saw that they were the rear lights of a state trooper's cruiser, and we drove behind him for a while. I couldn't believe it, but Harvey started tailgating him. And then he decided to pass. Once we pulled in front of the cop, the inside of our car flashed with a red strobe.

We were going about seventy-five and I thought Harvey might jam on the gas and rage blind down the highway. The red light pulsed into the car like pumping blood. My heart started racing as everything flashed red. There was no quiet assurance. If I grabbed the wheel, we'd just crash. Harvey stared straight ahead and slowed to pull over.

The trooper gave Harvey a field sobriety test. He failed. As the officer clicked cuffs on Harvey and pushed him into the police car's back seat, Harvey kept shouting, "I've got a good lawyer!"

The trooper ignored me while he filled out paperwork. I stood within the glow of his taillights but peered into the unending dark.

After a long time the trooper walked back to me. "What's the deal here?" He sounded genuinely baffled. With my frizzled hair, overalls, and backpack, it didn't take much to convince him I was just hitchhiking.

"He's a boozer," I said. Then I thought of the black barrel pointed at my head, the sound of Harvey's flat tone as he spoke. I didn't mention anything about the gun under the seat. With only one road, and no control over when I'd leave it, I didn't need Harvey looking for me.

The trooper asked if I wanted a ride into Phoenix. That sounded reasonable, but now, surrounded by silence, the desert didn't seem as formidable, just infinitely quiet.

"No thanks. I'll stay here."

The officer's voice popped up an octave. "You sure?"

"Yeah." But I wasn't.

I asked for water, and the trooper watched, half laughing

in disbelief, while I filled my plastic bottle from a large jug in his trunk. As his taillights drifted into the darkness, I took a deep, deep breath and walked into the desert.

6

Mojave Morning

		MARCH				
			1	2	3	4
5	6	7	8	9	10	11
12	13	14	15	16	17	18
19	20	21	22	23	24	25
26	27	28	29	**30**	31	

As night dragged on, the desert's frigid grip tightened. I found some flat ground hidden from the road and kicked aside fractured shale to smooth a small plot. When I packed I'd thought about bringing a tent, but my tent was too big to carry easily on the small pack. So now, without any grass or moss, or even a sleeping pad, I'd have to make do with a mattress of cold rocks and a roof of empty sky. I laid my sleeping bag down and knew that my hip and shoulder bones would press hard against the shale. In no time, I lay shivering in the fetal position. I knew the vodka I'd been drinking all day was sapping my core body heat by transferring it to my skin. My shivering intensified.

STEVE THEME

In time—I don't know how long, a couple hours maybe—I couldn't touch my thumb to my pinky finger. I knew this signaled an early warning of hypothermia. But since I was at least twenty miles from the nearest anything, all I could do was keep shaking, my joints grating against the rock. *Don't fall asleep.*

Without any distractions it became too easy to focus on my cramped muscles. I made a conscious decision to think about something pleasant, something warming, and Katie walked into my thoughts again. I remembered when our paths crossed at the main entrance of Nathan Hale High School. We each held campaign posters for our respective runs for senior class president, and we both wanted to hang them in the same place, centered over the entryway. My knee-jerk reaction was to tell her I'd designed this sign specifically for this space and that it should rightfully go there. But before I opened my mouth, I looked into her eyes. Mistake. She glowed—not the generic way many young women can radiate life, but a kindred spirit glow.

"So, uh," bumbled from my mouth, "we're running against each other."

She smiled. "Kind of looks that way, unless you're hanging that sign for another guy named Steve Theme."

"Yeah, there's a bunch of us." We both stepped closer. "What do we do now?"

She came closer still, so that I could hear her hushed words. "I could hang my poster and you could tell me if it's level."

I slid forward more so that our faces, our lips, were

only a hand's width apart. "You're picking up on this whole politics thing pretty quickly."

We agreed neither of us would hang our posters there. I didn't make it through the primaries—Katie won the election.

For the following several months we'd end up at her house after school nuzzling on the couch. Even though I'd lost the election, badly, with each passing day I grew more glad that I'd run. Sitting in each other's arms, we'd talk about our world that seemed drowning in problems: pollution, overpopulation, crooked politicians—Nixon had resigned because of the Watergate break-in, and his VP Spiro Agnew had resigned under charges of extortion, tax fraud, bribery, and conspiracy—fighting in the Middle East, starving African children, the ongoing gas crisis, the lingering sting of Vietnam... Talking about these miseries grew old for her, and she said we were becoming maudlin, but at least I could relax in her arms.

I mashed my shivering face into the crook of my elbow, trying to hold in heat. Each exhale forced a wisp of warm air back against my cheeks.

After a few months, Katie decided to attend a clown school at night so she could perform for kids in hospitals. One day when it was just the two of us, she put on a green jump suit, blew up two balloons, stuck them in her shirt like boobs, and danced around. She looked pretty good like that. But I wasn't the only one who thought she looked good.

Katie became interested in a guy she'd met at clown school and started dating him. I'd been replaced by a clown.

He was taller, darker, and older—not to mention he

owned a cool clown van painted with graphics of circus scenes and balloons. The van had no windows except in the front, so I assumed it functioned as a four-wheeled bed.

But even with that clown, Katie and I continued seeing each other as friends, remaining closer than I expected, considering she was dating. She still wanted to see me, and all I wanted was to see her.

While waiting for the sun to trek around the earth and bring some warmth, I fell into hallucinations. I was standing next to a crackling campfire that sounded like a theater filled with clapping hands. Its warmth loosened my clenched fingers and blanketed my face. I turned and stuck out my butt, happily standing as close to the fire as the heat allowed.

My head would snap back, making the flames fizzle, and then I'd reenter reality lying on the ground, alone, shivering. I thought of building a real fire, but I knew that if I rose from my bag, the cold would bring me to my knees. Plus, I hadn't brought a flashlight, so I couldn't see firewood in the dark, but that didn't matter since there wasn't any wood anyway. Moving any part of my body released heat, so my throbbing shoulder still pressed against rock. The hallucinations became all too welcoming.

After many trips between the illusory campfires and my frigid sleeping bag, I saw light on the tops of distant mountains—mountains that had been hidden in the dark expanse. I watched the line of sun spend an eternity moving down the slopes. Eventually, the light graced me, and I pulled my bag even closer.

It took an hour of lying in the dawn sun before I no longer feared the air and stood up.

Plants with a single wiry green shoot, about a foot high, supported bright yellow flowers with orange centers. Spiny cacti took shapes and sizes I had never seen. Some had long, gently bending limbs covered by gray fuzz—thin old women waving. Others bore single straight stalks with pipe-cleaner spikes. Several looked like white fan coral I'd seen on TV. But the smallest plants put on the biggest shows: fire-red petals honed to sword points, yellow stems with hot-pink veins strung through them, blue buds and round purple leaves. Lowering to my knees, I touched them. Some petals felt velvet delicate, while others seemed forged from orange iron. Bluish tufts of grass a couple feet high and wide were interspersed throughout the myriad of flowers. Colors surrounded me as if a rainbow had fallen and shattered.

After my breakfast of a hoagie roll smeared with peanut butter and layered with thick slabs of cheese—shopping for food was simple—I looked far across the hills: no roads, not a single path, no evidence that even foot trails had ever cut this expanse.

I pawed through the thin wardrobe in my pack: denim overalls, one pair of cutoffs, a green flannel shirt, two T-shirts—one imprinted with the cover from the Eagles' *One of These Nights* album featuring a bleached cow's skull like you'd find lying in the desert, and the other with Led Zepplin's *Zoso* album showing an old man bent over carrying a bundle of firewood. I also riffled through a hand towel, one pair of wool socks, cotton socks and boxers, a toothbrush, a wool watchman's cap, my worn suede jacket/pillow, glacier goggle sunglasses, flip-flops, and boots. I lacked for fashion but not for style.

Since I commanded all the horizons, I dressed in sunglasses and boots.

I walked about a mile but stayed clear of rock outcroppings to reduce my chances of coming across snakes or Gila monsters. At my farthest point, the air temperature and my skin struck a perfect balance so that I felt nothing separating me from the atmosphere—I'd been incorporated. Before turning back toward my pack, I stood still, struck by how rarely we have the opportunity to be only ourselves and, through complete lack of structure, build who we are.

The stillness eventually called out for a ruckus: I sang, flapped my eagle arms, ran around, faced the sun while I thrust my arms above my head and yodeled like a fiend.

Not a soul on earth knew where I was, but I felt surrounded by a band of friends, as though I were sharing the experience in a joyous crowd, and that sensation made me want to reach out. I looked to the sky, focusing hard on the empty blue.

"Why was I so calm last night when that guy held the gun to my head?" I was a speck on an empty earth. "If you're there, uh...I'm still here. And thanks. A lot." *What in the hell am I doing? Who the hell am I talking to? Shit, I've already gone crazy.*

I started walking again.

Beauty sang from the valleys to the mountains, and I didn't wish to share the morning with anybody. This huge expanse held only me. With no judgments or prying eyes, I stood naked to the world, and I reveled in my solitude.

Hours later, I dressed and walked back to the road.

While waiting for a ride I thought about the night before and how, even with a gun to my head, a gentle assurance had given me the confidence to remain still. I should've been scared shitless.

Nothing added up. The only indisputable fact was that I'd somehow held a hummingbird.

7
Body Language

Another 390 miles had ticked by with half a dozen rides when I landed in Las Cruces, New Mexico, and decided to tilt south. The allure of Mexico pulled: señoritas, tequila, mariachi bands. But my attraction stemmed from romantic songs that varnished poverty, like James Taylor's "Mexico"—a good song, but not a good enough reason to cross the border.

By the time I'd reached the border on the outskirts of El Paso, day had run deep into night. Standing at a truck stop, I watched a cloud of bugs swarm the light above a phone booth. Beyond that I could see into a small diner through windows yellowed with grease. I was hungry and stepped inside, not knowing if I'd eat there or not. Once in I noticed a sign, *Showers*, above a hallway toward the back. That made me feel comfortable knowing the place catered to truckers and vagabonds. I took a seat at the green Formica counter pockmarked with brown cigarette burns. For a moment when I opened the menu and a waitress walked toward me I felt like a normal customer. We made eye contact. The food wasn't pricey but with limited money, and no idea when I'd earn more, I shook my head and closed the menu. She turned away. That thin sense of belonging shifted to disappointment that I didn't fit in, even here.

Behind the diner, an empty railway switching yard stretched into the featureless night. I walked into the darkness until I reached a low stack of railroad ties and sat with a thud. The scent of their creosote crept around me. I saw myself as if from above: sitting hunched next to empty train tracks, in the middle of the night, alone, casting a silent shadow from the diner's distant light.

My harmonica called. The tracks wanted to hear the blues, and I delivered. Slow, quiet notes emerged as a prelude to alert the dark. Gathering steam, I blew lone coyote howls. A bass line emerged, my boots marked time, and a muddy river flowed onto the tracks. I hunched over, rested my elbows on my thighs, and just kept playing. The sound wrapped around me and I didn't feel so alone. Finally, dirty guttural rolls roamed across the dark switching yard. This wasn't a performance; no applause rose as I blew the last growling notes—only tumbleweeds rustled on their journeys to nowhere. I felt validated. The music belonged.

Whenever I was at a truck stop, I tended to walk in

front of the rumbling line of semi cabs, where I could look through the windshields, maybe ask for a ride. After crossing the expansive parking lot and noticing how tired I was, I decided to take a shortcut between the trailers and walk back to the rail yard in hopes of finding a place to bed down. With all the trailers lined up next to one another they formed rows of thin dark alleys. I disappeared into one of the corridors where rumbling engines echoed off the metal walls.

When I was about halfway into the slot, a black silhouette of a man appeared at the other end. He stood still for a moment facing me. His stooped shoulders, arms at his sides, and feet spread apart for extra stability gave me an ominous feeling. The trailers were parked so closely together that my shoulders nearly touched both sides, so I figured he'd wait until I emerged before he entered. Instead, the form started walking toward me.

This doesn't seem right.
Why doesn't he just wait?
I was on the Mexican border.
Where's he going?
There's nothing back here.
I knew desperate people with little or no money crossed illegally into the United States. The rumbling engines amplified the thoughts pounding in my head.
I'm sure he can see me.
No one could see us.
Why is he still walking?
I stopped, but he kept coming.
I need to do something.

Turning around entered my mind, but I didn't want to lose sight of him.

He closed to within about ten feet but was still silent. I slid my right hand over my knife sheath and unbuckled it, knowing it'd take only a second to open the blade. Fixing my eyes straight ahead, I bent my knees, lowering my center of gravity.

I felt a shock knowing I was about to draw my knife in self-defense but didn't linger on the thought. Even though it was night and we stood in deep shadows, he could see as I unclipped the leather flap and placed my palm over the knife's brass butt. Just before I started the well-rehearsed routine, he turned without a word and quickly left. I took my hand off the knife but left the sheath unbuckled. When I emerged from the alley, he'd already vanished.

I patted my knife and thought again of Katie. The knife had become my best friend the summer before while fishing in Alaska, and now it took that role again, in part because it was a touchstone. She knew it stayed strapped to my side virtually all the time, and that made her worry less. "It's kind of a selfish gift that way," she once said. I decided that whenever I made my way back to the Northwest, I'd pass through Pullman and see her at WSU. My muscles relaxed.

No one should be without a knife. Mine spread peanut butter, cut cord, opened cans of peaches, pared corn kernels from the cob, sliced sausage, carved wood, and cleaned under my fingernails. And now, it helped to keep me whole.

While I walked back to the rail yard my sharpened senses registered only slow-rolling tumbleweeds. I hustled down the tracks away from the lights to a shallow gully where I decided to spend the night. I wanted camouflage, so I gathered some tumbleweeds and piled them over my sleeping bag, pressing the spindly branches together to build a loose cocoon. At the head of my bag I placed the branches within inches of my chin. That way, if they started to blow away in the night, they'd probably poke me in the face and I'd wake up. I deviated from my standard nightly ritual of placing the folded knife under my jacket pillow. This night I kept the blade locked open and set it next to my jacket.

Staring into the blank sky, I again questioned why I'd decided to take this journey. Was this gully dust better than the life I'd left behind? For that matter, was I leaving something behind or searching for something greater? What something? Was I a running coward or a brave seeker? Had I found anything? *What am I even doing on this planet hiding under tumbleweeds in a ditch?*

The questions seemed both monumental and meaningless. No matter what answers I came up with, they wouldn't last; life changed too quickly.

I jostled the weeds. They didn't fall off, so I drifted into sleep.

DAWN REVEALED PILES OF BLACK rotted railroad ties; no flowers like my previous morning in the desert. I didn't waste any time before rolling up my bag and hitting the road.

"Hi," I said, climbing into a lopsided pickup covered in dents.

The driver smiled.

"Where you headed?" I asked.

No response. The driver sat thick and brown. Black hair stuck out from under his faded baseball cap and short sleeves revealed muscular forearms. Cracked calluses extended beyond his palms and rounded up the sides of his hands. Small clods of dirt covered the cab's floor, and yellow scraps of notebook paper lay on the sun-cracked seat.

The driver didn't speak English, apparently not a word. Before stopping for me he probably understood there was only a slim chance I spoke Spanish. It seemed he knew we wouldn't be able to talk, that we'd just sit, but regardless, he overcame the pending awkward silence to help a stranger. Riding in that dusty cab, I realized I probably wouldn't give someone a ride if I thought they didn't speak my language.

From the rearview mirror swung a cross on a silver chain where Christ hung. I'd never liked seeing those in cars. I would picture the driver yelling, "Just in case you didn't notice my Christian glow, I've got Jesus a-swingin' in my windshield!"

After a long stillness, I began to wonder if he'd hung the figure there not to impress others, but to remind himself.

The man pointed to a small business as we passed it. I assumed it was where he worked, or maybe made deliveries. I nodded. For the next hour, we didn't say a word. Good people come in all languages.

8

Gentle Direction

	MARCH / APRIL					
			1	2	3	4
5	6	7	8	9	10	11
12	13	14	15	16	17	18
19	20	21	22	23	24	25
26	27	28	29	30	31	1

West Texas makes the moon look like Eden. The only thing that made crossing the scabland bearable was my companion—a big, black, badass, U.S. Marine. I don't recall his first name, but his last name was Studmire.

"Just call me Stud—everyone does." Stud packed himself into a two-door Honda Civic. The size of his hands made the steering wheel look as if it belonged in a toy car, and his flattop buzz cut brushed the ceiling. As he turned toward me, his square jaw jutted out from a neck wrapped in ropes of muscle. Stud was dressed in street clothes, but when I threw my pack in the back I noticed his olive green duffle bag with the insignia of the eagle, globe, and anchor.

"I'm based at Camp Pendleton," he said once I'd turned to face forward again. "Been in the Corps three years and it's been damn good. I like the mother fuckers, even my CO, and he likes me." Stud sat quiet for a moment, as if listening to his own words. "So what the hell are you doing?"

"Traveling."

"No shit."

I wanted to say I was headed south, but that struck me as vague enough to touch on pathetic, and it wouldn't have made sense since we were going northeast just then. "Guess I'm not really sure what I'm doing."

"I hear ya." His voice trailed off.

I got the feeling we shared vague futures. To get us out of the sudden pall that filled the car, I asked, "Were you ever shipped overseas?" anticipating a story or two.

"I wish." He perked up. "Nam ended just before I got out of basic and they say they can't just fly us all over the fuckin' place for nothin'. I'll go anywhere they tell me. There's just no reason to go."

He turned sharply to face me. "I didn't enlist to sit on my ass.

"If there's no war that's great," he continued. "Hell, I've even talked with guys who were at Iwo. That was one brutal motherfuckin' rock. But this is starting to get old. There are other things to do." He stared out of the window. "I'm just not sure what."

Stud was facing the end of his hitch and had only two weeks left before deciding if he would re-up. "I've got to talk it over with my wife. She's been back in St. Louis for the last six months." He smiled slightly. "Nobody does me like mama." His next words rolled out of his mouth like heavy stones. "I'm gonna try to save my marriage also. Man," he pursed his lips and slowly shook his head, "I don't know what's gonna happen."

As we crossed the featureless plateau I pictured myself wandering out there, walking toward a vague horizon. I thought maybe Stud saw himself out there too.

Stud was driving to St. Louis. After looking at my map, I told him I'd ride to Memphis, where I'd once again head south. He seemed satisfied with that, and we agreed that we'd each roll down our window as soon as we farted, even if it was silent, since we were going to be in close quarters for the next thousand miles.

"Look at that motherfucker," Stud blurted, holding up his left arm. He rolled his forearm, showing me a thick gold watch on his wrist. "On base there's this motherfucker who sells 'em on the side." Stud swore the way people shake salt on food. Maybe he learned swearing in the Corps; maybe he taught it.

We drove through Pecos, Odessa, Midland, and Sweetwater, miles and miles of miles and miles. This geology was the ugly sister of the high desert, a landscape distinguished only by telephone poles and power lines. Over several hours my stomach started burbling and my head sloshed in a slow spin. The back of my mouth started to water and taste metallic. Then, just outside of Abilene, "Stud! Pull over!"

We skidded to the side of the road. I swung open the door, leaned out, and threw up breakfast. The cheese had tasted off, but I figured it was time to eat the greasy chunk since it wasn't getting any fresher.

"Ain't that a bitch," Stud said. "It ain't life threaten', man. You just probably ate somethin' bad."

We both stepped out for a stretch. Walking around, I tried to clear my head, but it fogged more. In only a few minutes, I began to shiver.

"For a white guy, you're looking extra white," Stud said with a little jab. "But really, man, you look fuckin' sick."

My mouth filled with saliva, anticipating more vomit, which followed.

"You need a doctor?"

"I don't think so." I wrapped my arms tight across my chest to reduce the shivering. "Breakfast didn't taste right. It'll pass."

Before we got into his car again, Stud flipped down the back seats and rearranged the bags so I could crawl in through the hatchback to lie down. There wasn't enough room to stretch out, so I curled into the fetal position. After half an hour my clammy shirt stuck to me. I lay there shaking in the middle of a full-blown case of food poisoning. Adding to my sickness, I felt guilty for morphing into a blob of Jell-O unable to help Stud stay alert, but that may have been for the better. My silence gave him a chance to air his thoughts.

"You know what I like most about the Marines?"

"No," I squeaked, attempting to hold up my end of the conversation.

"We've all got each other's backs. My ass is covered all the time. We're all trained, and we know what to do." He arched around so that he faced me in back. "And we'll do it. Fuck yes." He turned back to the windshield. "I trust those fuckers with my life."

I moaned to let him know I was still listening.

"I barely made it outta high school, but now I'm a field radio operator with a security clearance. You give me any type of radio and I'll make that fucker sing."

"That's good."

"But it's been three years now and it's starting to feel like the same shit every day. When I first got in, everything seemed new and I ate it up. But now...I don't know. I think I want out, and I can leave with an honorable, but the damn thing is, I don't know what else to do." The uncertainty in his voice seemed a rarity. "I've never had to look for a job. Hell, I've even prayed about it for a few weeks, and I'm not a guy who's prayed much these last few years."

I thought of my words from two days before, when I'd spoken to the desert sky, *Was that you last night?* That still struck me as weird, even desperate. I knew people prayed, but I never thought about any god answering. I didn't want to make light of Stud's prayers, but felt compelled to asked. "So what's god say?"

"It's like talking to a fuckin' wall."

Big surprise.

Then, almost sheepishly, "There haven't been any bolts of lightnin' or anything like that. But to tell you the truth, little by little I'm startin' to figure it out. When I was growing up, the reverend always said most of us would never get a burning bush, but that we'd all get gentle direction"—he paused—"if we just asked for it."

One second at a time, the hours passed. I'd never experienced food poisoning but figured that was the only thing that could've caused this. Convincing myself this was just sour cheese calmed me and reduced my fear that this might be something more serious. All I remember of Dallas and Fort Worth is looking up through the windows of Stud's Civic and watching a thousand orange-tinted freeway lights streak by.

We finished the eight hundred miles across Texas to Texarkana, Arkansas, mostly in silence. Around four a.m., on the outskirts of Little Rock, I started drinking from my water bottle and felt well enough to crawl back into the passenger's seat.

"You didn't miss a fuckin' thing," Stud said.

When we reached Memphis I felt like I'd spent my entire life in that car and was uneasy about leaving its protection. The sun was barely above the horizon when we pulled into a parking lot.

"So, where you goin' now?" Stud asked as I reached for the door handle.

The thought of trying Stud's method, praying for an answer, occurred to me. "I don't know—south, I guess."

This felt minuscule compared with the decisions Stud faced—whether to divorce, maybe enlist for another two years in the military. I carried the weight of a fruit fly and felt nonexistent. But he looked at me and seemed to draw some comfort that he wasn't the only person unsure of his future. He nodded, held out his hand, and we shook.

"Thanks, Stud. This was a huge ride. Sorry I wasn't better company."

"Don't worry about it, man. Everything worked okay." He rubbed his eyes with big palms. "I'm goin' to get some rack time."

STEVE THEME

I stepped out, and after shrugging on my backpack, I bent to look through the open passenger's window. "Good luck with your wife." The words felt trite.

"Yeah." He exhaled slowly. "We'll see."

I thought of asking him if he'd decided about reenlisting, but didn't. He had enough on his mind. "Maybe you'll get a little of that gentle direction."

He put the car into gear. "Got some last night."

9
Holes in the Sky

The wait began like any other while standing at the intersection of I-55 and I-20 in Jackson, Mississippi. After a while, I pulled out a harmonica and played as people drove by, my right hand in the air, thumb up, left hand holding the harp to my lips. Some people smiled and waved as I played, and I'd wave back. Eventually my mouth dried out.

After about two hours of standing in the relentless sun my face started burning. At hour three, I noticed how white the skin was under my watchband when compared to my pink forearms. I knew my arms would still have that burning feeling when I would later lie in my sleeping bag, and that left me with dread. Four hours of standing on the hot concrete made my ankle and hip joints feel like they were lined with sandpaper, and my right shoulder pinged with pain when I held out my arm. To stay a bit cooler, I poured some of what little water I had over my head and worked it into my hair. I didn't want to use too much or I'd look like some wet-head lunatic. Plus, eventually I'd have none left to drink. Hour five left me mesmerized by the waves of heat rising from the road. My face felt crinkly, and I wished I'd brought a hat. I thought about walking away from the highway and sitting under a tree, but that would mean I might miss a ride and my wait would be even longer. Fantasies of a white bird shading me with its wings began to float through my mind.

"Man! I've been standing here forever," I said in a rasp while getting into a four-door sedan.

"Pretty hot today," the man said, hitting the gas hard to get us back into traffic. Then, in a tone someone might use to give a legal deposition, "My name is Sam Andrews."

Sam sat tall and trim, probably in his mid-fifties. Deep lines furrowed his face. He wore his salt-and-pepper hair in a crew cut resembling my father's. His glasses had thick black rims. Once we stopped accelerating, he turned toward me and, without any prompting, said, "I'm a rocket scientist."

"That sounds interesting." I wasn't sure if he was joking, but he didn't say it like he was trying to get a laugh.

"I work at the Stennis Space Center for NASA; been there fifteen years."

Now I was actually interested.

"Before NASA I did a stint at McDonnell Douglas, most of the time working on propulsion systems, jet engines mostly."

"Which engines?" My words implied I might know something about jet engines, which I didn't.

"Ended with the J79. Those were for the F-4s, you know, the Phantoms." He swigged some air. "They're a hell of a fighter. Those and the 52s, they were the backbone of the war. At first I didn't think the Viet Cong had a chance." His words fired like defiant rounds. "If the goddamn government just used more of them instead of sitting on their posh political asses we could've won." He took a deep breath, slowed himself, and his voice took on the tone of demoralized resignation. "Our guys just didn't get the support they needed."

Interstate 55 rolled out straight and flat, and the trees that lined both sides of the road blocked anything that could be considered a view. Because of something, probably an accident, the traffic was backed up for what seemed like miles, converting the front seat into a park bench, giving Sam a chance to crank back up again.

"Hell, the Viet Cong called it the American War! We didn't start it!" His voice lowered. "But we didn't finish it either." Sam shook his head. "Communist containment policy? That's a worldwide joke now. If that's how we run our policies, I want out. We didn't contain squat." He looked at me with a *well, duh,* expression, as if he had just stated something so obvious he was an ignoramus to even mention it. "We could've sent twice as much firepower and Saigon wouldn't be goddamn Ho Chi Min City today!"

The war more or less started when I was eight years old. The first impact I felt happened when a young lady who'd been our next door neighbor and my babysitter—she spent a lot of time helping me sound out words so I could spell them—found out that her fiancé's plane had been shot down. I pictured a plane trailing smoke as it lost altitude until it hit the ground, like in the movies. He was flown back to the States to be treated for burns, and I was sure the doctors and nurses at the hospital would fix him. He lived two weeks.

When my mother told me he'd died, my stomach dropped and churned in a way I'd never known. I had planned—mentally and emotionally—that he would be fine, that she would be fine, that they'd still get married and she'd get to teach her own kids how to spell.

Sam's tone began sounding like my father's, and he started getting on my nerves. They both knew what should be done and exactly how, when, and where to do it, and anyone who didn't agree was a garden-variety idiot. My father and I had disagreed enough times that I felt he didn't want me to return—one less idiot he'd have to deal with. And I wasn't sure I wanted to return.

I decided Sam—or mostly me—could use a change of topic, so I asked him about NASA. He moved his hands from gripping the top of the steering wheel to let them hang from the bottom, and he gave a bemused smile, apparently recognizing what I'd just done. He said he was part of the team that answered JFK's challenge to send a man to the moon and return him safely.

"I worked on the Apollo program." His voice took a measured tone. "Stennis was built to develop the rockets we needed. Some of us thought it was crazy to even attempt a moon shot, because it wasn't possible. Others thought it was crazy because it was possible." He chuckled. "I just knew funding had been allocated and we had a clear goal—send a man to the moon and bring him back alive... pretty straightforward. We kind of did it."

I expected greater joy in his voice when he spoke about one of humanity's greatest achievements. "It was practically a miracle," I said, no longer annoyed. "The whole world watched. You guys did do it."

"Of course we did it," Sam said. "But the price came high. And I don't mean money. People look at Armstrong and Aldrin and hold them up, and they should. Those guys did a bang-up job. But we didn't keep everyone alive. Grissom, White, and Chaffee didn't make it."

The names sounded familiar, astronauts, but I wasn't recalling why I recognized them.

"A month before launch, a number of us were down at Cape Kennedy for a plugs-out test of the command module to make sure everything could run on internal power alone." He sucked a breath between clenched teeth. "When I heard that first call of 'Fire, fire, fire',"—his gaze dropped—"I knew they had no chance." The cars ahead of us were motionless. "The command module guys pressurized it with oxygen. Jesus, at that pressure, with pure O-two, an aluminum bar burns like wood." His face contorted. "Over the comm, all we could do was listen to them scream. Sounded like they were burning alive in hell." Sam turned toward me. "And it wasn't quick."

He didn't say so, but as he stared quietly out of his side window, I got the impression he felt lingering guilt from his complicity in a mistake that killed three men. Seeing this chink, an acknowledgment of his fallibility, I let go of the annoyance I'd felt during his tirade about the war.

"That test showed us a lot, really forced our eyes open. Even the hatch swung inward, so there was no way they could get out fast. We changed that in a damn hurry. And those nylon suits, they were nothing more than plastic wrap." He took another long look out of his side window. "Gus and Ed ended up melted together."

I rolled down the window for some fresh air. I pictured myself listening to the three men's wails as they burned—imagined the surreal feeling of time slowing while understanding the inevitable outcome, and thinking, *This can't be happening. This can't be happening!*

WE RODE INTO THE NIGHT, passing our time talking about his family and my high school sports.

"Bill graduated from Florida State about two years ago, with honors." Bill was Sam's only child. Once again, Sam stared into the distance. "We didn't always get along, but he made me proud. Really proud." His eyes brightened. "We used to take flying lessons together. It was great getting our licenses. He'd quiz me to make sure I knew the material."

Sam's son would only be a few years older than me, and I guessed that he'd moved out and was living his own life.

"We started in ground school when Billy was only

sixteen. We got our licenses and Bill certified as a P-I-C, that's Pilot in Command. After he logged about a hundred flight hours he went for his instrument rating so he could fly in the dark, during bad weather, you know, extreme conditions." Sam smiled. "He one-upped his old man. I always figured he would."

"He sounds really accomplished."

"He was."

With those words the already pronounced lines on Sam's face deepened, and I suddenly understood that Bill hadn't merely moved out. The hum of the road filled the silence before Sam's voice locked into a well-rehearsed monologue.

"My boy was taking a sightseeing flight with a couple of his buddies..." Sam's body became a marble statue staring straight ahead. "They had been water-skiing earlier that day. The weather was sunny, calm, a good flying day. Just a sightseeing flight." He paused, letting out a gentle breath. "They were over the De Soto National Forest." Each word now received its due. "The witnesses said the plane flipped. It started spinning. Toward the ground."

From watching Word War II documentaries, I knew pilots called that a death spiral. Sam avoided the words.

"In the end no one could say what caused it. There was no autopsy. The fire made that pointless. But no alcohol or drugs were involved."

He slumped, and his sigh sounded like a lone note from a cello. "They were just young men, hadn't even left their marks. Bright, good, young men." His eyes moistened.

Mine too.

"But I'm certain there were no alcohol or drugs. I'm certain."

The setting sun's immense silence filled our car.

Sam invited me to his house for dinner and said I could sleep there. We both knew what he was attempting and I felt happy to serve as a surrogate son for a night, to let him help another young man. Sam lived northeast of New Orleans in Slidell, Louisiana, just off Bayou Liberty Road. Once we parked in his driveway the dark bayou surrounded us. I imagined living in the abyss of the swamp where every dense night closed out the world. That probably comforted Sam.

We walked into his home where beige colored everything: walls, rugs, furniture, appliances. There wasn't much art—a few pictures of airplanes, and a picture on the mantel of his son wearing a cap and gown as he wrapped one arm around a woman I assumed was his mother and the other arm wrapped around Sam—three smiles in a row.

"That's a nice picture."

"Yep, that was a happy milestone," Sam said. "I've made peace that there'll be times every day that I'll miss him, probably for the rest of my life. So now I'm not surprised when I do." He turned away.

I wanted to decompress, so I walked out a sliding glass door from the living room into the backyard. A bulkhead at the end of the yard held back the bayou. Channels of water wandered out to the darkness. On the heavy air I smelled a hint of flowers mixed with rotting wood, and I listened as ripples gently splashed off the bulkhead. They sounded like the tiny waves I'd heard lapping against the hull of my grandfather's forty-four-foot sailboat when there was no wind.

For nine years, my father, my grandfather, his crew of old friends, and I raced that boat on Puget Sound every Sunday in the winter. Most races happened on blustery days with waves exploding across the bow, but a few of the races were windless snoozers.

On one of the early races, when I was nine years old, we were heeled over and I asked my dad how the boat could sail almost straight into the wind. "Why doesn't the wind just blow us backward?"

"See the sail?" He pointed to the jib, its foot fastened to the tip of the bow and its leading edge rising to the top of the mast. We had it pulled in tight so the third corner was back by the cockpit. "That's a wing."

"What do you mean?"

"I mean it's a wing. See how it's shaped? Curved out just like a wing."

I tipped my head sideways to alter my perspective. Sure enough, there was a big white wing.

"The air pressure is less on the outside, basically the same as the top of an airplane's wing, but instead of holding us up, it pulls us forward. It's like we're flying, but just a bit slower than an airplane."

My first duty on Gramp's boat was to pass sandwiches from the icebox up to the men on deck. When the wind became angry, I wasn't allowed on deck at all because my dad was afraid I'd get swept over. The boat had been built in the '20s, when hulls curved low to the waterline—a classic design, but when the sea stacked up, waves washed over the boat and through the cockpit.

After two years I became a grinder, a deck monkey, cranking on winches to trim the sails. When my grandfather said crank, I'd crank, and when he said stop, I'd stop. A couple years later I worked the mid-deck, next to the mast, raising and lowering the sails. After eight years I worked the foredeck, rigging the sails, clearing jams, calling to trim the sails, and being the last one into the cockpit during storms.

One February afternoon we were racing into a gale. I gripped the base of the mast as spray hit my face like buckshot. The sea kept building, so I got down and lay at the foot of the mast, holding fast to a winch and looking at the teak deck only inches from my nose.

Barely audible over the riot of wind, my father shouted from the cockpit, "Watch yourself!"

Boom!

The boat shuddered, slamming my face to the deck as our jib split down the middle and a million frayed whips of canvas cracked. I was rattled, but one look back at my father showed he was terrified, and not for the boat. Where a strong sail had just flown, all that remained was a hole in the sky.

10
Integrated Discrimination

New Orleans pulled me west from my momentum east. I wanted to stroll down Bourbon Street, enjoy some jazz, and gawk at the famous French Quarter. I'd read, heard, and imagined too much about Mardi Gras to miss this opportunity to visit the apex of American debauchery. After catching an early-morning ride to the north side of town, I decided taking a city bus would be the easiest path to Bourbon Street.

The morning rush hour brought an onslaught of people to the bus stop. Every person was black. I'd never been the only white person in a crowd before. I'd probably never experience this in Seattle, let alone at the UW, and that spurred a feeling of accomplishment.

I fancied that I'd become racially integrated. But as more people arrived, I began feeling uneasy. No one seemed to take notice of me or act like I stood out, but I felt like I did. I'd always thought integration was about how I viewed others; it now included how I perceived myself. We were all simply waiting for a bus, yet I started feeling conspicuous and awkward.

The bus filled to standing-room only and I was one of the last to board, which left me by the front door. Looking back through the sea of bobbing heads, I searched for another white face. I'm not sure why—maybe I thought it would make me feel more comfortable—but I remained the only white person. Unable to congratulate myself for being integrated, I did take quiet credit for merely being there.

Humidity and heat began to take their toll on all of us. I knew I smelled, but the air became thick with body odor, more than just mine. Many factors can impact how we smell: diet, hydration, personal hygiene, general health, and more. But the bus smelled different than I did and reminded me of a conversation I'd had one afternoon in a locker room.

While playing football in high school we all sweated, especially under pads on hot days. In the locker room one day after practice a teammate, Greg, and I wondered why we smelled different. Greg's skin was smooth as a night pond and the same color. He started at fullback, and I started at guard. First I'd slam a defensive lineman out of the way, and then Greg would come through the hole and bull over a linebacker, clearing a path for the running back.

"Man, you stink," he said as I pulled off soggy shoulder pads. "Like a wet dog."

"Ever get a whiff of yourself, pretty boy?'

We agreed nobody would want to smell either of us, but the difference remained, and we wondered why. Greg said that's how god made us, so there was nothing we could do about it.

"Doesn't make sense to me," I told him.

We debated who stank worse but agreed it didn't matter. Winning mattered. Working together mattered. That year we hammered our way to a 13-0 championship season.

At every bus stop, I needed to move my backpack so people could pass to the door. It wasn't a big pack, but in a jammed bus it might as well have been floppy bagpipes, and I received a few glares as if I stood threatening to play them. I didn't feel the glares were because I was white—although realistically some might have been—but rather, every time I moved my pack so one person could get by, I had to push up against another person and ended up inconveniencing pretty much everyone around me.

As people came and went, I started thinking about the civil rights movement: school busing, Reverend King, the Black Panthers, the Freedom Riders, the Watts riots, the Civil Rights Act, protests, and the list goes on. These seemed far removed from the bus I was riding. But I probably wouldn't have been on that bus without the sacrifices made by so many people over the previous decades. How could the civil rights movement of the fifties and sixties have helped a white boy in 1978? I couldn't pinpoint why I wouldn't be there, just that I wouldn't.

In one sense it seemed the country had come a long way; in another sense it seemed segregation was still strong. I suspected few, if any, whites typically rode that bus. As I looked around, I couldn't see the people's pasts but was sure the older ones had experienced serious discrimination when they were younger, and more of them than I realized probably still did. If I had been told that because of my white skin I couldn't eat somewhere, couldn't get a job, couldn't go to school or live where I wanted, couldn't develop a relationship with who I wanted, or even get a drink of water—I wasn't sure if I could ever rid myself of that bitter taste.

As I continued through the South over the following weeks, I came to learn that my thoughts on that bus reflected little more than an intellectual exercise. I'd get multiple opportunities to experience racism, toward both blacks and whites.

By mid-morning I had finally reached the French Quarter. I wandered down Bourbon Street along the squat architecture that lined its sidewalks. I'd expected gilded hotels and chic bars. Instead, rows of low brick buildings the color of worn wallet leather held up balconies with endless black iron railings—nothing shiny, no glass or stainless steel facades. The street looked too small to support its reputation.

Wilting balloons tied to lampposts hung as the only indicators of recent revelry. A few tourists wandered the streets looking around like they were in a museum. Even though the city remained loved by many, I couldn't shake the feeling that New Orleans had become a dead town walking, these buildings its future ghosts.

Each time I inhaled the hot air I felt as though bread dough filled my mouth. Hiding from the sun under a balcony, I pulled off my smelly shirt. I wished I'd packed deodorant and decided that as soon as I could I'd buy some.

On Burgundy Street I heard jazz marching from a bar. I've never been a big fan of Dixieland jazz, but it's a music of zesty life, and to honor that I stood and listened. Once I'd absorbed enough clarinet notes, and since I didn't have the money to soak in any boozy frolic, I decided my New Orleans experience was as complete as it would get.

At a gas station, I checked a map with local details and decided to walk to Highway 90, which would carry me along the Gulf Coast. I made it to a nondescript on-ramp where I ate yet another peanut butter and cheese sandwich. I'd just seen New Orleans but felt I hadn't really been there.

By the time I'd caught enough rides to reach Biloxi, Mississippi, a short thin guy named Clint picked me up and asked if I wanted to get a tour of bayou back roads—see the deep, rural, real South. He was a few years older than I was and I couldn't picture his straight dark hair as having ever been out of place. Since I was touring, and he was offering to give a tour, I accepted.

We drove down muddy roads passing swayback shacks. One was built on a flat island half the size of a football field. A black stovepipe jutted from one of the walls.

"People live out there?" I asked, not believing anyone could live on just that dab of land.

"Oh yes," Clint said. "There's folks who've been in this country for generations, since the first Cajuns. These places go back for miles. No neighbors, just the bayous. That's how they like it."

At the front of many of the homes small porches had wicker chairs and torn couches. Behind the houses, rows of corn and a variety of low green bushes marked garden plots. Chickens roamed.

"A number of years back, there was bad leaf blight on the corn. Some people called it ear rot. I prefer leaf blight." He looked at me with a furrowed brow. "A lot of these people suffered mightily. They went hungry more than usual."

I rubbernecked as we drove past each family settlement, hoping to register the images permanently. "What do these people do, I mean, for a living?"

"I know some of them hunt gators—there's plenty—then they sell the meat and hides. And a lot of them harvest Spanish moss from the oaks. It's used in pillows and put into packing crates, those sorts of things. And they like their moonshine." Clint took the tone of a teacher trying to explain a simple concept to a dense student. "Basically, they raise or kill what they need. These aren't college boys."

This was the type of area that state tourism boards don't want people to see. The ingrained poverty and lack of any new development had stagnated the area for probably a century. At the time I naïvely thought that U.S. living standards like this existed only in history books.

We turned down a long dirt road that eventually became overgrown with green. As Clint drove, the front bumper became a ship's prow cutting through waves of fronds. We stopped when the waves grew too high to drive through. When I pushed open my door, it cleared a space among the reeds and grasses. I wondered why he chose to drive here.

Not sure what to say, I blurted the obvious. "We've got to be pretty deep into nowhere."

"Yeah, there ain't much here but the breeze."

I felt like an ant lost in a lawn. Behind us, reeds we'd driven over had sprung back up, obscuring our path.

"You know," he said, stepping close to me and lowering his voice, "If two men are caught having sex in Mississippi, they'll go to prison for ten years." His eyes darted as if searching to make sure no one, except me, heard him.

Despite our isolation, I didn't feel threatened—Clint was smaller than me, showed no signs of aggression, and my knife, as always, was strapped to my side. He seemed to be the frightened one.

His eyes darted around again while he pressed his palms together. "Can I feel of you?"

I thought about his phrase, *feel of you*, and wondered what he meant, but I didn't ask him to elaborate. Clint seemed unable to ask explicitly for what he wanted.

"Just to feel of you, that's all." His cadence quickened, punctuated by shallow breaths. "That's all I want. I'm not going to get this chance again." He extended his arms toward me, as a beggar might plead for food.

STEVE THEME

"You're perfect. People here don't understand." He stood motionless, staring me in the eyes.

My words came out hushed. "I think this tour is over." I continued facing him for a moment, feeling compassion, then turned and walked to the passenger's door.

On the drive out Clint repeatedly talked about a house owned by a friend of his. "He's out of town and the house is empty, but there's a cot."

A cot? Not that I was about to change my mind, but if I had been interested, a cot wasn't exactly a huge incentive.

"It's in a nice room. Upstairs. With a door."

"No."

We drove in silence for a while before he turned to me. "I don't want to be damned to hell."

"What?"

He raised his voice, but the words slowed. Each stood on its own. "I don't want to go to…hell." He peered down for a moment. "Everyone says homosexuals go to hell. Preachers say it's a sin, one of the worst, an abomination against God, against Jesus and Mary, against the entire human race."

Hell couldn't be real, nothing more than a scare tactic, but the tactic was working.

"It's just in me. I've tried to get rid of it, but God knows I can't." His tongue flicked, wetting his lips. "You're the only one I've told."

Once again, my purpose was to not interrupt.

"Even thoughts—just thoughts—are a sin!" He pounded the steering wheel. "Why? I don't deserve this!" He wasn't talking to me anymore. "I've been good." His eyes began to tear. "I've been good! Damn it! Why?" He pulled over and came to a slow stop, then hung his head and began to cry. After a bit he wiped his eyes. "I'm sorry." Sucking the snot back into his nose, he gave a weak smile and a short cough. Then he shook his head and laughed, that weak self-conscious laugh people use when they know they've put someone else in an awkward situation. He talked through his last dribbles of tears. "I bet this isn't what you expected."

"I never know what to expect," leaked out.

We drove back to Highway 90 without a word, and as I stepped from the car Clint slumped.

That night I bedded down in a clearing next to a brackish stream. I liked reading, especially before going to sleep; I typically had several books going at once. But on this trip, since I had no flashlight, there was no way to read after sunset. And I hadn't brought a book anyway. So every night it was just me and my thoughts.

Lying there, I reflected on laws and their power over people. I'd just seen that power rack a man with fear as he reached out, trying to be authentic to his nature. Until then I'd interpreted laws as a simple set of rules—driving the speed limit and not stealing—ones I mostly followed.

It seemed unfair to me that lawmakers would legislate who consenting adults could have sex with. I didn't know the Bible, but lawmakers did, and as a faithful people they worked to enforce its will as they understood it. In a history class, I'd learned some southern states even codified appropriate sexual positions between men and women. I envisioned bills passing through the various legislatures with diagrams of the missionary position—each state ratifying a one-page Kama Sutra.

STEVE THEME

I lay down under an oak tree and thought about the opposition between human nature and the Ten Commandments, of which I could think of four: don't kill, don't steal, don't bone your neighbor's wife, and honor your mother and father. I'd never killed anyone, but on the rest, I was a little shaky. Human nature and the Commandments appeared at battle with each other, but that god didn't seem in any hurry to negotiate a truce.

I envisioned Clint's face from earlier in the day. His understanding that he wouldn't get what he so desperately hoped for seemed to be a sadistic trick god had played on him. *Or was it the legislators who were cruel? Or could homosexuality just plain be wrong? Why would a god give people longings against his will? Did those desires come from the devil? Is there a devil? Is he winning?* I kept staring into the night.

In high school during a World History class, I'd learned that for more than a thousand years the Old Testament's stories were passed down orally—and I assumed that more than once they'd been told after a few glasses of wine, maybe more than a few. Much of the New Testament wasn't written until hundreds of years after the death of Jesus. For another thousand years after that, the only way to create a Bible was by writing every copy by hand, each scribe potentially incorporating his biases and cultural norms. The texts had all been translated from ancient languages by countless unknown people.

Did what remained amount to little more than tall tales? The miracles of Saint Paul Bunyan? The proclamations of sex-starved old men? At first I felt weak, even stupid, for considering such grandiose questions.

Looking into the sky's black ink, I overcame my reluctance to rely on anything other than myself for answers; I didn't have any. I remembered that as a child lying in bed, I wanted to believe in some god. A little faith felt comforting, but as I grew, faith fell away, replaced with the pillars of facts and proof.

I realized the clarifications I was seeking were new to me, but not new to many others. I restated my questions, some only mentally, others aloud, and I tossed them up for God, Vishnu, Allah, Yahweh, Jehovah, Superman, whoever, in what I thought of as a prayer. Lying alone on damp ground, I felt part of a greater whole. Physical solitude didn't keep me from connecting with the legions of people who'd asked the same questions and shared the same uncertainties. I couldn't point to them, but I understood they were out there, and I came to believe that even if the seekers didn't find answers, they'd find each other.

11

Hospitality and Hurricanes

	APRIL					
						1
2	3	4	5	6	7	8
9	10	11	12	13	14	15
16	17	18	19	20	21	22
23	24	25	26	27	28	29
30						

"Cousin Les and us is headed down to Gulf Shores to my grandpap's place," twanged one of the guys in the car. "I'm Bud and thiz'ere's my brother Bo." Bud and Bo sat in back while Cousin Les drove. I rode shotgun. Bud leaned in closer. "We're headed for sun, beers and swimmin'."

Cousin Les cracked a smile. His blond hair was cropped neatly over his ears and he wore light-gray shorts with a sun-faded blue T-shirt. "Gulf Shores is on the coast, real nice place. I'm on a break from the University of Alabama for a few days, and we're headed to the family beach house.

We all share it." Les cocked his head toward the back seat. "So when was the last time we all came out here together?"

"Geez, we was in junior high," said Bud.

"Yep," Bo agreed.

Les turned to me. "We've all been out here since then, but not together."

The boys in back sported long shabby beards and their overalls were splotched with grease stains. They struck a delicate balance between hillbilly, redneck, and swamp rat—teeth optional.

"Heck, we ain't hardly even seen you since then, Cousin Les," Bud said.

While Les talked about studying to become an architect the brothers played some punching game: the one who took a punch would shout an elaborate curse—something like, "You goddam rott'n hog," and then it was his turn to punch. They were shouting enough, it became hard for Les and me to talk. As we neared Gulf Shores, Les gave me a quick slap on the knee. "How'd you like to come with us for a couple days?"

I thought he might ask, since that would give him a chance to get some breaks from the prize fighters. But I wasn't in a position to spend money on partying, so I didn't answer immediately.

"I'll pay for your food and beer."

"Oh." I twisted my arm behind my back, giving yelps of mock pain. "Okay, okay, I'll drink your beer." I then settled in with the feeling of three-day permanence and understood my role. An expenses paid weekend vacation on the Gulf of Mexico sounded exciting, even with the Bud-and-Bo package.

Bud was a talker. "Yeah, Cousin Les, I gotta tell ya, I knocked up this gal. Jus' found out a couple weeks ago."

Les shook his head.

"I'm figurin' on marryin' her one of these days." Bud gave a clunky chuckle and leaned forward to slap me on the shoulder. "One of these days!" He laughed louder.

I didn't like Bud.

We drove onto a low jetty with a lagoon on one side, the gulf on the other, and the noon sun above. The lagoon looked cool, smooth, and dark, while the coastal beach radiated light as if each grain of white sand were a polished mirror.

We headed back to the lagoon side, driving by long, thin waterfront houses. Most had private docks.

"It's just down this road a ways," Les drawled." "Man, I can't wait to hit that water."

"Hey, Cousin Les?" Bud called out. "Remember when that ol' barbecue tipped over on yo daddy?" The brothers cackled.

"Yeah, that was pretty exciting," Les said flatly. "He still has scars on his belly." Les paused for a moment. "Hey, Bud, how about that time you lit the shed on fire trying to burn a *Playboy* so the grown-ups wouldn't find it."

"Boy howdy. I got a whoopin' fo' that."

"Yeah, we saw."

"Dummy." Bo punched Bud. "That was a good *Playboy*."

"So y'all had a lot of adventures out here?" I asked. Since Memphis I'd been practicing a southern accent, so I'd fit in better with my rides. Once I'd managed to slow my cadence the accent became passable.

The three quickly started shouting over the top of

each other about pit roasting, family gatherings, aunts, uncles, drinking too much, and grudges.

As we neared the house, Bud said, "My gramps bought this place. Jeez, it's great. We'd barbecue. An' I mean barbecue! Barbecue like a mother!" He thrust his arm up as he howled and pounded the roof. "Hell yes!"

"Hell yes!" Les shouted. "It was great!"

We zipped into a sand driveway next to a narrow pink house with clean white trim. Right as we stopped, the boys jumped out of the car. I noticed Les kicking off his sandals and then running toward the long finger of a dock that extended into the lagoon.

Bud tossed off one boot and then the other. Bo followed suit. They fumbled while squirming from their overalls.

I wasn't going to be left in the dust, so I kicked off my flip-flops, tossed my wallet toward my pack, and started running as I pulled off my T-shirt, so all I was left wearing were my cutoffs. My legs kept pumping as I sprinted down the dock shoulder-to-shoulder with Bo, who was wearing only his boxers, which would inspire anyone to run. I launched myself off the end and stretched out to an arcing dive while Bo curled into a cannonball.

As I sailed through the air, watching the water pass below me, thoughts raced that I'd be spending three days here, food and beer paid for, sleeping in a real house, and tagging along with some guys who seemed well practiced at having fun. But once I slid under the surface, my thoughts evaporated, and I submerged into cool silence.

Throughout this trip, each morning, I consciously warned myself not to burden the day with expectations. If I didn't remember on my own, the day's surprises usually reminded me. So even though theoretically I had no expectations, this day was developing better than expected.

After we finished flailing around in the water, we walked to the beach house and claimed sleeping spaces. I landed in a semi-private side room, an office without a door. After dropping my pack in a corner, I walked to the kitchen to join the other guys. "Goddamn, boys! What're y'all doin'?"

Bo froze. "Whatta ya mean?" He was holding a salt shaker over his bottle of beer and appeared to be shaking salt into the golden jubilation. I supposed that was better than peeing in it, but not much.

I didn't want to sound too critical, like some control freak, but I blurted, "Are you *trying* to ruin your beers?" These guys weren't perfect, but I thought they at least knew how to drink a damn beer.

"It's good for ya," Les said. "Helps restore the salt you lose to the heat." He fluttered his hands as if to show the salt floating away.

When in Rome… Luckily, it took only a few swallows for me to realize Southerners had devised the perfect remedy to replace precious lost salt.

Les turned to Bud. "So this gal's really knocked up?"
Bud smiled. "Yep."

Bo looked up from a chair he'd flopped into. "She gonna shittify yo life."

"I want me a son, and I'm gonna raise me a good'n," Bud spouted, while sitting at the kitchen table. "And I'll know I done good when I cain't whoop him anymore an' 'stead he can whoop me, jus' like I whooped my daddy."

Bud was thin, scraggly, like he'd have trouble whooping anyone. But not a boy.

Bud blabbered on while I lost myself in memory. I was about ten years old and setting our kitchen table before some of my parents' friends were coming over for dinner. I accidentally knocked over a pitcher of water. The white tablecloth and napkins got soaked, and water started dripping over the side and onto the floor. While I stood frozen and looked at the soggy mess, my father grabbed my neck from behind and then clenched the waistband of my pants. He lifted me over his head; I could see the texture of the popcorn ceiling only inches from my face. Instant fear. I knew this one was going to be bad. I couldn't run, or block, or anything. I could only wait.

The ceiling pulled away as he slammed me to the floor; my lower back screamed with needled pain as I writhed and cried out that it was broken. In my agony time slowed. *Now he's done it.* Though I'd been thrown down stairs, kicked across floors, knocked to the ground, this would be the one that was going to send me to the hospital. I was afraid that I would have to tell the doctors what had happened. I'd have to tell them while my father would be standing there. Then I'd really get it. That seemed incomprehensible—I'd never told anyone.

My back wasn't broken.

The memory ended, and while Bud sat describing his eagerness to continue his family's cycle of violence, I silently vowed to break mine. I hadn't been beaten for a few years—I'd grown stronger than my father—but I still needed to put distance between us; the emotional abuse hadn't stopped. And I believed that the farther away I got, the less likely I'd be to repeat the past. As I stared at the kitchen table, I felt a life-changing resolve that I'd never strike a child.

That afternoon, the boys and some neighbors threw a backyard barbecue, cooking brisket, ribs, and chicken. Each cut of meat was put on a grill at a different time so they'd all be ready together: first brisket, then ribs, and finally chicken. Just inhaling the all-encompassing aromas of meat caramelizing made me hungry. Ribs straight from the gill, slathered in sweet smoky sauce, were the first hot food I'd eaten since leaving Seattle more than a week before. Earlier in the day a neighbor brought over a pony keg of beer, and we'd all had a few. Bud had a few more than a few.

As I sat across a picnic table from Bud, I noticed that he was staring at his food, and Bo, who was sitting next to him, was staring at Bud. Bud squeezed one eye shut, bent down to within inches of his brisket, and swept his head back and forth, examining every fiber of the meat. He looked like a scientist—a drunk hillbilly scientist—squinting into a microscope.

Bud let out a "Hmmm."

"We like to barbecue," Bo said.

Bud straightened up, extended his right index finger in a slow and ceremonial gesture, and pushed it into the brisket. Then he didn't move. Maybe he was balancing himself so he wouldn't tip face first on to his plate. "Ma finger knows."

"Your finger knows what?" I asked.

"Ma finger knows when meat's cooked right."

"Yur finger only knows yur nose," Bo said. "Yur drunk."

"Ma finger has its own mind." Once again, with ceremonial slowness, "It has been many places."

I didn't doubt that.

"Why don't you stick that finger up yur butt." By now Bo was well into a chicken thigh.

"You don't understand, you ignoramus." He then pointed his well-traveled finger at Bo. His words took on that struggled articulation when a drunk wants people to grasp the gravitas of his statement. "It is our family honor."

"So, what's your finger say?" I asked. Family honor and all aside, I wanted to know what his learned finger thought.

"It's time to eat." The finger had spoken. And it was a good thing that's what it said, because everyone else had already started.

We reveled in the sun, cooled off in the lagoon, played music around a beach fire, and worked hard at relaxing. Over the next days, Les and I ate in several seafood restaurants overlooking the gulf. Shrimp and crab made for a nice break from peanut butter and cheese. True to his word, Les sprang for everything. I felt somewhat guilty, but I understood, and acted on, my role as an outlet for him to escape Bo and Bud. For the most part, I avoided the cousins and frequently called Les away from them. He gladly came each time.

On our last night together, we took a short drive west to Bon Secour, Alabama, a town of about three hundred people on the coastline of Bon Secour Bay, which is on the outskirts of the larger Mobile Bay. As drainage for two-thirds of Alabama and parts of Georgia,

Tennessee, and Mississippi, Mobile Bay is a huge swath with a bounty that supports thousands of people. In Bon Secour shrimping is the main industry, which is fortuitous, because the owners of the Riverside Inn Motel had invited the boys, and indirectly me, to their shrimp feed. I love shrimp, but they don't love me.

"Sounds too dang good to be true." I told Les. "I mean really, way, waaaay good."

As we drove to the feed, I shared with Les how I'd grown up around saltwater and how I'd fished for salmon, shrimp, and halibut in Alaska. "I got to tell ya, Les, I'm always fish hungry."

"Well then today's your lucky day," Les said as we pulled up. "These folks are old friends. They're one of the families that were always at the house when we were kids."

From the parking lot, I could see the Riverside Inn was a single-story motel with about a dozen rooms side-by-side.

As I walked around the inn, a scene unfolded that I recognized, but only from history books and movies: deep green grass cushioned a couple acres of pasture; in the middle of the field a large water oak draped in Spanish moss supported a rope swing; a chestnut mare languidly grazed on the rich grass; and people dressed in white congregated in small groups sprinkled across the green velvet. The field ended at the banks of the river, where broad willows lined the flow's path, as if showing the river where to go. A gently rocking shrimp boat was moored at the family's private dock.

Our hostess glided toward us, smiling from under a white lace hat with a broad brim. Her cream-colored dress accented with pink roses flowed down to her ankles in several layers of billowing cotton. She looked like clouds during early sunset.

She gave Les a hug. "Aren't you a sight for sore eyes? It's been years." She took a step back while still grasping his shoulders. "Good lord, you're a man." She then motioned to me with a smile. "And who is this gentleman?"

"I'm Steve, ma'am," I delivered in my best southern drawl. "I'm on a trip 'cross America an' spendin' a weekend with Les and the boys."

"I trust they're treatin' you right." She gave Les a wink. "Where you from, son?"

"From Seattle, in Washington."

She looked perplexed.

"Next to Canada." I'd learned to add the part about Canada because when I said Washington to people east of the Mississippi they generally assumed I meant Washington, D.C.

"Well, you had me fooled! I thought you were one of us." Approval permeated her voice. "Well you make sure to eat plenty of those shrimp." She then reached out and took my right hand warmly between both of hers and leaned forward as if to tell me a secret. "I don't want any of those little creatures left." Then she spread out a silk hand fan, waving it to create a puff of breeze that carried her to the next guests.

I'd never seen hospitality flow so easily. "She sure knows how to make you feel at home," I said to Les.

"Yeah, it's part of our culture. My momma always said that after the War Between the States all we had left were our memories and our manners, and by God, we're not going to lose those."

Two five-gallon aluminum pots filled with boiling water sat over rosebud propane burners ready to turn pale shrimp into pink delicacies. Wiry fishermen tended the pots, their weathered forearms etched with muscle. At the dock, their boat bore jagged rust stains running down white flaking paint.

While I watched the shrimp boil, ears of corn floating with them, one of the men pointed and said, "That there's my boat. She ain't much to look at. But she can fish." Then, further defending her honor, "We ain't movie stars here. In this business, being pretty don't make any extra money."

He grabbed a slotted spoon and scooped a couple shrimp from the deep pot. After blowing on them he handed me one. A few minutes later the fisherman shouted, "Come on y'all. Time for the blessing." Everyone walked toward picnic tables and formed a circle. The strangers on each side of me reached out to hold my hands. I felt welcome.

The fisherman began in a booming voice thanking God for the good shrimping season and for the food we were about to eat, asking protection for all the men at sea, and giving thanks for the opportunity to gather and enjoy fellowship. As the prayer ended on amen, the people next to me each gave my hands a slight squeeze.

This was a first for me—people joining hands in prayer. I thought about how at Thanksgiving each year someone in my family would get tasked with reciting the same short mechanical prayer. *God is great. God is good. Let us thank Him for our food. Amen.* That satisfied our annual prayer quota.

After many y'alls and all y'alls, Les and his cousins

headed north to Mobile. I decided to stay since I planned to continue traveling east along the coast. As darkness cupped the sky, I walked down a dirt road, found an old wooden tool shed, and bedded down behind it.

Since those welcoming days, I've followed Bon Secour when it's in the news. But the town captures headlines only when hurricanes hit. The following year, 1979, Hurricane Frederic, a category three, leveled much of the Bon Secour waterfront. It was the first major storm to hit the area in fifty years, and it ravaged land the way a wildfire destroys a forest. Almost half a million people were evacuated along the coast. The people rebuilt.

In September of 2004 another hurricane, Ivan, made landfall west of Gulf Shores, right on top of Bon Secour. A report from the National Hurricane Center described it:

> Ivan weakened only slowly and made landfall as a 105 knot hurricane...just west of Gulf Shores, Alabama. By this time, the eye diameter had increased to 40-50 nautical miles, which resulted in some of the strongest winds occurring over a narrow area near the southern Alabama-western Florida panhandle border.

Ivan resulted in twenty-five deaths in the United States. It barged through with malicious winds, ocean surge, freshwater floods, and pounding surf, ringing up a bill of $14.2 billion of destruction. At one point, 1.8 million people across nine states lost power, but the small towns of Gulf Shores and Bon Secour took the brunt of Ivan's rage. Again, the people rebuilt.

STEVE THEME

Then came the most destructive natural disaster in the history of the United States: Katrina. That fury drove twenty-two-foot swells into Bon Secour Bay; the town's elevation is only ten feet. I don't know if the Riverside Inn survived. I just hope the people did.

12

Guide My Feet

	APRIL					
						1
2	3	4	5	6	7	8
9	10	11	12	13	14	15
16	17	18	19	20	21	22
23	24	25	26	27	28	29
30						

In the early morning I found myself on the western outskirts of Panama City, Florida. I wasn't having any luck landing a ride, so I started walking east as the sun rose. The temperature was mild and the air smelled honeyed from flowers that grew on both sides of the road. After several miles I reached the thick of town and stopped, figuring that getting a ride there'd be easy.

Hundreds, maybe thousands, of people looked at me as they drove by, most of them neutral, others with curiosity, some with disdain. I'd become accustomed to people staring as they passed and no longer felt like a storefront oddity. Since I still wasn't having any luck getting a ride, I walked more. It didn't take long before the afternoon heat started swarming in. The perfume of flowers that had filled the morning gave way to greasy exhaust from hamburger stands and the oily scent of baking blacktop.

I'd covered about seven miles when I stopped at a gas station to drink from a hose on the pump island and fill my water bottle. Then I hunkered in the shade of some palms to let my sweat dry. Cars drove past, and I wondered if I was missing a ride. Throughout the trip if I wasn't in a car, or asleep, the thought of missing a ride gnawed at me. To minimize downtime I often pulled food from my pack and made sandwiches while I stood on the roadside. Then, holding food in one hand, I'd hold out my arm and hitchhike with the other. If a car stopped, depending on the size of the remaining sandwich, I'd either stuff it all in my mouth or jam it in my backpack, figuring people wouldn't want a stranger eating in their car. It wasn't a comforting way to eat, but it was better than feeling I might miss a ride.

With a slow moan, I stood up from under the palms, sandwich in hand. I persisted for another steamy hour holding out my thumb. No ride. It became time to make a strategic decision: would I keep standing, or would I walk all the way across Panama City? According to my calculations I'd already crossed half the city. Standing was exhausting—not only physically but also emotionally, as each passing car shaved another sliver off my optimism. Many of the people driving by were senior citizens, and I knew these northern retirees weren't keen on picking up some scruff. I decided to walk.

There were a few sidewalks, but mostly I walked on thin dirt paths next to busy roads. I stopped at several gas stations to refill my water bottle and make sure I was headed the right direction. By late afternoon the sky had yet to produce a single sun-blocking cloud.

As I reached the east end of town, near an Air Force base, I figured my luck would improve. Standing with my thumb out, facing west toward traffic, I was again staring into the sun. Another agonizing hour passed. My face felt tight. I needed more water.

A café close by looked cool. Once I sat down and the waitress looked at me, I knew something wasn't right.

"Do you want some water?" she asked, bending toward me and holding out an arm to steady me, as if approaching a person after an accident.

"Yeah, ice water. A 7-Up too, please." The voice I heard surprised me, it sounded like an old man's, weak and hoarse. With my face radiating heat, I walked to the restroom. In the mirror, my forehead and cheeks looked plastic, reminding me of a toy fire engine. They shined and covered the beginnings of some swelling. When I splashed my face with cold water it felt so good I stuck my entire head under the faucet. Water tumbled over my neck, scalp, and face, caressing me with its cool fingers. Bent over with my eyes closed, I felt woozy and held on tightly to the sink. I didn't care if someone walked in on me.

Back at the booth, my hair continued dripping onto my shoulders.

Bringing the drinks, the waitress asked, "Are you okay?"

"Yeah, I'm okay. Thanks."

She walked away but kept looking back.

When I left the café, I bought sunscreen and headed out for more road time. I wanted to shave myself bald to release heat. The sun hung low enough that as I looked west, each car became little more than a blinding glare.

To the side of the road, broken asphalt had given way to grasses sprouting through cracks. I lowered onto one knee to examine how these delicate green blades that swayed with the slightest breeze could push through the asphalt. Lost in that wonder, I noticed that I wasn't hitchhiking. Just kneeling there seemed okay, even though potential rides were passing behind me. I gently ran my palm over the tips of the grass, watching them bend and spring back up. The motion became a game. I'd swoosh my hand across the grass, and it would bounce back up. Every action was the same, but each one struck me as completely new. I felt like a child playing repetitive rounds of peek-a-boo, and I started laughing.

It's okay to take a break. That hit me like the sun. Two thousand miles had passed before I let myself feel this. Up until now, every moment I was within reach of a roadside had been spent standing with my thumb out. Now, cars whizzed behind me, and I couldn't care less.

This isn't a race. Many times on the trip, I'd imagined myself with a giant screw in my back. The metal twisted into me, building up pressure to shoot out flames that propelled me forward like a rocket—my back arched and my limbs splayed out, thrashing like ribbons in the wind. But each time I stroked the grass, my momentum slowed and the screw backed out a turn. Finally the image dissipated. *I've made it. I've escaped.*

I was beyond the reach of any ghosts that had chased me, and I inhaled with the gasps of a newborn.

Rides didn't matter. I slowed through the Florida panhandle—walking only—accepting a pace to accommodate my interests. When curious side roads attracted me, I walked them, granting myself the freedom to saunter. This was my leave from the bombardment of strangers.

Nursing my face and staying out of the sun became priorities. When I felt hot, shade trees protected me; all I had to do was seek them out. Over a few days, I strolled about twenty-five miles.

One Sunday morning I walked through a small township, more like a village: no stores, no gas station, no signs; just small, white clapboard houses lining a single dirt road. Most of the houses had front porches enclosed behind screens. Cinder blocks placed under the floor frames propped every house off the ground. This didn't fit my stereotypical image of a small southern town with yards that had become a menagerie of rusting trucks surrounded by garage sale junk and plastic kiddie pools full of fetid water—this was just white houses.

Walking down the street, I could hear gospel music pouring from a church. The building looked to be a single room, slightly larger than the homes around it. Its white paint clung loosely to the siding, peeling in spots. A wooden cross rose from the roof peak above the front door. Cars weren't parked around the church. There wasn't even a parking lot, but the church sounded full. As I neared, a young woman not quite my age, in her white Sunday dress, walked out from behind a hedge next to the road.

"Whatcha doin'?" she asked, approaching quickly, like a child reaching for a novelty. "I'm Cil." She wore her hair in a short Afro that topped her trim frame, her face a satin black. "We don't see people like you jus' walkin' through here."

I assumed she meant white people.

She smiled easily and walked up close. "Where ya goin'?"

"I'm not sure." She was so pretty. "Any suggestions?"

"Oh, I don' know. Not all that much 'round here." Her voice bounced. "You could try goin' to the beach."

We walked together down the main street, and she suggested that we sit on the church steps. I laid down my pack and took a seat. She planted herself next to me, close enough that our shoulders almost touched. We didn't know each other, but it felt reassuring that another person would choose to sit close to me, especially a pretty girl. Being alone so much, even if others were around, often left me feeling like I was background clutter.

By now, the church shook with the voices inside, and I could hear every word.

Guide my feet, while I run this race,
Guide my feet, while I run this race,
Guide my feet, while I run this race,
For I don't want to run this race in vain.

"Is this hymn called 'Guide My Feet'?"

"You must be a mind reader." She smiled. "You never heard this?"

"I'm not up on all my hymns."

"Where you from?"

"Pretty far away, Seattle, Washington." I paused and got the typical blank expression. "It's next to Canada."

"Are you some kind of crazy man? That is a long, long ways away." Her face lit up more. "What's it like?"

"Well…" I took in a slow breath, smelling dense vegetation, not flowers or a deep forest humus but a constant balm of plants growing and dying without distinct seasons. "Well… it's not like this."

"And?"

"I guess it rains mostly. It's usually cold, generally pretty crappy, but there are mountains everywhere and a lot of blue lakes."

"I never seen a mountain." She looked up and down the street. "We don't have any of those. What's their names?"

"The biggest is called Mount Rainier. You can see it from almost a hundred miles away, and it's a volcano."

Her eyes tightened into slits. "I'm no fool. Don't tell me you got some red hot volcano in your town."

"No, really." Suddenly it dawned on me how unimaginable this must sound to a person who'd only lived on flat land amid dense trees, someone following generations of people who'd lived on this land only. "It hasn't erupted in probably thousands of years, so it's not red hot, and it's not right in the town. It's just a mountain." I tipped my head back, as if staring up at something high and huge. "But it's a really big one. And you can see it from a long ways off."

Her face softened as my story sounded less far-fetched. Cil and I talked more about the differences between our hometowns, and about some of my travels. Once she heard I'd spent time in college, she told me her dream.

STEVE THEME

"A school teacher, that's what I really want to be, teach elementary school kids. Teach 'em reading and all the subjects." She fell silent. The smile left her face. "No one here has ever been to college." Her hands fidgeted. "We just an ol' slave settlement." The momentum of history always runs long into the present.

She gazed up. "I'm going to try, don't know how, but I want to be the first." She managed a timid smile, and then looked into her lap. "All I'm sure of is it costs a lot more than we have."

"Have you heard about this new thing called a Pell Grant? I'm going to apply for one when I get back."

She didn't move, as if I'd said nothing.

I raised my voice. "It's free money. You don't have to pay it back."

She slowly raised her head, turning toward me, but didn't speak.

"Basically it's for the poorest kids." I didn't want to insult her, but I wanted to let her know she might be a good candidate.

"You're not lying, are you?" Her voice became a straight line. "Who gives away money?"

"The federal government. They can afford to throw a few crumbs our way." Our eyes met, and we held our gaze. Typically, when I sat that close to a pretty girl and looked into her eyes, I followed the look with a kiss. Instead, I lowered my voice to little more than a whisper. "There's money begging to find good people like you."

"I don't know if you're right. Still sounds crazy to me. But I s'pose if you say so." The hymn continued rolling between us. "We've got a county library, maybe they know something about this free money."

The song came to a soulful end, and I could hear the pastor telling the congregation to go in peace. Cil gave a panicked glance toward the double doors behind us. Her face stiffened. "It's time for you to go—right now." She could tell her sudden change disappointed me. "If they see us here, me with a white boy, there'll be trouble for both of us."

My feet got lively.

13

Worlds Away

	APRIL					
						1
2	3	4	5	6	7	8
9	10	11	12	13	14	15
16	17	18	19	20	21	22
23	24	25	26	27	28	29
30						

*B**efore the sun sets, I'll have crossed a continent*—that came to me once the driver told me where we were going.

"We's headed fo' a hootenanny," one of the six teenagers said as I sat on the floor of a cleared-out painter's work van. They were all a year or two younger than I was and on their way to St. Augustine Beach, Florida, on the Atlantic.

A couple sat up front, and in back were three boys and two girls, all sitting on the floor. To hear each other over the rattle of the well-used work van, we needed to shout. "Last night we jus' won the basketball championship," one of the guys said, slapping up a high-five with me.

"Y'all did?" I asked with exaggerated surprise, pointing my finger around the group.

"We been waitin' and waitin'." One girl grabbed her friend's shoulders and shook them. "Waitin' all year. Dis our celebration."

Everyone seemed to be talking and their voices blossomed in all directions.

"Whatcha doin' here?" the driver shouted back.

"I ain't doin' nothin'. Just travelin' and don't even know where."

The guy next to me said, "I let you know thiz some special day."

"'Cause you won the game?"

"Nah, 'cause we partyin' wid a white boy!"

We high-fived again and I swiveled my head around as if trying to find the white boy. *Could this be the first time they've hung out socially with a white kid?*

Nothing could stop us, and with the coast about a hundred miles away, we bounded toward the beach. One of the guys pulled out a joint, and it didn't take long until we were rolling across the floor each time the van rounded a corner, piling on each other, laughing. When the driver accelerated from a green light, one of the guys in back let the momentum rock him toward the rear of the van, placing him close enough to plant a kiss on one of the girls. This wasn't a peck, but a nice smooch on the lips. As the driver took his foot off the gas to shift gears, the lapse of acceleration pulled the boy forward again. The girl gasped and raised an open palm as if getting ready to slap him across his fresh face, but she still had the hint of a smile. She let her hand drop, but not before delivering a thwack on his shoulder.

He laughed as he rolled back. "Gotcha!"

She shared a wondering glance with the other girls.

"You got some style!" I cheered.

After a while we left the main road and pulled onto a path worn through thick palm fronds. About a quarter mile later, the path opened to a grassy field with little more than a clay trail leading to a cabin with a tin roof. I noticed there were no power lines, no other driveways, no fences, just a thick green field and a square home with a lot of peeling white paint. The driver honked, and a teenage girl popped through the front door, sprinting toward the van. We now made four couples, not from a romantic standpoint, just nicely balanced.

As we kept driving, they spoke of eating hamburgers, swimming in the waves, and being able to someday tell their children, and grandchildren, that they were champions. When the topic turned to life after high school, they sounded like many kids, not sure of what they wanted to do.

"We gots a big chicken factory 'bout fifteen miles out," said one. "My uncle works there, maybe he get me a job." Other than that, none of them had plans; no mention of college or trade school.

Next to them, I felt pompous for leaving school, even ashamed. Yes, I'd needed a change, and I planned on returning to the University of Washington, which I didn't mention to the others, but the ease with which I left made me feel spoiled. I'd spent my days on campus looking down on everyone, feeling that those around me were taking the experience for granted. Mighty Me sat in judgment, but I hated myself for sitting there. I'd earned the opportunity to attend school, but abandoning that opportunity now filled my pinpoint of self with doubt. By leaving, was I squandering one of the greatest fortunes that could be afforded to anyone? Had I simply been too immature to let others be themselves? Did I despise them just because they weren't me, because they hadn't arrived by traveling my path? *Am I that small-minded?*

The only way I could redeem myself was to make that rusted, rattling van my classroom.

We drove past shacks that were being slowly devoured by tall grasses, moss, and the smothering green of kudzu. Front yards had faded FOR SALE signs made of cardboard or plywood propped against used tires, bed frames, or refrigerators. Entire homes were made from sheets of corrugated metal, and many were covered with a jigsaw of plastic tarps. One shack, with nothing more than glass shards clinging to its window frames, formed the backdrop for a three-hundred-pound woman sitting on a tree stump and resting her feet on a freshly cracked case of Budweiser. Outhouses looked like they were sinking into the holes they covered. The kids in the van didn't comment on any of this. Could this be America, the one I thought I knew, equality and justice for all?

Years later, I learned the Peace Corps sends recruits to clinics in that area to prepare them for assignments in the third world.

Once we reached St. Augustine Beach, and after hearty goodbyes, my friends headed north and I continued south—still my direction, for no particular reason. Cultural whiplash hit when I stepped out of the van onto a white sidewalk next to a set of beach volleyball courts groomed to perfection. The people wore bright beach clothes and were walking with friends, playing, or just sunbathing.

When I was standing on the roadside, I didn't mind that people stared at me as they drove by. But when I was walking amongst them, passing just feet away, I hated it when they stared. And they did. Wearing overalls and road boots at a tony beach like this, shouldering a worn pack and sleeping bag, I felt like a freak people gawked at. In their eyes, I mostly noticed uncomfortable distaste. *Don't get too close. He might be rabid.*

Assessing myself, I didn't see a freak. I saw a young man trying to expand his awareness and heal himself in the only way he could figure how. As random as it was, my journey didn't feel random. So far, many different people had felt I was a safe audience that let them talk about their fears and frailties. My awareness was broadening as I learned how similar we are. Even those kids back at school I considered brat fucks probably harbored all kinds of emotions similar to the ones I felt.

I didn't feel lost, spending my effort on a haphazard folly—I was on a mission.

But those connections I had made were in cars as I talked one-on-one. Here, I saw a world of activity where I was only a spectator—a spectator that the participants actively ignored. That total lack of connection flipped me to a sense of being nonexistent. In all directions, the world moved past me. What was I doing standing next to the Atlantic Ocean? Just standing there? Was I a coward running away? A bold explorer seeking knowledge? A sick person trying to get well? I had no answers. Maybe I'd become nonexistent to even myself.

Mission deflated.

Navel gazing was getting depressing, and I needed a shower: days of dried sweat meant my skin was sticky, my hair was stiff, and I stunk like a homeless person. Searching around, I found a public bathroom with showers. I walked in and stripped, and as I lathered up I noticed a guy leaning out from one of the toilet stalls. He sat there, staring, fixating on me, apparently getting his jollies. I faced the wall and closed my eyes, imagining myself rising up through waterfalls of the Cascade Mountains back home. But when I opened my eyes the waterfall was a black iron pipe jutting from a concrete wall.

When I turned off the water, the jolly guy was gone, and I emerged with flexible skin, imagining I was a crab that had molted its old shell.

After drying with a hand towel, I put on my cutoffs and the Eagles T-shirt—dirty and smelly, but better than going naked. I then headed over to a bank of sinks to shave. Because I had no shaving cream or soap, I spent extra time bent down at the faucet splashing water on my face to soften my stubble. Then I straightened and looked in the mirror. *Where's my reflection?*

A stranger was staring me in the eyes, and I startled.

This person resembled me: bushy blond hair, about nineteen years old, stubble, the hint of a sunburn lingering on his face. *His face? Whose face? What the fuck is going on?* I felt awkward looking into his eyes. We were standing too close.

I turned away and focused on the row of toilet stalls.

They looked normal. *Okay, things are normal*, I reassured myself. So I looked back into the mirror.

The stranger watched as I froze in blank bewilderment. *Oh shit. I'm freaking out! What's happening?* I didn't even know his name.

Mirrors don't lie. But I felt no comfort of familiarity, no connection with that person. *Mirrors don't lie. Mirrors don't lie. Who is that?* Fear, confusion, and loss filled me. My legs felt weak.

I passed on shaving—on looking in the mirror. As I walked back to the wooden bench where my pack lay, I couldn't help but wonder if I was drifting into some psychotic rabbit hole. I sat down, completely still, and didn't want to look at anything. What if more of the world had changed? What if I started to appear like something else? What if I glanced at my hands and they became crab claws? What had snapped in me? I hadn't taken any drugs. I looked around slowly to make sure that I was still in a public bathroom, that my surroundings hadn't morphed into something different—maybe a carnival funhouse of mirrors with a pipe organ pumping as a sunken-eyed carny called me in.

While sitting on the bench, I conducted a quick examination. By this point I'd been gone a little under three weeks and had experienced around a hundred rides, probably more. With each person who picked me up, I became a chameleon, adapting to reflect their personalities. If someone acted formal, I acted formal; if they were funny, then I became funny; if desperate, then I showed my desperation; morose, confident, hyper, spaced out, intellectual... I didn't even sound like myself anymore since I'd taken on a southern accent. I'd adopted a hundred rapid-fire personalities. Mimicking the drivers put them at ease and made the ride more comfortable for them and me. But now, by myself, I didn't recognize which personality, if any, was mine. The chameleon had eaten my identity.

The hard panic lasted only a few minutes; at least that's what it seemed like. Getting away from the mirrors helped, and I sought refuge at the beach, where I sat cross-legged in the sand. The only explanation I could think of was that seeing no reflection of myself in others left no validation that I impacted the world.

Months later I'd do some research in the *Diagnostic and Statistical Manual of Mental Disorders* and would find that psychiatrists call this an episode of dissociative fugue:

> The loss of one's identity, or the formation of a new identity, can occur with sudden, unexpected, purposeful travel away from home. Symptoms can last from hours to months.

But all I knew on that beach was that I was scared. I, my true self, no longer existed.

To regain my bearings, I thought writing a letter would help straighten me out. Bull crap—that wouldn't be strong enough medicine. So I exchanged three dollars with an ice cream vendor for a palm full of quarters and walked to a phone booth, where I gave Mark, my bass-playing best friend since sixth grade, a call. As each of the dozen quarters clanked into the machine, I started to feel like paying was going to last longer than the call.

"Hello?"

"Guess who?" He'd know.

"Oh man. I thought you were lost on the moon." Mark's voice let loose with jovial relief. "You been raped yet?"

"Not yet. You?"

"Yeah, right. So where are ya?"

"Sunny Florida. Funny, sunny, losing-my-fuckin'-mind Florida."

Mark seemed to immediately understand I needed support. He'd never taken the strength of our friendship for granted.

"Go on."

"I'm cracking up, man." My words scared me. "It's like a bad acid trip without the acid."

"You freakin' out? Sure you're not on acid now?"

"Yeah, I'm sure. But a weird thing just happened…I looked in a mirror and didn't recognize myself."

"Don't bullshit me, man. You're on acid."

"I'm not. All right!" This therapy wasn't helping as quickly as I had hoped. "I just wanted to check and make sure this isn't some Twilight Zone where my whole life is an illusion."

"No, Captain Crazy, you're not made up. I'm here. You're there. And we're talkin'. You may end up in the loony bin, but I'll get you out."

Relief started filling me, not from Mark reassuring me my life was real, but simply because he knew who I was. "I know you'll get me out, buddy. That's why I called. Just hearing your voice is helping." My death grip on the phone started loosening.

"So fill me in," he said. "What's been going on?"

"It's been wild. A drunk mafia hit man held a gun to

my head and told me he'd kill me. I wandered around naked in the desert. Crossed Texas sick with food poisoning with a Marine, spent a night in a rocket scientist's house, partied for a few days with some southern guys. And that's not even scratching the surface." In a mocking tone, I asked, "So, what've you been up to?"

"You left out going crazy."

"Yeah, but that's just today, and it's not over yet." I made my voice a higher pitch, sounding like a girl. "Toto, I've got a feeling we're not in Kansas anymore."

"Little Stevie goes to Oz and freaks out. We should make a movie."

"Sounds good, but I'm not wearing a dress." An older gentleman who had been waiting patiently behind me quickly walked away.

"For me it's pretty much same-o, same-o," Mark said. "Cooking at the Spaghetti House, doing some kickass biking. They extended the Burke-Gilman Trail, so I can slap on the Walkman and ride through two Aerosmith albums."

A mechanical voice butted in. "Please deposit another one dollar and twenty-five cents for the next three minutes." This always came on after the first minute of a long-distance call from a pay phone.

"So, you're doing okay now?" Mark asked.

"Yeah, I guess things are back to the way they're supposed to be."

"Of course they're the way they're supposed to be." He paused for a moment. "I'm still shooting thunder and lightning from my penis."

"And mine still eclipses the sun." These had been our

bragging rights since junior high school. "But don't go kiddin' yourself, I've still got the bigger—"

Click.

The call worked better than a prescription or sitting alone writing would have.

There was still some daylight left, so I decided to toss the dice again and catch a ride heading south, and before long I was skirting the coast on Highway A1A. There were no majestic mountains with earth-encompassing vistas, but A1A lolled in its own beauty and calmness. Breezes from the sea carried spring's warmth, and the rich blue that flowed in from the eastern horizon drew a clean line along the white-sand beaches that ran without end.

Several rides later, evening came, and I walked off the road and found a grassy hollow surrounded by palm trees. Short grasses, most of them dead and turned to straw, lined the ground in a soft warm mat. Flowers lightly scented the air, reminding me of a sophisticated woman who knows how to wear perfume. I'd reached home for the night. Laying out my sleeping bag, I envisioned myself a character on *Gilligan's Island*. Two trees stood perfectly spaced for tying a hammock, and I could see myself reclined under the canopy of palms. Maybe I'd scale one of the trees and bring down a coconut for dinner. The ocean wind kept bugs away, and the foliage took on richer shades of green as the sun arced further west. My hideaway offered secluded, gorgeous perfection.

Nothing pressed in with due dates, expectations, or babble. Daily racket cleared from my mind, and I became even with the world. Lying on my back, I let the air breathe me as I stared up and could see only deep blue mystery.

I wondered about purpose—my purpose, everyone's purpose, the lack of purpose. Haphazard events seemed to reign over everyone, and this only magnified beneath the lens of hitchhiking. Days had no pattern: I rose from a different spot every morning, had no plan for nightly shelter, and only random actions filled the gaps between. Where's the purpose, the plan? Maybe our plans lay hidden in that deep blue mystery. Maybe the plan is to have no plan. Does purpose even matter? Why do we thirst for purpose?

I fell into a deep serenity when I realized I didn't need to know the answers to any of the questions, understanding that the breadth of my life would be based upon what mattered to me. Then what mattered to me?

Everything mattered: family, friends, education, money, safety, society, books, dogs... So why did I leave them all? The question was way too big. Maybe I'd unravel it later, so I edged out my grand intellectualizing and brought my thoughts back to earth. Dinner mattered.

Propping myself up to sit against a palm, I skipped the fantasy of climbing for coconuts and pulled out a meal of bread and cheese—thought I'd switch things up and not have peanut butter. While pleasantly munching, I felt something on my forearm, and then something else. A few more drops of rain found me—not a problem. I snuggled up to the tree trunk, figuring the fronds could act as my umbrella. More drops, more snuggling. Within about five minutes, fat drops battered me. Fresh gusts kicked up to a squall, causing the palm fronds to extend like blown-out umbrellas.

I assumed the deluge would pass quickly, the same way a full pitcher empties when it's tipped over. After all, the sky could hold only so much water, so I decided to wait out the torrent. I rolled up my cotton sleeping bag, already a heavy red sponge, and lashed it to my pack. My comfy hollow became a pond an inch deep, quickly getting deeper. Looking around, I noticed high ground in short supply, so I slogged around the thick undergrowth hoping to find anything dry. In the dark, my pack kept getting caught on branches that I couldn't see. I hunched over as I walked, using the pack as a rain shield, and tried to minimize the number of blowing fronds that slapped me in the face. It didn't take long before I thought of Don Quixote searching for the nonexistent Dulcinea. In the book, though, the search was funny.

Finally, I walked back to the exposed highway. Looking north, I could see only a little way into the murky expanse. I stood in the sideways deluge and alternated between casting my eyes down to protect them from the rain and glancing up in hopes of seeing headlights. Half an hour passed with nothing but pounding, dark rain. Not a big surprise—I couldn't imagine anyone wanting to drive in this. I felt foolish—no, closer to moronic—for standing in the rain, for bringing no rain gear, for leaving on this trip, for gazing into the stupid blue mystery.

To the south I saw an almost imperceptible, hazy dot of light on the horizon, diffused by the billion drops separating me from the glow. I guessed that possibly, just maybe, it came from a neon sign in the shape of an arrow pointing off the road. A motel?

Nearby shelter was nonexistent, and if I continued to stand wet in the wind, waiting for morning, my body heat would drain away.

I thought of the prayer the man had said for me on my first day out, asking for God's protection, and I started walking toward the dot. Maybe it was nothing more than a streetlamp.

My shriveled fingertips trickled water like leaking faucets. With each sloshing step, I swore I could feel my toes wrinkling to white prunes. I kept walking and simply accepted the drenching. Everything I carried would get saturated, except maybe my journal, which I'd sealed in a plastic bag.

After about forty-five minutes of plodding, my head, neck, arms, hands, thighs, feet—everything—felt chilled. Shielding my eyes from the rain, I continued walking toward the glow. I couldn't believe my luck. It was an arrow pointing to a motel. But I couldn't make out if it read Vacancy or No Vacancy.

Vacancy! And it looked cheap! Of the two hundred dollars I'd started with, I still had about seventy-five. Opening the office door triggered a dull buzz from a back room where a TV droned.

"Be there in a second," croaked an old woman. She crept out to the counter with her head bent toward the floor. As she reached down for a registration card, she didn't bother to look at me. When she finally did her eyes jolted.

I stood motionless, dripping on her floor.

"It's a rough one out there tonight." She wasn't doing such a good job of suppressing a laugh.

"Yes. You are correct."

She seemed at a loss for words, but managed her standard "You got a license plate number?"

"Nope. I'm walking."

She eyed me. Maybe the storm swayed her, or maybe it was the cash I started counting. After paying her forty bucks, I walked across the parking pond to my room. There I saw what looked like an alien environment—a dry space carved from the storm—where a white bed billowed comfort.

14

Bloodshed

	APRIL					
						1
2	3	4	5	6	7	8
9	10	11	12	13	14	15
16	17	18	19	20	21	22
23	24	25	26	27	28	29
30						

After eating a peanut butter breakfast in the motel room and packing my mostly dry clothes that had spent the night hanging from lamps, the closet door, the shower curtain rod, and a few rusty hangers, I set out, clean and full. The sky had returned to an ocean of blue, and rides came easily.

Shortly before noon a middle-aged couple pulled over in a rickety sedan. I hopped in the back door on the passenger's side, and the man driving gave me a panicked glance. Something wasn't right.

With tires shooting gravel, we sped onto the road. I noticed that the woman was rocking back-and-forth, side-to-side, writhing and moaning. In a moment I saw leaves in her hair and the back of her neck streaked with blood.

"I found 'er like this jus' a minute ago on the side of the road," the man blurted in a high-pitched rattle.

She reached out to him, but he recoiled from her bloody palms. "Thank ya sir. Gawd, thank ya fo' pickin' me up."

"We need a hospital," he said to the windshield.

I peered over the seat. The woman wore a white sleeveless dress that drew sharp lines against her black skin. At first I thought the dress had a pattern of roses, but I soon realized these were blotches of blood soaked through from underneath. Her face and exposed arms showed ripped skin, some surrounded by caked dry blood, others fresh and weeping. The wounds I could see were about two inches long and a half-inch deep, each one ragged and pink. These weren't created with a knife—maybe a hook twisted in and pulled straight out. Several gashes streaked her face, maybe four or five on each arm, and more on her exposed calves. They led up under her dress.

Who is this guy?
What happened to her?
Why?
What's he want from me?
Where's a hospital?

His black hands trembled on the steering wheel, and it seemed he was grasping for emotional support. Maybe that's why he picked me up; I'd simply appeared as the first person available to share his burden.

"I'll keep my eyes open for a hospital sign." I tried to sound reassuring, but my voice shook. "You just drive." I placed my hand on his seatback. "You did the right thing picking her up." I felt like vomiting.

She moaned, curled over, hugging her legs. "They strapped me to a chair laz night and cut me everywherz, bad." Then she sat up and turned toward me; her grimace pinched sharp wrinkles from the corners of her bloodshot eyes. "But they didn' do *that*. No, they didn' do *that* to me." Her crying became louder. Her rocking sped up.

"I don' know what happened to her," the man said. "My wife'll kill me if she sees me drivin' with another woman."

That struck me as an odd thing to say. This was no romantic situation. Maybe his wife had caught him pursuing other interests. Apparently he had even more concerns beyond our circumstance.

We kept driving but saw no signs—not for speed limits, exits, towns, or mileage, let alone for a hospital. On a normal day, highways are choked with signs, but during that tiny eternity, none appeared. Even though I told the driver I'd look for the signs, his head swiveled back and forth, scanning for anything.

"God, I hope my wife don' see me."

We kept searching, the car swerving some each time he'd twist his head looking for a hospital—or his wife.

I couldn't believe we weren't seeing anything other than open road. A shape caught my eye on the left of our car, and I turned to look. Three boys in a new four-door pulled up next to us. The one in the back on the passenger side rolled down his window. He shouted, but I couldn't hear what he was saying. For an instant, wishful thinking made me hope he'd tell us where a hospital was. The driver in our car rolled down his window to hear the boy.

"Niggers! Niggers!" The kid in back hollered, pointing to us, and glaring at me. In case we didn't hear, the passenger in front rolled down his window, and the two shouted in unison. "Niggers!"

The guy in the front seat threw an empty whiskey fifth at us, but the wind caught it, and the glass shattered on the road. They flipped us off and sped ahead laughing.

"Are those the ones who did this to you?" I asked the woman.

"No." Her sobbing intensified.

Hospital Next Exit.

Finally! I didn't feel relief, just more urgency.

Our driver stomped on the gas. When we pulled up to the emergency room, the woman remained bent over, hugging her knees. I jumped out and opened her door. The driver and I, one of us on each side, held her up by placing our forearms under her armpits as we walked in. We didn't need to get far past the sliding glass doors before two nurses lifted her from us.

The driver and I stood together without the bloody woman for the first time and just stared at each other. His short gray afro blended with gray sideburns that ran down his gaunt face. Thin red veins spidered across the whites of his eyes, and his cheekbones angled sharply to his jaw. Deep creases, the ones long-time smokers have, radiated from the corners of his mouth, which drooped in sad exhaustion.

Maybe he didn't feel hollow, but I did. Reaching inside, there was nothing to grab, just hot haze. As my adrenaline began to subside, I noticed we were still standing in the doorway. When an admitting nurse called us to a desk, we pulled two chairs into a space designed for one.

"What is your relationship to the victim?" she asked, pen in hand, poised over a form. Neither of us could say much.

When I told her I was hitchhiking from Seattle, she didn't ask me anything more and relied on the driver for information. He asked if he could get a coffee and offered to stay—talk with police. The nurse told me I could go.

"There's nothin' more you can do here, son," the driver said, laying a hand on my knee. "Thank you mightily." He mustered the weakest of smiles.

Standing up, I gave his shoulder a gentle pat before walking away. I found a bathroom and washed the woman's blood from my hands and forearms. While rubbing paper towels over my skin, I thought of the many news reports I'd heard about cruelties people intentionally committed, but that I had seen one of those cruelties—was washing its blood from my own skin—hit me in the gut harder than anything I'd seen in the media. I wondered if this story would be on the local evening news. *If it bleeds, it leads.* I figured the reporters who doubled as ambulance chasers wouldn't be able to resist. Maybe this would be juicy enough to make the national news.

The sky was still blue, but everything seemed distant and foggy. Green leaves waved frantically in the wind like a crowd of people signaling from a sinking ship.

Removing my pack from the car, after glancing at the stains where the woman sat, I began a shaky walk back to the highway, replaying images in my mind. They weren't the images I'd seen in the car, but those of what must have happened the night before: seeing her strapped to a chair, being cut, taunted, tortured, probably gang raped.

What causes people to inflict that kind of suffering? How much anger filled them? How much remorse? Any? Years from now, will they look back on that night as a low point in their lives? A high point? Nothing special?

Brambles, insects, white lines in the parking lot, a brick wall—I looked around at anything that could fill my vision with normalcy. With a deep breath, my thoughts briefly stopped.

I never doubted that our driver had nothing to do with the crime. He overcame the paranoia that his wife might see him, that he might get pulled into something dangerous, and he stepped up when he was needed. My hands still shook, but thinking of his compassion slightly steadied me.

The images came back; she turned to me, her face only inches from mine, her grimace squeezing blood from ragged wounds. *Help me!* I shook my head hard, inhaling all the air my lungs could hold, and then let a slow breath drain until I emptied. The images dissipated, and I squinted into the sunlight.

Gun-shy. That's how I felt about taking another ride, any ride, ever. It was like I'd been playing Russian roulette. I didn't want to step into another car, but I couldn't live in the hospital parking lot.

Highway 1A kept heading south, so I did too.

As each car approached, I peered through the windshield, to check for hair caked with leaves, maybe someone rocking in a seat. I couldn't stop inspecting.

A car slowed. I stared hard into the passenger compartment. Only a driver; that helped. It pulled over in front of me. Approaching the car from behind, everything looked calm, so I kept nearing. As I reached for the door handle, I imagined it as glowing hot, that I should recoil from the car. Instead, I crept in.

Norman Jessup, a chiropractor from Johannesburg, South Africa, sat in the driver's seat. He was taking a vacation, touring the East Coast. Norman sat tall with an elongated head and an aquiline nose, probably in his late twenties. Bold prints punctuated his shirt. "I'm an Afrikaner," he said proudly. "My family descended from Dutch emigrants to South Africa." He faced me. "This is my first time to the States."

No blood on the seats or dashboard. Just him and me, no trembling or crying. My eyes darted, and I swiveled my head to check the back seat. All clear. My chameleon took over.

"That's great that you know where your family comes from." I paused for a second, clearing my head. "I'm an American mutt." The pride in my voice surprised me. "Have a bit of German—well, probably more than a bit of that—French, English, and some Norwegian. Maybe some Jewish too—at least one uncle thought so, but I really don't know much about it. Even my great-grandmother can't say exactly where we're from." I'd often yearned for some pure ancestral roots—my people.

But when I realized they had been lost to history, I became just fine with recognizing my roots as American. Not genetic roots; American genetics don't exist. Several days before, I'd gotten one ride with a couple from New Hampshire. On their license plate was the state motto that reflects the entire country: Live Free Or Die—my people.

Norman didn't have any schedule to keep, so we decided to tour Palm Beach. Eventually, we parked and walked around looking for some lunch. A warm breeze carried the scent of fresh bread, and we stepped into a café. Norman bought us lunch: an antipasto plate of sausage, cheeses, olives, artichoke hearts, and peppers.

While I dipped the torn edge of a sourdough roll in olive oil, my mind alternated between the present moment sitting in the café and the horror of the morning; Norman and me drinking ice water from crystal glasses and a whisky bottle shattering. White napkins. The red blotches on her cotton dress.

I envisioned Life standing on a pitcher's mound and hurling all the tricks it could. But I wasn't the batter, just a confused catcher, absorbing every pitch. A vision of the woman appeared. She was also squatting behind home plate as she held up her mitt in hopes of shielding her face. The ball flew so hard.

Images replayed in my mind even as I maintained my chameleon act. There was no point in telling Norman about it all. That would just sicken his afternoon.

As we left the café, Norman grabbed a map of Palm Beach from a rack of brochures and then plotted our tour. The Palm Beach Country Club made our list as the first stop—not that we could get in but just to drive around, get up to the clubhouse maybe. Arriving, we drove onto a scrubbed-white entry lane. I'd never seen a white driveway before. We drove through the porte-cochere, which funneled us back to the road, a polite way of giving us the bum's rush.

From there we headed along the coast on South Ocean

Boulevard, the high-rent district—heliports in front yards. The boulevard was lined in an unending string of Mediterranean mansions. After a while, it became boring looking at red tile roofs, tall green hedges that hid brick fences, pillars and gates, snaking driveways, and swimming pools.

"What's that?" I asked Norman, pointing to a yard with a perfectly flat and obsessively manicured grass rectangle surrounded by a white line. It looked too big for tennis, too nice for volleyball.

"It's a croquet lawn," he said without skipping a beat. "Vicious game. Looks genteel with everyone wearing white suits and all, but the good players are calculating. It's more of a blood sport."

Once we moved past the ultra-high-end homes and entered a part of town for lesser millionaires, I felt like I was bathing in irony and had to ask Norman about his experiences with apartheid. South Africa's apartheid government was alive and well at the time. I didn't feel like debating, just listening.

"I didn't see many coloreds growing up," he said comfortably, as if that would be a given. "There were some servants, but they needed passes to get into our part of town. It's not America, where anybody can wander anywhere." His ease when describing segregation left no hint of guilt. "It's always been like that. I was just born into it." Then he added philosophically, "We're all born into something."

Even with America's imperfections, I felt incredibly lucky I'd been born here—not to mention as a white male. I thought about my parents, far from perfect, but they had provided for my material needs and I assumed they tried their best. The Pacific Northwest offered a green chunk of the globe with as much bounty anyone could ask for: plenty of water, mild climate, jobs, clean air, distance from war, abundant food, and for me a select crew of lifelong friends.

Why am I trying to escape? Maybe my life had become too uniform, and I squirmed in my own skin. Had this journey become my elite classroom, where tuition consisted of relentless danger and loneliness? Or was that just a way to rationalize running away from my problems?

I thought about Cil and her village where no one had gone to college, about the black kids I'd ridden with to the coast who saw little for their futures except menial work, about my New Orleans bus ride. America no longer legislated segregation, we just lived with it—not everywhere, not everyone, but it was more prevalent than I had thought. Segregation remained alive within the grain of society's hardwood.

"I never really thought about apartheid as a kid," Norman continued. He looked silently at several more mansions as we passed. "I could have gone anywhere on this trip, but I wanted to come here because I know the States are different.

"I don't think it's going to last," he said. "The government, that is. It's antiquated, and the people see changes in other countries." He lit a cigarette and rolled down the window to spit out a fleck of tobacco. "They know about Martin Luther King. South Africa is bound to change." Norman faced me, no more smile. "It's just a matter of how much bloodshed it's going to take."

15
While We Can

"We been savin' up for two years to see Florida," Cindy said with a clothes-pin-on-her-nose Midwestern accent. Cindy and her friend Mary Ann were young waitresses on their first big vacation. From Cincinnati, and in their early twenties, they decided to stop for a hitchhiker. I hopped right in. They were nearly identical: long straight brown hair, trim figures, floral print short-sleeved shirts, white shorts above tan thighs. The volley began:

"Where ya from?"

"How'd ya get here?"

"Why'd ya leave?"

"Where ya goin'?"

"What's ya favorite food?"

They outplayed me at my own game. I was the question guy, not the answer guy. After surviving the pair's initial interrogation, I found out they wanted to see Miami.

Cindy drove and spoke through her gum chewing. "We been best friends since junior high, and after graduatin' we started waitressin' at the Tic Toc downtown."

Mary Ann chimed in. "It's okay, but there's more—a lot more—outside o' that town, and who knows when we'll have a chance to do this again? What's gonna happen when we have kids? What then? We won't be able to just leave when we feel like it."

Cindy bobbed her head in agreement.

We drove to the center of Miami Beach and left the car to walk. Once we were on the beach, Mary Ann said, "What the hell is this? It's just a bunch of old people sittin' around doing nothin'." There were a few younger people, probably in their forties, but overall this was a crowd of tan wrinkles.

"We didn't drive a thousand miles for this," Cindy said.

The ladies tramped back to the car, and Mary Ann pulled a rumpled map from her purse, spreading it on the hood. We discussed several destinations reachable before nightfall, but only one seemed intriguing, even mysterious.

We saw a highway that fell off the bottom of Florida and lay like limp yarn dangling into the Gulf of Mexico. At first we thought someone had inadvertently scribbled on the map. There couldn't be a road that just left the land and continued into the ocean. With her face pushed down to read the small print, Mary Ann announced it was indeed a road, stringing across islands until it ended on Key West, which, on this map, was the size of a flea. She crumpled the map back into her purse, and we sped off.

As we left the mainland on the Overseas Highway, there were plenty of signs that said No Hitchhiking. Those in authority clearly wanted to keep out the riffraff, and it appeared hitchhikers topped their list.

Reaching Key Largo, we landed on a planet I'd never visited—the Planet of Bridges. Miles of concrete roadway were elevated above the green sea and intermittent mangrove swamps as impenetrable as Superman's chest.

"Wow," Mary Ann said.

"It's scary," I said. "It's like we're driving off the end of the earth."

"This is why we traveled for vacation," Cindy said, gripping the steering wheel with both hands and pulling herself forward. "Get the camera, get the camera!" The straight road ahead of us wedged its way into the horizon between the sky and the sea.

Shallow water reflected light green and merged into deep blue. Surrounded by water, with almost no land in sight, I became a stowaway on an ocean crossing. We were tempted to stop at each dot of land along the way, but the sun kept sinking and we wanted to reach Key West before dark. Night got there before us anyway

"Steve, you wanna get a motel room?" Cindy asked.

"Sure." I didn't expect this. *Who am I to argue?*

As we entered the room, Mary Ann said, "Now, Steve, we're on vacation for a good time, not a loose time." Cindy gave me a look that said she felt the same way. They were like bookends—unfortunately, I wasn't a book.

We talked more and got ready for bed. After unrolling my sleeping bag on the floor, I took off my overalls before lying down. Cindy elbowed Mary Ann. "Look at that." She then pointed to my abdominal muscles, each distinct, with the lines of my obliques leading down under the waistband of my boxers.

Another slow "Wow" came from Mary Ann. "You've even got muscles there."

I felt both awkward and flattered, but mostly awkward. I wasn't trying to flash any skin or strike a pose, and I wasn't sure how to answer, so I didn't say anything, and just got into my sleeping bag.

Once they were in their beds and we were lying in the dark, Cindy spoke up. "Ya know…we won't ever get to do this again."

As I lay there, everything seemed right: my pack next to me, boots next to the door, a little food, water, and money, and my jacket rolled up for a familiar pillow. I felt an order, a messy, uncertain order that let me know things were as they should be—a simple acceptance that even though I didn't know what I was doing, it was the right thing to do. That motel room floor felt like the only place I could possibly be.

Mary Ann said, "Ya know? Really, we don't get to do anything again. Even showin' up to work every day, we don't get to do again. Sure, some stuff's the same, but really, every day is new. We only get one chance to do something right now, and it'll stay that way forever."

"You're babbling," Cindy said, as she rolled over. "But you're probably right."

"Don't worry, ladies. Carpe diem, that's Latin for 'seize the day,' and you've done a great job doing it." My day had begun with a trip to the emergency room. I was afraid that when I closed my eyes, I wouldn't be able to get the vision of the bloodied woman's face out of my mind. But I just fell asleep.

Eight hours passed in a blink. Waking before the girls, I gave each a tap to say goodbye and thanks. Maybe I could have stayed with them for another day or two, but I didn't want to horn in on their vacation. Once outside, I inhaled the soft humidity of a day that would never come again.

16

Tropical Claustrophobia

	APRIL					
						1
2	3	4	5	6	7	8
9	10	11	12	13	14	15
16	17	18	19	20	21	22
23	24	25	26	27	28	29
30						

Key West is the largest dead end in the world and is the southernmost point of the continental US. As I stood in the morning light, I thought about the day I'd left Seattle, talking at the kitchen table with my mother when she asked me where I was going. "South." My entire plan consisted of that one word. In its immense vagueness, I thought *south* would never run out. Now it had.

Finding an obscure palm grove, I hid my pack in a spot where I'd be able to sleep that night and then spent the rest of the day walking. This was nothing like the trudge across Panama City, though. It was more of a light-footed saunter.

Downtown Key West reminded me of the architecture in the French Quarter of New Orleans: streets barely wide enough for two-way traffic, wrought-iron railed balconies hung over broad sidewalks, and none of the immediate buildings rising over two stories. But that's where the similarities ended. New Orleans seemed hung over. Key West buzzed with a compression of people and a hundred small shops; the island felt almost big enough to hold itself.

The most noticeable group of people were wide-eyed tourists adorned in shiny clothes and poking their heads into bodegas. I walked by numerous bars, but I when peered in the windows, I saw only men—maybe the women hadn't started drinking yet. Then I started to notice groups of lithe men walking in short shorts with pastel shirts knotted to show their belly buttons, and I figured it out. The rest of the people blended into the island, regular working folks who seemed to revel in the quirkiness of their town.

Duval Street, the tourist hub, rang with activity. Pizza joints squatted next to pricey boutiques, and every business seemed no larger than a living room. Throngs of people strolled through thick aromas wafting from candle shops, bars, Cuban delicatessens, and bevies of men wearing too much cologne. Cool air seeped from art galleries with glistening doors, and through their windows I could see sculptures of marble and bronze. Plenty of shops sold tacky T-shirts, costume jewelry, gum, and sunscreen.

For lunch I walked up to a window that sold pizza by the slice. Even though a slice cost only a couple of bucks, I had to think twice. My money had worn down to a dog-eared twenty, a five, three ones, and some change. I was plenty hungry, but my pack was on the other end of the island with only warm cheese and stale rolls. I splurged.

While I sat on a bench eating my slice, I wondered how anyone could ever afford to vacation here, in posh hotels, wearing designer clothes, and eating in restaurants—my imagination couldn't stretch that far.

By early evening I found myself sitting in Sloppy Joe's Bar. Ernest Hemingway, who called Sloppy Joe's his home away from home, even used it as the setting for his story "A Clean, Well-Lighted Place." As subtle reminders of its literary pedigree, the owners covered every flat surface with pictures of Hemingway: Hemingway on the walls, on the tables, behind the bar, near and far. I half expected to see portraits of him on the floor, looking up dresses. I silently toasted him—that seemed like a good enough excuse for a drink.

But when a person is alone, toasting invites specters. That night's ghosts came and reminded me of my utter singleness, disconnected from every soul on the island—disconnected from every soul for thousands of miles. I'd known I would feel this way sometimes, but the feeling was becoming more frequent. I'd catch myself looking for a familiar face but never find one, so I'd look at my hands, checking my palms for familiar creases.

After wandering until midnight, I decided Key West would become my new home.

I needed another treat, a pick-me-up from my loneliness,

and ordered a spicy beef sandwich from a Cuban deli. I sat and ate at a nearby picnic table so I could still smell the deli's roasting beef, for free.

"Hi," a guy about my age said as he walked up in khaki pants and a button-down short-sleeved shirt. He sat on the tabletop, placing his feet on the bench. Skinny and with every hair in place, he asked, "Where you from?" Then he looked me up and down.

"Seattle. Just got here last night." I took another bite of the sandwich.

He slid closer. "How'd someone like you get here?"

"Hitchhiked."

"From Seattle? Are you crazy?"

"Mostly not."

"Hitchhikers don't make it to Key West," he said with authority. "The cops are all over them, since there's only one road in." He tipped his head and looked into the black sky. "But when you're leaving, they won't hassle you." He peered at me with a detective's intensity. "How'd you get down the highway?"

"A lucky ride." I couldn't tell where this guy was trying to take the conversation.

"I've been here about three months," he said, but I noted his skin was pasty white.

He asked if I liked my sandwich, and I held up what little remained. He said he'd eaten there often and started listing his favorite items. We talked about food, the town, weather. This struck me as an unusual amount of chitchat.

"I've got a friend with a nice house that has an extra

bed." He glanced down at the ground and then back at me. "You need a place to stay tonight?"

That one caught me mid-bite. This had been another long day and I was exhausted, especially now that the sandwich had started settling in my stomach and the drinks were wearing off. Some more chewing gave me a chance to think. "Two beds?"

"Well, yeah ...of course." I couldn't tell if he felt insulted, disappointed, or neutral.

"Yeah, a place to sleep would be nice."

After a short walk we stepped up to a large white house with a stained-glass front door that looked like cockatoo feathers of red, orange, and yellow. Blue Spanish tiles led to a sunken living room with potted palms that reached two stories before touching the ceiling. On the first floor, the rooms were separated by arched passageways covered in mauve stucco.

"Jack just bought this place and had it remodeled. He's always talking about how he's become accustomed to the splendid."

"Is he here?"

"No. Thank goodness." The boy shook his head. "He's on a business trip to New York."

Now I felt uncomfortable, since this guy didn't seem close to the owner. We walked up a white curved staircase and entered a room with two beds.

Half-open bamboo blinds took up one wall and let in long slits of dim light. Without turning on a lamp, my host said, "That's your bed," pointing to the right. As I walked across the room, stripes of light and dark shadows scrolled over me.

As he climbed into his bed, I heard, "You didn't have to wake me up. Damn it!" Sounded like a man.

The room suddenly seemed smaller. Before getting into bed, I ran my hands across the top cover, checking for an occupant. Finding none, I had to decide if I was going to stay or leave. I stood for a moment, feeling heavy. I climbed in and watched the ceiling fan swirl in languid rotations.

For a while the original occupant of the other bed grunted and yanked blankets around. Once he settled, the two began to talk. The one who brought me there spoke up and sing-songed, "I know, I know, who stole, who stole, Jack's coke."

"That was worth ten grand," came the flat reply. "Are you going to tell him?"

"No, he'd have them killed, and they're friends of mine."

Great. *Now I'm about to fall asleep in some violent rich guy's house, apparently a drug dealer, and he didn't invite me. Not to mention the guys in the other bed.* I didn't feel like listening to grunting and moaning all night and thought about leaving. But that would mean getting up and walking all the way to my pack. All it took was the fan's breeze to hold me down.

"Do you love me?" asked the one who brought me there.

"Hell no! I barely even know you."

The lovelorn one then started whining for sex. The answer was definite. "Look, I've been used three times today. I've got to save myself for dates tomorrow."

"You may be used." Sheets rustled. "But you're not used up."

"For tonight, I am," the prostitute said. Then, changing his tune, he asked across the room, "You want to join us?"

"No, thanks. That's okay." As I spoke, my eyes stayed closed. In the morning, I walked by more rooms, with more beds, with more guys—Jack's harem. Apparently my night there had been a recruitment effort.

I left, hungry only for breakfast.

17

Shorty

	APRIL					
						1
2	3	4	5	6	7	8
9	10	11	12	13	14	15
16	17	18	19	20	21	22
23	24	25	26	27	28	29
30						

Stepping out of Jack's harem, I pulled out a harp and started blowing a staccato rhythm, echoing my brisk pace. The streets weren't awake yet, and the notes clipped through my thoughts as I wondered if staying in Key West was such a good idea.

After several blocks I came across a guy leaning against a fire hydrant. I guessed him to be about seventeen. "Hi, don't suppose you know where there's a grocery store?"

"Nope, just got here," he said.

"Yeah, me too."

We started talking and he called himself Shorty, a

fitting name; he and the fireplug looked like they could have come from the same mother. He smelled boozy, and his small deep-set eyes peered from a round face splattered with pale pock marks. His head was topped with a rough buzz cut.

"I had long hair," he said, rubbing a hand over his scalp while wincing. "It was cool, but I needed to cut it. Cut it myself this morning." He stared silently at nothing and seemed to be looking for some response.

I could tell this was transitioning into a situation where I'd become the outlet for a pent-up need to talk, like so many times on this trip. I had left hoping to learn more about people, and about more people, so I took on my role as a confidant. I'd come to believe that the one contribution I'd been making was giving people the rare opportunity to open up and know that no matter what they said, there'd be no repercussions: secrets told to a ghost are forever safe. At times, it even seemed like they were seeking absolution and viewed me as their indigent priest. "Why are you here?"

"Well," he said, looking down and kicking at the ground. "I'm from Oklahoma, and a guy back home started messin' with me. Messin' with my head. And the asshole wouldn't quit. He started screwin' with me in front of other people. Tryin' to act like some big fuck.

"Then he started messin' with my car." Shorty stopped kicking and stared at me. He shook his head like a principal scolding a student who had done something unbelievably stupid. "So about a week ago I knocked on his door." He was talking to his frayed tennis shoes. "And when he answered, I blasted him twice with my three-fifty-seven. After he hit the floor, I got him once more in the face." Shorty glanced at me and then looked up to the clouds while his words echoed in our heads.

My chest thumped, but I didn't react. He began to fidget, and I suspected this was the first time he'd heard himself say those words.

"So I've been runnin'." He moved to walk away, but before leaving, he said, "It's been worth it, so far."

Later that morning I walked to the beach and sat under a palm. Not knowing where my mind would go, I ended up replaying my conversation with Shorty. We both knew he'd get caught. I pulled out my journal to scratch down some entries, and realized we don't write our histories in pencil.

18

Dead Man's Float

	APRIL					
						1
2	3	4	5	6	7	8
9	10	11	12	13	**14**	15
16	17	18	19	20	21	22
23	24	25	26	27	28	29
30						

Spectacular, yet intimate, the one public beach I found was ringed with palm trees and plush with silky white sand. Standing chest deep in the gulf one windless afternoon, I had the entire beach to myself. I watched glassy waves roll on a indolent sea, and I imagined the ocean as a mirror where the sun could watch itself. I let my knees buckle and slipped below the surface, face down. My limp arms and legs hung under my hunched back that bobbed dutifully to the surface—the dead man's float. Floating in this position took no effort and breathing was easy, since I only had to tip my head up for air. I'd learned this several years earlier as a survival technique while training to be a lifeguard.

My mind quieted. After lifting my head just enough to draw in a slow breath, I dropped my face back into the water, releasing any will over my body. Repeating this technique took me deeper into nothing. There were no pressure points on my body, and I continued the slow breathing until I didn't feel my arms or legs, didn't see anything, didn't think. After several minutes, I stood up and wondered if I'd just experienced the sensation of death. Many times I'd imagined death as being like my self-awareness before I'd been born. Each time led to a void where even black didn't exist. That grew to become my definition of nothing, and it satisfied my need to understand death. Heaven didn't make sense, and hell was little more than a nun's knuckle-smacking ruler. Death existed as nothing: nothing to fear, nothing to miss. Nil.

I swam a few strokes toward shore and then stood up to shake off my hair. After the past several weeks in the sun, my hair had bleached almost white and the beginning of a deep tan covered me. I turned back to the sea and saw something riding the low waves.

A small, transparent pink sail appeared on the surface attached to a jellyfish as wide as a drink coaster. In the Pacific Northwest, I'd seen hoards of jellyfish similar to this lying on the beach at low tide, but they were blue. Since they were harmless, I'd picked up many of them for close examination and to toss at my sister. When the tide came back in, hundreds, maybe thousands, would float away.

But this one drifted alone. Its pink sail darkened as it extended from the jellyfish until along the outer edge it became opaque, a sharp line of neon pink against the

STEVE THEME

soft-blue sea. To get a closer look, I waded out to where the water came up to my chin. Royal-blue tentacles dangled from the pink body and undulated with a fluid ease.

I reached out to run my finger along the pink sail and trace its iridescent outline. The jellyfish bobbed like a bathtub toy. I reached for it again, but this time a wave raised the delicate body, pushing it up around my hand.

Slam! Pain ricocheted between my fingers as if they'd been hit by lightning. The alien blue tentacles clung to my knuckles, so I thrust out my free hand to scrape them off.

Slam! Now both hands roiled with pain. I thrashed my hands through the water to remove the tentacles, but the damage had been done and I couldn't shake the fire.

Now a bolt of panic hit—I realized I'd just received dozens of injections from a man-of-war, one of the sea's most poisonous creatures. *Fuck, I'm stupid.*

I gasped, and in the process sucked in saltwater. Coughing it out sent the rasp of brine into my sinuses.

The cough emptied my lungs and I wanted more air, needed more air. My sinuses and throat burned. I instantly wanted to get rid of the salty sting by inhaling, but my lips were even with the waves and breathing would only suck in more of the harsh sea, which would begin the uncontrollable coughing cycle that would fill my lungs with water.

Stay calm. Stay calm. Don't inhale yet. Just get to shore. Stay calm. While suppressing the impulse to gag, I thrust my burning hands into the water as paddles and then kicked and lurched toward shore while sipping air.

Once I got waist deep, I stood coughing convulsively, shaking my hands, trying again to sling out the pain.

When I made it to the beach, I dropped and sat in the sand, flopped my limp hands into my lap, and waited for the fire to extinguish. Long, thin welts showed where the tentacles had stung me. After a minute I could feel my wrists heating up, ringing to a hot numb sensation, but the welts were only on my hands. I thought there must be a few stingers in my wrists that I couldn't see. *Smooth move, Einstein. What kind of nimrod pets a poisonous jellyfish?*

I searched my memory for what I knew about man-of-war stings. From training I remembered the effects could range from very painful to fatal. All I knew for sure was that the tentacles had lodged tiny barbs in my hands. Soon my lower forearms started tingling, which led to sharp burning and finally a hot numbness.

The poison was traveling up my arms. Both arms progressed at the same rate. I figured in about ten minutes the poison would reach my chest, meeting at my heart.

I need to do something. Right now.

No one was around, but there was a phone booth down the road. Balancing the desire to run but trying to keep my heart from racing, I walked with a steady purpose. The 911 system didn't exist in Key West in 1978, and at the booth the phonebook had been ripped out, leaving only scraps of yellow paper on the floor, so I dialed zero. At least I could ask an operator for a number to a poison control center.

"This is the operator. How may I help you?"

"Yeah, hi," I said in my best calm voice. "Can you give me the number to poison control?"

"Where are you, sir?"

"In Key West," I said, hoping she understood that I had an issue, without going into details.

"Oh, it's so nice there," she began

Hurry up! No time to gab.

"Here it is," she said with crisp efficiency. She understood my urgency, and I was grateful.

Searching through my pockets with jittery hands, I found a nickel and a penny, not enough to make a call. "I don't actually have any money with me." Time to plead. "I was just swimming and got stung by a poisonous jellyfish. I need to get some advice, quick."

"Okay, I'll put you through. Stay on the line."

Although I was scared, I felt a calming presence, the same calm that had assured me Harvey Pinkerton wouldn't pull the trigger while he held the gun to my head. My panic quieted, slowing my heart.

I had to tell the operator, just in case she became the last person I'd ever speak to. "It started in my fingers, and now it's in my forearms." I hesitated, not wanting to hear my next words. "The poison is moving toward my chest."

"I'll stay on the line with you."

I heard ringing and a recorded voice click on to tell me the attending nurse was busy. They'd get with me as soon as possible, the answering machine assured.

"It's in my elbows now. They're both burning."

"I hope you don't die."

"Me too." This struck me as the type of dialogue from a cheesy TV sitcom. But no one was laughing.

In the following silence, with the poison advancing, I lost any semblance of the calming presence. My breathing became shallow and fast. It dawned on me that I could actually die in a dirty phone booth. *Where's my ID?* I'd left my wallet in my pack, hidden in the stand of palms that was blocks away. *If I die, no one'll know who I am. I'll be a John Doe.* The pain and doubt I'd inflict on my family will live in them for decades. The worst scenario I could think of was becoming a reality; I was dying anonymously. *Oh shit, this is serious, and there's nothing I can do.* Poison continued pushing the pain steadily up my arms. The Plexiglas surrounding me was cracked and yellowed, making the world look out of focus.

I wanted to live. My heart sped up. Rather than my past flashing before me, the future played: friends, graduating college, laughing, crying, success and failure, marriage, kids. I could practically see them, feel the touch of a wife I had yet to meet.

Life meant everything, to everyone, everywhere.

My recent thoughts of death being a void meant nothing. No comfort came from my intellectualizing. An intrinsic desire strained toward life. The force was overpowering and undeniable.

At last, the nurse picked up and I told her what had happened.

"I don't think it'll be fatal."

Closing my eyes, I let out a sigh.

"Unless it builds to anaphylactic shock."

I opened them.

"That's unlikely, though," she said, "or you'd already be unconscious. How long ago did this happen?"

"About five minutes."

"Umm...you're safe." She gave me warning signs to watch for. "You should put steak tenderizer on your hands."

"Steak tenderizer? Are you sure?" *This just keeps getting more weird.*

"That's about all you can do, sir. It neutralizes the venom."

I drew a blank.

"Do you have any steak tenderizer with you?"

"No, none." Up to that point, my need for steak tenderizer hadn't been pressing. "I was swimming."

"You might want to try a restaurant."

My chest loosened until I could inhale normal breaths, but I couldn't help feeling she was shooing me off the phone with her steak tenderizer remedy. I thanked her as my arms burned.

"Hello? Operator?"

"Yes."

"Thanks for putting my call through, especially for free. You helped a ton."

"Sounds like you're going to be okay. I bet you'll be fine by dinner." Her words provided more comfort than the nurse's.

The pain grew. My skin felt both numb and burning, getting more intense as it penetrated my biceps.

Relieved, a little, I struck out to find a friendly restaurant. After a few minutes, the first restaurant I came across said Steakhouse—an interesting coincidence. The place looked nice, not somewhere they'd appreciate a soggy, shirtless, teenager wandering between patrons. To improve my chances that they'd help me, I went to the kitchen door in back, which was where the tenderizer would be anyway. The alley behind the place smelled like burned French fries, and smears of black grease streaked the concrete. Hearing voices and the hum of exhaust fans, I pounded on the steel door.

The door swung open. A heavy man wearing a white apron with pink stains looked at me. "What?"

I explained what had happened, as briefly as I could, and then asked for some tenderizer.

"You want it for what?"

I explained again.

"No, we're not going to do that." The door shut with a thud.

Even though my arms still burned, I could feel the symptoms subsiding. Down the street, I didn't see any place that looked like it would carry steak tenderizer. So instead of continuing my search, I walked back to the beach and sat in the shade while the pain quieted.

What didn't quiet were my thoughts about a life force. Only moments before I was stung I had death figured out and was at peace with its nothingness. But with the real possibility of dying placed before me, all I wanted to do was survive. What well did this universal desire spring from? I sat, watching sand fleas hop onto my legs and pelicans fly above the water.

19
Mallory Square Bongo Boy

	APRIL					
						1
2	3	4	5	6	7	8
9	10	11	12	13	14	15
16	17	18	19	20	21	22
23	24	25	26	27	28	29
30						

Every evening in Key West herds of people migrated down Duvall Street to the west end of town. It took a few days, but I followed the flow. Crowds were congregating in Mallory Square, a concrete slab where anybody could do anything—and did.

As I approached the pandemonium, a calypso band pounded steel drums in a pelvic-thrusting beat and a girl in an orange peasant dress cartwheeled across the entrance: orange dress—white panties—orange dress—white panties—orange dress.

I made a circuit around the plaza, which was a little larger than a football field. One of the long sides was supported on pilings and extended beyond the shore into the Gulf of Mexico. The other long side faced town. Waist-high concrete planter boxes that held large ferns were spread in no particular orientation. In several places the ferns doubled as leafy curtains, providing sporadic intimate spaces.

Once in the thick, I saw vaudevillians performing slapstick routines, fire blowers, and self-proclaimed seers using tarot cards to unveil the future. A harlequin dressed in a black-and-white-checkered bodysuit wore a pointed bell-topped hat and held a wand tipped with a creepy little harlequin head wearing the same pointed hat. Pottery hawkers sold glazed pipes, bongs, turquoise jewelry, and cheap sunglasses; members of a frayed folk band cradled guitars, dobros, mandolins, and a miniature accordion; tin cans, open instrument cases, and upturned hats dotted the concrete to catch dollars and change. A street preacher chastised the wicked and hollered for repentance, while next to him a mime appeared to be plucking a chicken. Cinnamon incense alternated with the scents of warm salt air and pot. A raver shouted at demons only he could see. Street magicians executed flawless illusions; a couple dressed in purple robes deftly tapped mystical tunes on dulcimers; a belly dancer stood on a small mat scattered with cash. Tourists wandered, some paunchy in plaid shorts and others lanky in sheer dresses and holding crystal wine glasses. Dogs roamed.

But all of this was only half the show; maybe less than half. The real show, the force that drew the people, was the sun. At sunset, the endless sea reflected crimson clouds, and once the sun rested on the oceanic horizon, it became a blazing portal leading to infinity. On cue, just before the last slice of sun dipped into the sea, the calypso band sped to a frenzy, and a number of people kicked off their shoes and ran wildly through the crowd. At top speed they—and I—hit the end of the square and flung themselves into the air, landing in the water below.

Once back on the dock, I laid a bandana on the ground, seeded it with a few quarters, and then pulled out a harp and started blowing—my livelihood as a busker began.

The harmonica isn't intended to be played continuously. It's an instrument used for punch, and after several nights my two-hour solos were turning my lips into old fisherman's hands. I needed a partner.

The guy who sold pizza slices through the window on Duvall Street also played guitar at the square. We started talking and teamed up. He came from Canada so we caterwauled Neil Young tunes: "The Needle and the Damage Done," "Old Man," "Heart of Gold," and others. For a few songs as we got deeper into the verses we'd start winging the lyrics, hum-mumbling. When we ran out of improv lyrics, we'd play blues and even some Beatles' songs.

Most nights brought in about twenty bucks, and we'd split it half and half. Sometimes the conditions were just right, and we'd get a crowd rocking. On a good night, we could make fifty. Playing kept me from stealing food.

On nights when the Preacher followed us, we'd bring in almost nothing. We called him that because he mostly talked to the ground but occasionally would snap his head up, stare at a person, and start yelling a hellfire sermon. After about five seconds, his head would drop back down. He wrapped himself in a black blanket that looked like a monk's robe. No matter how hot the night, he stayed cloaked as he roamed. On those few nights when he attached himself to our act, he wouldn't face us but stood as if we were a trio. We'd relocate, but it wouldn't take long for the Preacher to again make us the three amigos—a baritone, a tenor, and a guy screaming threats through his spit.

One night after the square fell quiet, I noticed the Banana Bread Man relaxing on a bench. The dusk hid any wrinkles on his black skin, but I guessed him to be about fifty. Music from bars mixed in the creamy air.

The Banana Bread Man had been at Mallory Square longer than anyone could remember. He carried thick slices of pudding-rich banana bread on a platter that hung from a strap wrapped around the back of his neck, like a peanut vendor at a baseball game. He'd shout, "Git yo banana bread!" Then, in an almost irritated tone, "Don' blame me when it's gone." Every night the Banana Bread Man sold out, and when his last platter emptied, he'd walk to his yellow Caddy parked just outside the square, pockets bulging with rumpled cash.

"Nice night," I said as he propped his feet on a cardboard box he used to store his bread. I figured he'd recognize me because he stopped to listen one night while I played some blues.

"Well, hello," he said while putting away his cash.

"You mind if I ask how long you've been selling banana bread?"

He rocked back. "Oh, 'bout five years now, off and

STEVE THEME

on. It's a pretty good livin'." He patted his pockets and pulled out a pint of sloe gin.

I asked what he'd done before selling banana bread.

"I was a train cook. Traveled across America—Chicago, St. Louie, L.A., the Big Apple. You name it, I been there. Good money, but it only took a couple years and I started gettin' lonely. You know, always travelin' and such."

"Yeah. I know the feeling. I've been traveling some myself." I sat down next to him. "Nothing like a couple years, but I've hardly seen a single person two days in a row—Jesus, even two hours in a row." I faced him. "That loneliness has been creeping in."

"So, when you playin' the blues, you mean it? You feel it?"

"Plenty."

"Well, don't worry. The blues is just a good man feelin' bad." He rubbed a hand along the top of his thigh as if massaging a sore muscle. "It'll pass. But I hear ya. I finally took a job cookin' in a diner. Felt I needed to slow down, plant some roots, and I got to know some fellas. We'd have a hoot in the ol' days, that's for sure. Cattin' around clubs. Walkin' up to women. Makin' introductions. Dancin'. Maybe a scuffle here an' there."

Then, with no hint of regret, "But I'm a married man now. She's from heav'n above. Been twenty-five years, and them roamin' days is long gone." Before we parted, he clapped his hands together and pointed a quick finger at me. "But I tell you what, you ain't lived till you been a black man on a Saturday night." I suspected he was right.

Several days later while I was playing in the square, I looked to the setting sun and was overcome by a memory. I was about thirteen years old at my parents' house and lying on the family room floor, ducking under a cloud cover of cigarette and pipe smoke, watching the TV news program *60 Minutes*. The segment was about Key West, and they showed a young guy playing bongos at Mallory Square as the sun set behind him. He became an energetic silhouette that looked to be emitting rays of sunlight. I remembered thinking I wanted to do that, feeling a pull toward the adventurous life I imagined he lived—he wasn't lying on his parents' floor watching TV. While I continued to play my harp, a clap of realization hit that I'd become that *60 Minutes* bongo boy. For the first time on the trip, I felt concrete accomplishment.

20
Attempting Normal

I'd been in Key West about two weeks and had spent my nights sleeping in a stand of palms at the back of a vacant lot. I could lie down in overgrown grasses without being seen, something like camping in a wilderness the size of a basketball court. Unfortunately, my roommates were mosquitoes and ants.

A nearby beach had restrooms and an outdoor shower with a steady stream of people pouring under it. Between spending time in the Gulf of Mexico and showering, I was constantly clean—I even washed my clothes under the shower, generally while still wearing them.

Each night I remembered the downpour that had

flooded my Gilligan's Island hideaway on Florida's Atlantic coast. But now if a storm hit, I didn't have enough money for a motel, so I decided to take a stab at living like a normal American—getting a job and renting a room.

I asked around at some restaurants to see if they needed a dishwasher or other help. After several days of rejections, I walked into yet one more restaurant but saw nothing more than a large empty room. Some hammering came from the kitchen, so I walked back. The building was under renovation, and I wound up as a part-time carpenter's helper. I'd pounded nails on a framing crew before and had used plenty of power tools, so the work wasn't foreign. The carpenter and I built hangar doors that raised, opening the dining room to the sidewalk, and we installed huge windows in the roof that could be cranked open. I made molding, helped install a new mahogany bar with brass railings, and repaired the hardwood floor.

My fun meter hit zero when the carpenter told me to paint the interior of a walk-in freezer. The freezer needed aluminum paint, a silver liquid made of skunk grease and sulfur pulp waste. Even with the freezer door open, the combination of no ventilation, the heat, the humidity, and the aroma caused me to nearly vomit. I don't think puke would have made the smell any worse. When I could feel the acid creeping up my throat, I'd dash out to settle my stomach and clear my head and then march back in.

During my days walking around town I'd noticed a house with a sign: ROOMS FOR RENT. The sign was made of worn plywood with black hand-painted letters, and it hung from a rain gutter. Beneath the sign was a sprawling porch. An old Cuban woman sat squat and brown in a wicker chair next to the front door.

"Do you have any rooms available?"

She silently eyed me. The longer she stared, the scruffier I felt. I gave her my best I'm-not-going-to-stab-you-in-the-middle-of-the-night look. It worked.

"You pay cash each week, seventy-five dollars on Sunday," she said while leading me down a skinny corridor. It had once been a wide hallway, but now yellowed newspapers stacked almost to the ceiling narrowed the passage, doubling as cockroach skyscrapers.

"There's the bathroom," she said, pointing down another narrowed hall. "No friends spend the night or you leave."

My room was on the first floor, but rent didn't include a window. The room had a twin bed with sheets as yellowed as the newspapers, a brown dresser, a light bulb dangling from the ceiling, four beige walls, and a door.

As long as I was earning $3.55 an hour, the room was all I could afford and still save some money to thumb back to Seattle. At least I didn't need to worry about downpours, and the cockroaches were on par with the mosquitos and ants outside. Plus there was a bathroom down the hall, rather than down the street.

On my first night, I noticed gaps between the walls of my room and the ceiling, which let light—along with a woman's voice—leak down from the room above.

"I know you're there."

Is she talking to me?

"I know you're there. Why don't you stop? I said stop goddamn it!" She started sobbing. "Stop spraying at me! Stop spraying!" She cried softly, for a moment.

"You'll never get me! Never! Why do you come to scare an old woman?"

And come they did, every night, from behind the walls and up from the floor to steal her clothes, money, or soul. I thought about complaining to the Cuban woman, who spent her days sitting in endless silence staring straight ahead. But I didn't think complaining would do any good; it might have just pushed a mentally ill person onto the street. During my stay, I never saw anyone in the house, not even the woman upstairs. I never heard the toilet flush, never heard a door open or close, never heard a conversation. After a while I felt like the only ones living there were me and a tortured ghost.

Every night I listened as the woman's inconsolable fears rained down through the ceiling. She pounded on the bed and walls and stomped on the floor to keep down the spraying demons. She became more frantic as the hours stretched on. At times I felt acclimated to it, and at times I almost cried with her. On one night when it sounded like she might be hurting herself, I wanted to go up to check if she was okay but realized even knocking on her door might send her through the roof—or more likely lunging at me. I thought about walking upstairs during the daylight and talking with her, but I had no idea what I'd say and was afraid of what I might find. I felt impotent.

One night while listening to her, not knowing what to do, and having thought about the situation for a week, I tried my first attempt at a last resort—prayer.

The morning I'd spent in the Mojave, I'd looked up and said thank you for the desert's beauty and for still being alive. But I wasn't sure if that counted as a prayer since I didn't ask for anything; I assumed you were supposed to ask for things. Now, I wanted to start by saying, "To whom it may concern." That felt appropriate. Instead, I started with, "God, can you help this woman?" My words were little more than whispers. "If you can let her know you're with her—if you are—that might help."

Her shrieking grew louder.

While god ignored us, I felt like screaming, *Are you fucking deaf?* But instead I lay back on my bed, numb. I was a fool for thinking anything would come from a prayer, but I was also strangely proud that I'd opened myself to try something new, even if it was pointless. Most experiments end in failure.

As I lay on the bed my body went slack. I closed my eyes and was free from my obsession about the woman, or god, or anything.

THE HOUSE DIDN'T HAVE A kitchen, so I made the dresser into my pantry. On the top, I placed perishables: avocados, bananas, bread, so I could see how they were aging. Cans stayed in a drawer. I didn't care much if I ate the food warm or cold, which was good, since I had no way to heat or cool anything. My knife became a can opener, a spatula, a zester, a slicer, and a scoop. I also had a spoon and fork. Although my favorite meal was still peanut butter and cheese sandwiches, I branched out to kippered herring, hominy, matzo balls, and salads made from canned spinach mixed with packets of mayonnaise. Some concoctions I ate with gusto; others, not so much.

The house had a shared shower, but it was dank and scary. Every day after work I'd take a swim. No matter how dirty the day, the sea always held enough water to clean me.

One day after swimming, I was standing at a street corner while next to me a young woman stood hugging a large bag of groceries with one arm and a watermelon in the crook of her other arm. When she pushed the bottom of the bag up, the melon began to fall. She gasped. I jerked and caught the melon before it hit the sidewalk.

With my hands cupped under the wayward fruit, I said, "I guess it was trying to escape."

Her face broke into a wide smile, and she gave a quick roll of her eyes. "Yeah, I was getting the feeling it didn't like me." She blushed. She was older than I was, maybe in her mid-twenties, and petite. Long brown hair flowed down her back, and she was golden tan. She wore blue-jean cut-offs and a bikini top.

I wasn't wearing a shirt, and my blond hair, still wet with saltwater, hung down in ringlets to my shoulders. Our eyes met, and I lost any ability I might have had to make a clever comment. We stood in silence. After a moment the silence tilted toward awkward.

"You saved my day," she said through a half-nervous laugh.

"At the least I saved your watermelon's day." My cheeks tingled. "You want a hand carrying this?"

"Oh no, that's okay. I'm just heading down this way."

"That's the way I'm going." I wasn't going anywhere.

She paused a moment, glanced around, as if looking for an answer. "Sure, that'd be nice." We started walking.

From her tan I suspected she lived in Key West, but asked anyway. "So, what are you doing in the Keys?"

"Diving."

"Diving?"

"Yep, I work at a dive shop in Daytona Beach but the water here is soooo much better."

"I swim every day but try to stay on top." I glanced at my hands and remembered the tentacle welts.

"Have you ever tried scuba?"

"No, but I've watched a lot of Jacques Cousteau specials. So, you know, I'm pretty much an expert."

"No doubt." Her voice lilted, playing the next question as a melody. "And so what are you doing here?"

What do I say? Telling her my main goal was to avoid sleeping in the bushes would make me sound like a deranged indigent. Saying I was on a trek to expand my horizons would've sounded grandiose. Worse yet, telling her I might be running away from a crappy situation would've made me a loser unable to cope with his own life. "I'm just on a trip."

"A trip?"

"Yeah, kind of." I felt lost. So while we walked, I just gave up and told her the truth. I shared that most of the time I felt confused, not knowing what I was doing or what I'd do once I was done doing this. The only thing I was sure of was that, for now, I needed to explore.

"You're more mature than most nineteen-year-olds," Sophie said. She brushed her hair from her face as she looked at me. "I'd never have the courage to just leave like that, especially hitchhiking, even if I was a man."

"I don't know about courage...maybe I'm just running away."

"You'll figure it out."

We held our gaze for longer than a moment; her eyes were an eternity of blue.

When we walked past my boarding house I told her that's where I lived. "See that lady sitting on the porch?" Sophie nodded. "I think she's a mannequin. Half the time I don't think she's even breathing."

"The place looks creepy."

"It is." I almost told her about the frantic woman and that I'd tried praying to help her, but I was afraid that would make me sound like the crazy one.

We kept walking and reached a small motel where she and a girlfriend were staying. Sophie unlocked the door and we both stepped in. Propped against one wall were polished steel scuba tanks, hoses, black flippers, and orange buoyancy vests. I set the watermelon on the counter.

"You want to sit down?" she asked. "I've got a little time before I've got to get ready." She lowered herself into a chair next to the bed. "My friend and I are driving to Big Coppitt Key, but you might like a little air-conditioning before you go back to that haunted house."

"Definitely." I took a seat on a small orange sofa.

She talked of scrimping to save money. This trip was her one extravagance. "By next year..." She faltered, took a deep breath, and then her words rushed as if she where an excited child. "By next year I'll own my own shop. Whatta ya think?"

"I think you sound like you know where you're going and you're determined to get there."

"Oh, hell yes, I am." She leaned forward, resting her elbows on her thighs. "I know I can run a business, been doing that for five years for someone else. And I know diving. So why not? Why not shoot for that dream?"

"How's it feel?" I was envious. "I mean, to know what you want?"

"Scares the crap out of me." She sat back up and crossed her legs. "But that's part of the game, I guess. Seems unavoidable."

"I don't know if I'd have the courage to start a business. There's a lot at stake." I bent forward. "Now you're the brave one." We shared another gaze, longer than the last.

The phone rang, and it was Sophie's friend. She was on her way to the motel. When Sophie hung up, she said, "I've got to get my gear ready."

I wanted to ask her out but didn't have the money to take her anywhere. Before I could think of some way to see her again, she came to my rescue.

"You want to meet at Mallory Square tonight?"

Everything in me yelled, *Jump across the room. Kiss her neck, her cheeks, her full lips, stare into her eyes and tell her she's the most beautiful woman in the world.* "Yeah, that would be great. By the calypso band?"

She nodded and gave a smile that acknowledged we were both more than casually interested in each other. As I crossed the threshold, she reached out, placing her fingers on my forearm, letting them gently slide along until they reached my fingers. "Thanks for saving my watermelon."

"Anytime."

Heading back to the haunted house, I envisioned

Sophie's brunette hair tumbling over my tan chest while her naked arms wrapped around my back—hot breath, sweat, kindred spirits in an animal grip.

That was overly optimistic.

21

Fallout

	APRIL / MAY					
						1
2	3	4	5	6	7	8
9	10	11	12	13	14	15
16	17	18	19	20	21	22
23	24	25	26	27	28	29
30	1	2	3	4	5	6

I spent the afternoon daydreaming of what the night might bring with Sophie—lovemaking, an escape from the relentless loneliness; maybe I'd go back to Daytona with her.

A soothing sun pampered me as I strolled down the sidewalk. Passing a small shop, I noticed a belt buckle in the window. It was engraved with a sailing sloop heeled over and booming through the water. The brass glistened large and round. I stepped in to take a closer look.

When I asked about it, the owner placed the buckle on top of the glass case and then walked to the back of the store to help another customer. While she busied herself, I turned the buckle in my hands, admiring the details of the mast's rigging, the way the bow sliced the waves, like it had one blustery afternoon on the Strait of Georgia, in British Columbia, Canada. My father and I were in the cockpit of our 35-foot sailboat during a summer vacation. We were on a reach, the wind quartering from behind and pushing us across big rolling swells. Our sails bulged white against the blue sky, and we both sat with our legs locked straight, bracing against the low side of the cockpit. We leaned back and turned our heads forward to see above the high side of the hull.

"You want to take it?" my father asked. He was referring to me taking the tiller from him and steering the boat. "She has a pretty strong weather helm, so you'll have to hold on tight." A weather helm is when a sailboat reacts to all the energy moving it and makes it want to turn straight into the wind. If you're going fast, and we were, the pull is constant and hard.

"Heck, yeah." I grabbed the tiller, a polished shaft of wood that connects to a plank on the back of the boat that extends into the water, which turns, deflecting the water to do the steering. Immediately the tiller wanted to jump out of my hands and pull to the low side of the boat. "Jeeze, you weren't joking." It was all I could do to pull the tiller back to the center position and keep us going straight. I could feel the power of the wind, the sea, and the boat all working their forces as we rode up the waves and surfed down their backs. Our T-shirts rippled in the wind and the air smelled crisp, alive.

"Steve," my dad half-shouted above the wind, "these are the times you live for."

STEVE THEME

I thought of him working in an office for years and me sitting in endless classes, of mowing the lawn and him driving in traffic, of all the things that weren't sailing on a broad reach across the open sea, of all the things that weren't being together as a family, of all the things that weren't sharing a wonderful experience. I didn't say anything back to him; didn't need to. He was right and I owed him the exhilaration of that afternoon. He made it possible for me to grab the tiller and feel the power of the earth pull through my body.

I'd always wanted a sailboat someday, the same way Sophie wanted her business, maybe even more. To someday be able to hand my son the tiller, tell him he has a strong weather helm and let him feel the sea's command.

As I ran my fingers along the buckle's smooth surfaces, the owner stood with her back turned and talked with other customers. *Is she paying any attention to me?* The buckle's heft felt solid in my palm. *It's not like missing this is going to break her back.* I looked toward the back of the shop again. *I know something about sailing—a lot. I'm not some poser. I deserve this.* The owner was bending over, lifting a painting that was leaning against the wall. *I've done this before, nothing new.* My heart picked up its pace. *This'll be easy.* I took a shallow breath. *Now.*

I made it about ten yards down the sidewalk before a bony hand gripped my elbow. Turning, I saw the shop owner—a small woman with big anger. It would have been easy to break her grasp and run. But I didn't. She didn't deserve that and I didn't deserve the buckle, so I let her drag me back to the shop.

....

A SQUAD CAR ARRIVED. WITH my hands on the hood, feet spread, an officer patted me down. As his palms slid down my torso, I thought of Sophie.

While I sat in his back seat, my mind didn't race—the numbness of a dream engulfed me. I watched but didn't feel. The detachment lasted until the cop got in and we started driving to jail.

I was barefoot. I usually wore something on my feet, but that afternoon I'd felt light and springy with romantic anticipation, and flip-flops would've just weighed me down. Now my white soles pressed against the rusty floor.

The holding cell at the Monroe County jail, the southernmost jail in the continental United States, was a concrete box about twelve feet square with a continuously overflowing aluminum toilet bolted to the back wall. The two other walls were lined with concrete benches. Attached to the ceiling, behind thick wire mesh, fluorescent tubes cast a greenish-yellow tinge that exaggerated the cracks in the walls. My arms appeared jaundiced—gray veins running under yellowed skin—the same snot-yellow as the walls. Everything the light touched looked diseased.

The toilet had clearly been overflowing for hours at least, maybe days. The floor drain worked well enough to keep water from escaping into the hall but not well enough to suck down the mucus-gray puddle covering half the floor. I got on one of the benches: I sat on it, stood on it, and lay on it, trying to keep my bare feet off the floor. After several hours I had to pee. If I peed in the toilet, my urine would overflow and spread evenly across the lagoon. So I walked to the center of the cell, stood in the slippery water, and peed close to the drain.

Voices echoed down the hall, but I saw no one. I spent time replaying the mistakes of my life: ignoring people when I knew they needed help, causing car accidents, punching the wrong guy, smoking dope before work, shoplifting. *Who the hell do you think you are?* I was scared, depressed, ashamed, and locked in self-loathing.

Another hour or two passed when a guard pushed in the Preacher—the guy who sometimes stood too close when my guitarist and I played in Mallory Square. His black hair lay in mats and melded into his thick black sweater. Before placing him in the cell, the police took his blanket, revealing oily jeans and cracked boots. I envied his boots. Under those fluorescent lights, the collapsed dough of his face contrasted with his red, raw fingers. He didn't notice me but instead stood in a corner and talked to himself, letting out an occasional shout while staring at the ceiling and moving his arms as if he were climbing a ladder. Then he rotated and talked to different parts of the floor.

As a few more hours passed, the cell filled with ten guys. Everyone found common ground complaining about the slimy floor. I'd resigned myself to the guck, but some of the others shouted down the hall or peed on the walls. Luckily no one had to crap.

The Preacher continued to prattle until a drunk smashed him with a right hook to the temple, followed by a left hook. Letting out a quick whimper, the Preacher collapsed like a ragdoll, half in the water. I thought about helping him, but with his state of mind, and the others' moods, I stayed on the bench.

After another half hour, all of us were taken upstairs to the real cell blocks.

The sticky air hung hot and smelled of sweat, ass, and vomit. A guard issued me a mattress. I slung it over a shoulder and followed him. When he opened the cellblock door, he told me to find a bunk with no mattress on it. I stepped in, entering a world of forty-eight caged criminals.

The block was a wide hallway with a dozen cells along the right side. On the left side of the hall, an iron mesh ran floor to ceiling with two long horizontal slabs of concrete acting as a table and bench where inmates were supposed to eat. Behind the mesh, a corridor allowed the guards to patrol its length. Across the guard's walkway, another mesh held back prisoners housed in a similar cellblock.

All the cell doors were open. Each cell consisted of bunk beds on the left and right and a toilet bolted to the middle of the wall opposite the sliding barn doors. Walking into the only cell with an open bunk, I found a fat white guy in a grayish T-shirt, jeans around his ankles, taking a mighty shit. On the wall behind him was a life-sized mural crisp with a full palette of acrylic colors where a gaunt Satan stood wearing a loincloth, his stringy muscles running under crimson skin. One hand held a pitchfork, and the other extended out, palm up, beckoning three busty women, each dressed in a string bikini top and mini shorts. They gazed at the devil with seductive smiles, one licking her pink, shimmering lips.

"Throw some water on it!" came a holler from several cells down.

The fat guy didn't look up, just reached behind him and flushed as he sat. "Yessaday da was a skinny li'l fag in 'ere." He started laughing. "Ya could tell he'd given it up on da street, so some a da boys decided to do him in da ass. Dey took turns." A fart exploded. He looked up. "My 'pologies, but this un's soupy." He cackled loud enough so the men in other cells heard, drawing several inmates around the door.

"One of our guys went back fo' seconds an' had a seizure right in da middle of his fuck!" He roared, his face reddening. Those outside the cell bellowed with him. "Dat ol' boy started droolin' and fell right outta da bunk." My cellmate choked out a few more laughs.

I laughed with him. S*how no fear or you'll be the next kid to get his ass pounded.*

"After dat the guards took 'em both away." His voice rose. "An' you da lucky one." He laughed even harder and pointed at me. "It happen in yo bunk."

"Perfect." As I finished positioning my mattress in the rape bunk, the other men joined his laughter. But I looked strong, hadn't given it up on the street. It was obvious that getting at me would be no picnic.

The guy finished wiping his ass and took a square look at me for the first time. Assuming a more somber tone, he said, "But, man, you actually lucky dat you here."

I didn't feel lucky.

He walked toward the door and stood in the threshold, extended his arm, pointing across the mesh to the other cell block. "Dat's gladiator school. Someone gits carried out on a stretcher practically every day." The men in the doorway nodded in solemn agreement.

"So when do I get to make a phone call?" I'd seen movies; I should get a call.

One of the guys in the doorway said, "Phone privileges for uzz all was cut off yessaday, on account a da boy gettin' fucked." His gaze dropped to the floor. "They ain't told uzz when we get 'em back."

The following morning, guards passed breakfast trays through a slot in the wire mesh. I asked when I'd get to make a call.

"Don't know," the guard deadpanned. "Move on."

At night the cell doors locked electronically, four men to a cell. On my second night, I woke with a start when the intercom suddenly blared with an ad for Juicy Fruit gum. The noise woke up everyone, and I asked what was going on.

"Dey do this all da time, turn on dat fuckin' radio," the guy on the bunk below me said. No one knew why, but I thought it was to keep us awake so that during the day we'd be tired with low energy.

After a couple hours of hyperactive DJs, more ads, and rock 'n' roll, the Eagles' "Hotel California" played. All the men in the cell block lay quietly, no one snoring. Then, without prompting, everyone sang out, *"You can check out any time you'd like, but you can never leave."* Then the inmates fell back into silence as the lonely guitar solo played.

Time stood stale. My third day began, and I still hadn't been allowed to make a call or speak with anyone except inmates. I wondered when I'd get released, and my stomach churned every time I thought about it. Maybe my papers had been lost. Maybe no one in power even knew I was there. The soles of my feet and the skin between my toes had transmogrified from muddy brown to crusty black.

Each day I wandered up and down the aisle, just like the others. As I passed one of the cells, I noticed several guys listening to another as he spoke with fervor from an upper bunk.

"Come on in," the one sitting high said. "There's more room."

I stepped in.

"I've been telling these boys here the saving power of our Lord, Jesus Christ." He then pointed down to me and his eyes lit up. "You, too, can be saved." Considering the circumstances, he didn't seem the most trustworthy pitchman for salvation. "His forgiveness is absolute, and his love is unconditional."

"If you're so saved, what are you doing here?" I asked.

"I stole a car, clearly a bad decision. But I've prayed for His forgiveness." He turned his palms up and tipped his face toward the concrete ceiling, "And I'm forgiven!" This forgiveness seemed a convenience that allowed him to do whatever.

"Before landing here, I'd been going to church, almost every day. Now I love Jesus, and he's saved me!"

He reminded me of a Cheech & Chong skit where one of them says, "Before, I was all messed up on drugs. But since I found the Lord, now I'm all messed up on the Lord." Even so, this guy managed a positive attitude when the rest of us couldn't have seen one with a telescope.

"The only way to experience God's love and live the plan he has for you is to accept Jesus Christ as your

Lord and Savior," he said, sitting on his bunk with his legs dangling over the side. "Anything short of that condemns you to an eternity in the lake of fire and torment."

I pictured any door to god narrowing and then piped up a question that had been sitting in the back of my mind for years. "What about all the people born before Christ, or all those millions who never had a chance to hear about him because they were in other parts of the world?"

"They're in hell." His voice rang with clarity and conviction. His god now resembled a vindictive old man, not one with a plan of love for me.

"If God wanted them in heaven, Christ would have come at a different time or in a different place. What else could it be?"

I'd heard enough from this cookie-cutter Christian and stepped out. Inmates in the next cell were passing around a joint. I kept pacing.

On the third night a wiry brown guy—maybe he was Cuban, Honduran, Colombian; it was an international convention in there—sat next to me on the concrete bench during dinner. "You know," I said to him, "it seems only rednecks, dope dealers, and dope-dealin' rednecks are here."

"What the fuck you expec' man? This jail's the closest to the dope. Everything's smuggled through here—coke, heroin, weed." He scratched at himself. "Jus' don' get caught."

A minute or two later this man's spoon slipped from his hand and clanked on the floor. When he bent down to grab it, he suddenly jerked back up. "Man, your fuckin' feet are goin' to *fall off!*" As the guy continued eating, he'd periodically glance down at my feet and grimace.

By the fourth day, the black on my soles had grown up the sides of both feet. The discoloring worried me: was this a fungus, mold, or just scunge from the black floor? At least my feet didn't hurt.

I became despondent. I still hadn't been given the chance to make a call, so I convinced myself the police didn't even know I was locked up. Sitting hangdog—thoughts of Sophie were long gone—looking at my feet, I felt a hand settle on my shoulder, gently, in an almost fatherly fashion. It was a lanky man I knew had been convicted of smuggling three kilos of heroin and was awaiting transfer to a federal penitentiary. "Don't worry. You'll be out soon."

I nodded, but I also knew he was looking at a twenty-year sentence, and soon from his perspective didn't offer much comfort.

Later that day, a guard opened the main cell block door and shouted four names. Mine was one of them. *They know I'm here!* He led us down a hall saying, "You'll get your hearing now."

The four of us entered a small white room that was so bright, I had to squint and I couldn't figure out why they had to hyper-light the place. Maybe the police designed this blinding brightness to intimidate prisoners. The guard told us to sit on one side of a rectangular table where there were four metal seats facing one seat on the other side. After a few minutes, I realized there was nothing abnormal about the light in the room. Rather, the cellblock was in a constant state of dusk with no windows, and the only lights were on the ceiling in the aisle between the cellblocks. My eyes had adjusted to that. Eventually a man in a suit came and sat across from us.

"Where's the judge?" one of the guys asked.

"Who do you think I am?"

Great. Now this dope had pissed off the judge just before I was about to get sentenced. Did he think someone dressed in a black robe and a powdered wig would come strolling in?

The judge started at one end of the table and worked his way across, stating fines and the amount of time to serve if the fine couldn't be paid. I sat at the end, but when he reached me he broke his pattern. He asked that I stand and take several steps back from the table. *This isn't good.* I noticed him looking at my feet. He shook his head and let out a sigh.

"Sit down. Thirty days, minus time served, or one hundred twenty-four dollars."

"Can I get a phone call?"

"What do you mean?"

"I asked the guards, and they said I didn't get to make a call."

He furrowed his brow and glared at the guard. "Yeah, you can make a call."

Relief—then anxiety—I'd be calling my father.

During the short walk to the phone, I got lightheaded. I wasn't sure what I'd say, but I knew there'd be no pleasantries. My mother answered, and her voice brightened when she heard mine. I simply asked for my father. The click of another phone lifting snapped in my ears.

Shame and fear shook me. "I'm in jail."

He asked what I'd been arrested for. I told him.

"If there's a next time, you'll stay in and rot if that's what it takes."

My feet already looked rotted. I'd now suffered the worst part of my incarceration—humbling myself before my father, validating his view of me as Dopus. After thanking him, I wasn't sure the call was worth the subjugation.

Bail came via a wire a couple hours later. I crossed the courthouse lawn and checked my wallet, which had been stored. It still had the eleven dollars of life savings I'd entered with. Several days later I walked back to the shop and bought the buckle. It cost eight.

22

Infected

	MAY					
	1	2	3	4	5	6
7	8	9	10	11	12	13
14	15	16	17	18	19	20
21	22	23	24	25	26	27
28	29	30	31			

One minute out of jail and 3,500 miles from home: no friends, no food, no job, no shoes, eleven bucks. I didn't even know if I had a place to stay. Turned out, I didn't.

Since the Cuban lady on the porch hadn't seen me the day before when the weekly rent came due, she took my things from the room. She told me I needed to pay her the current week's rent or she wouldn't let me get my stuff. Rent was seventy dollars a week, but I was able to convince her to let me pay for just one day so I could take my things.

Next I headed to the beach to frantically rub my feet with sand and scrape off the encrusted grime. I soaked them in the water, wriggled my soles hard into the sandy bottom, and then sat on the beach and scrubbed sand between my toes. That night at Mallory Square I played so much that my lips started bleeding, but I earned twenty bucks.

I continued to play at Mallory Square over the next few days, which helped pull together cash for food but not enough to pay for a week's rent. Once darkness hit, I'd wander back to my overgrown stand of palms where I'd stayed my first days in Key West.

Eventually, I came across some men I'd met while I was a guest of Monroe County. Luke and Malachi were brothers from Savannah; John was an electrician from Virginia, and Jimmy Lee, the one who'd tried to explain god's love from a top bunk, said he was a bricklayer from Tallahassee.

We pooled our cash to squeeze into a single large room in another boardinghouse. The room was at the top of a long set of stairs and was furnished with a light fixture on the ceiling. The five of us stood in the room looking at the blank walls, the light, out the window. Stone-faced, we realized this was the best we could do. The police station was next door, and a parking lot full of squad cars spread out below our window.

Luke and Malachi were born a year apart but looked like twins. In their mid-twenties, their faces were mottled with blackheads, and their thin arms hung limp from slouching shoulders. With their brown greasy hair, wispy mustaches, and stained T-shirts, they could've been pin-up boys for trailer trash.

Stiffy (Malachi's nickname) broke the ice and drawled, "Las' time we tried to git this close to a cop shop was three years ago in Atlanta." He stared through the window at the police station, as if checking to make sure no one was listening. "We stold a narcotics cabinet from a 'ospital, and one of our wonderful partners foun' out. Well—he wanted the dope and knew we always kep' it with us." Stiffy turned from the window and gave us all a glance, and then he raised his voice. "We was drivin' down the road and noticed that SOB started follerin' us. Then at a stop light, he hangs his arm outta the window holdin' a gun and starts shootin'." He flinched. "We didn't expect that. Dis boy was crazy!"

"Shit Stiffy, you could duck down!" Luke shouted. "But I had to stay up an' keep drivin'." His voice implied Stiffy had planned it that way. "We needed to do somethin', and fast, 'cause I didn't know how many bullets that asshole had."

Everyone in the room nodded, agreeing fast would be good.

Luke could see he had our attention and kept talking. "I knew there was a poleese station 'bout half a mile down the road, so I told Stiffy I'd head for it. I figgurd"—Luke appeared to be the brains of the operation—"this bastard wouldn't foller us to the cops."

"Hell yes!" Stiffy interjected. Then they both were silent, bewildered.

"Anyways," Luke said, "so we come screamin' into the parkin' lot, and I slams on the brakes."

This was starting to sound suspect. It seemed too perfectly stupid.

Luke's voice quickened. "But that son of a bitch kept comin'...comin' fast! And I couldn't believe it, but he kep' shootin'." Luke extended his bony arms above his head in exasperation. "We thought, Jesus Christ! Now what? So we jumped out and ran into the station." He dropped his arms. "We knew we'd get caught but least we'd be alive."

Jimmy Lee slowed things down. "So you two had a stolen hospital narcotics cabinet, went and parked at a police station, and ran inside to the cops while some guy was shooting at you?"

"Oh yeah," Luke answered casually, like this happened every day. "Crazy, but 'xactly right. This ol' boy was waaaay too cranked on somethin'."

Stiffy pointed a righteous finger at us. "I guaran-god-damn-tee he woulda killed us." He stopped pointing. "As we was runnin' in some cops was runnin' out, and we heard more shootin'. Nobody got hit, but man I thought I was goin' to have a fuckin' heart attack!"

The rest of us shook our heads.

"The only good thang was we don't never use guns," Luke said, "so that helped with the sentencin'."

"You are some dumb sons of bitches," John let them know.

"Oh yes, we are!" Stiffy agreed.

We cracked up; the room seemed less blank.

Over the next several days Jimmy Lee began evangelizing again, this time with the story of how he'd become a heroin junkie a year before and then received salvation and a new life through Jesus. I couldn't help but discuss religion with Jimmy Lee. Our conversations occasionally made me feel uncomfortable; at times they were thought-provoking; and sometimes it seemed like I was listening to a man telling me about his talking dog—at first it sounded entertaining, but it quickly got weird.

"Addiction is a powerful thing," Jimmy Lee would frequently say. "A gift from the devil, that's all it is. I didn't have nothin' but my addiction and a junker car, and I got sick as shit of both. But with Christ, I've met people. You know, good people, who didn't want to screw me over.

"They took me in. Took care of me while I got dope sick and puked all over the place in withdrawals." His cadence slowed. "Then they got me goin' to a church next to the mission, and in a while I was back workin'."

His story of recovery was admirable, but what interested me more were the people who helped him. What sustained them to work every day with such a derelict and potentially dangerous person? I didn't have that in me.

Jimmy Lee parroted from the Bible. I was pretty sure that at times he was improvising on the passages, or at least customizing them, since many of them had men sharing a room in a boardinghouse. But, of our lot, Jimmy Lee appeared the most respectable. He sported a short haircut, wore cleaner clothes than the rest of us, and shaved every day.

One day I sat on my sleeping bag cross-legged, back propped against the wall, writing notes in my journal. Jimmy Lee was standing near the window looking at the police station.

"We are sinners!"

"No shit."

"Born with original sin." Then he shouted at me. "Born with it! I don't know why it's that way, but I know it is."

I'd always wondered why Christianity decreed that

our original (god-given?) nature is depravity that must be pried from us. Original sin seemed little more than a hot poker to herd people into a church cave. But in that boardinghouse room, we weren't experiencing any sin shortage. I asked Jimmy Lee, "You really buy into that original sin stuff?"

"I know I'm a sinner, can feel it in my very bones—even now."

WE'D TAKEN IN A COUPLE more guys to help with rent, and one hot afternoon, several of us were lying in the room. I'd folded a ratty blanket that I'd found by the side of the house under my sleeping bag as padding. Foam mattresses, dirty socks and underwear, food, and food wrappers made the floor a quilt of chaos. Smelly chaos.

We were lazy in the heat until Luke said he owned a white Cadillac with a white leather interior. "Rides like a dream," he bragged. "I made a couple good scores before comin' here and blew the cash on it."

"It doesn't ride like a dream," I told him. "It *is* a dream."

But then he walked me down the street, and there it was, with Georgia plates. The first time I rode in the Caddy, he asked if I'd like to drive. After adjusting the power seat, tilting the steering wheel up and gazing over the hood's white acreage, I took a self-satisfied breath and turned the key. The air-conditioning came on blowing sweet, cool air across my face.

As we pulled out, Luke said, "You're good. You drive this car like a white man."

His comment was intended to be racist, but I didn't

push back; nothing I could say would change him, and not many compliments had come my way lately.

The next time I took a ride, Jimmy Lee came along and Luke asked him to drive. After Jimmy Lee pulled out, Luke said, "You drive this car like a white man."

Then it dawned on me—Luke wanted others to drive the car because he'd stolen it. He was perfectly satisfied to send me, or anyone else, to jail for driving a car he'd stolen. As Jimmy Lee drove, Luke leaned back, kicking his feet up on the dash and clasping his hands behind his head.

My trip had started as a quest to seek new experiences, to broaden my horizons beyond what any university could offer—and I hoped to regain some self-respect. I'd needed a life reset that would help me live within my skin while not despising everyone else. Rather, I felt like a scientist who'd been working with a virus to find a cure but instead became infected. I simply scrounged for food and shelter and was now living with criminals. Most of the time, I was depressed as I watched the world progress around me as I slid backward into a hole.

How did I end up this way? Was I just a chronic loser? I wanted to blame this whole thing on having no money, but no amount of money could have changed how I viewed myself. Money could do a damn good job of changing how others viewed me, but others weren't my problem.

During the day I'd look for work. If I saw people working—building a porch, clearing brush, painting, anything—I'd ask if they needed a hired hand. I tried to maintain some distance from my roommates, but living with them made that hard.

Not long after we'd rented the room, Luke and Stiffy started bringing in their dope. It didn't matter what type they did as long as it made them feel different. After a week Jimmy Lee couldn't resist. He'd been saved, but not from them. A few days later, Jimmy Lee disappeared by stealing Luke's stolen car.

After we lived in the room about ten days, Stiffy scored some PCP, a livestock tranquilizer, from a pimp who called himself The Doctor and rented the room next to us with his three girls. Stiffy came into our room holding a hypodermic needle and said it was his treat. I cracked a beer to watch; car wrecks like this are too compelling to turn away from.

Stiffy played alchemist and mixed the PCP powder with drops of water and a ground-up Quaalude—a barbiturate, basically alcohol in a pill. With a match, he heated the milky liquid in a spoon, and then he sucked it into the syringe.

"My veins 'ave collapsed from shootin' up so much," he said while sinking the needle in his forearm several times, trying to find a decent vein. Once he hit pay dirt, he pushed in the plunger, and the chemicals invaded him. "It's waaaaaarm," he moaned. Not satisfied he'd injected enough, he pulled the plunger back out, sucking dark blood into the cylinder—this let his blood clean the walls of any residue before pushing it back in. When he pulled the needle out, he gazed at me, his eyes drooping closed. "Oh, man, you gotta try this. It's psychedelic but mellow. Really beautiful, man."

Luke grabbed the needle from Stiffy and pointed it at me. "Fire up, buddy."

The whole thing seemed easy: stick in, push plunger, feel mellow and beautiful. I couldn't remember the last time I'd felt mellow, let alone beautiful. Some escape wouldn't hurt, and this would be the only time I'd do it. I'd never heard of PCP being addictive. And I'd never heard of Quaaludes at all, but I figured if they were addictive, I'd have heard of them by then. I watched Stiffy with his grin and drooping shoulders. His problems were gone. He felt great. I felt terrible, but I also knew this would only make me sicker. "Thanks, but I'll pass."

Luke injected himself, and the same sense of ease flooded him.

Stiffy flopped back onto his blanket and then started giggling. "My life's a joke." His giggles morphed into hysterical laughter. "And I'm the punch line." He writhed like a worm as Luke sat motionless.

I'd seen enough and stared down at my watch. The date read May 9. It was my twentieth birthday. That took me off guard, but I felt nothing more than another tick of the second hand. I'd often felt compelled to tell people that being born isn't all that unique, let alone earned. This day confirmed for me that birthday celebrations are little more than self-indulgences for people seeking unwarranted praise. Then I did feel something— that same self-righteous disdain I'd had for what I called the pampered pets at college. But now that included everyone who celebrated birthdays. I left on this trip to get away from that sick attitude. *I can't escape. Is my whole miserable life going to be like this?*

Luke left the room, and I heard him tumble down the stairs.

STEVE THEME

I needed out. Finishing my beer, I walked down the stairs, where Luke lay splayed at the bottom with a cut on his forehead. I stepped over him.

23
Playing the Odds

"How'd you learn to play like that?" The young man's question came as a compliment.

Mallory Square's eclectic patrons were drifting off toward night activities, and I was blowing my last tune, eyeing the dollars and quarters on my bandana.

"I mean, with such feeling?" He fixed his eyes on mine. "You got right into me."

"I don't know. Just practice, I guess." My lips pulsed hot from ninety minutes of playing.

"I play the harmonica some, but nothing like you."

I let myself swell, but quietly—didn't want to appear pompous. "It's amazing how you improve when dinner depends on it."

"I've never played in front of people. That takes courage."

"No, just hunger."

"Oh, well then, if you're hungry..." He placed his index finger to his chin. "Why don't we grab some dinner?" He stood a bit taller than me and wore a stylish yellow shirt and terra-cotta-colored shorts. They draped around his slender frame like a flag in a languid breeze. His tan was impeccably smooth, and I guessed he was in his late twenties.

"Dinner?" I was wearing overalls and flip-flops, not even a shirt; I felt like a dirty fork. But my dinner plans were to sit in the boarding house with my ex-con roommates and eat spinach from a can. This guy seemed nice enough, maybe gay, but we could talk about playing the harmonica. "Some dinner wouldn't hurt. You have any place in mind?"

"How about the Green Parrot?"

I affected the accent of a British aristocrat. "Splendid choice, old chap." As far as bars went, the Green Parrot was one of my favorites. In a tourist town, it appealed to working locals. "Couldn't have selected a more appropriate establishment myself."

He gave me a high-five, introduced himself as Todd, and we set off.

At the table he told me how he'd grown up in Philadelphia but never felt like he belonged there—like he'd been dropped from a spaceship and landed in the wrong place. I could see that. Philly, or at least my impression of it, was a brash metropolis full of cabbies who called everyone Mac. Todd couldn't have been further from a Mac. He laughed easily, and we talked about music, our favorite books, the spirit of being a vagabond. He was a sculptor who sold his art in local galleries.

Sculpture is my favorite form of visual art. Paintings hang passively in two dimensions, not part of this three-dimensional world. They can be beautiful, but it's as if each holds an invisible sign saying, *Admire from a distance, and don't touch!* Sculptures live with us, viewable from infinite perspectives, casting shadows and creating textures that fill empty spaces with a bold presence.

"I've always wanted to create a sculpture. Work with my hands. Shape metal. Maybe use clay...something." I tipped back a beer from our second pitcher. "And besides, I can't draw worth a damn."

"If you want we can go take a look at my studio. It's just down the street."

When we met I'd given it a fifty-fifty chance that Todd was gay, but any homophobic tendencies I'd held before leaving Seattle had long since vanished. So many gay men had given me rides and tried to pick me up that I knew how to maintain a safe distance—how to enjoy their company while setting boundaries. So regardless of his swing, Todd was yet another interesting person I'd get to know a little. After a few more beers, I considered myself an art aficionado and was convinced I could offer lucid critiques of his pieces. This would give me an opportunity to return the compliments he'd paid me for my harmonica playing while dwelling poetically on the emotional nuances that each of his pieces evoked.

As we walked down the street, Todd peered at my pectoral muscles peaking from above the bib of my overalls.

"How'd you get such a developed chest?" The gay meter hit 80 percent, but he seemed harmless.

"From playing football. Fishing in Alaska. Things like that."

"They're beautiful," he said. The beat of silence that followed wasn't awkward—after all, we were artists. "I've never sculpted a human figure, but everybody admires Michelangelo's David."

David? Am I being compared to David? I could live with that. He clearly had a discerning eye.

We stepped into a modest single-level home. Accent walls of muted orange and yellow played off a taupe shag rug. Tall lithe sculptures, rods of twisting glazed porcelain, stood in corners. They were colored like vertical sunsets.

"Is this your house?" His pieces, although nice, didn't look like they commanded top dollar, not like bronze or marble sculptures would, and you needed a lot of dollars to own a house in Key West.

"No. This is Ronald's place." His words purred. "He's in Boston."

Time to find out for sure. "So, are you two lovers?" I felt mature saying the word lovers and for being so brash as to ask the question.

"You might say that."

"Is Ronald bi?" I wasn't sure why I asked that but felt even more cosmopolitan for using the term bi.

"Oh, yes—men and boys." He grinned at me, indicating that by boys he meant young men my age.

Now I knew what I was dealing with. "Let's see your studio." I figured Todd would be making some sort of advance fairly soon, and that's when I'd set things straight. I had this under control. The studio was a converted bedroom with cabinets, a plywood bench, and splotches of bright red and blue glazes on the linoleum floor.

Todd pulled out a joint. The joint had a wire that stuck out of the front and ran embedded through its length. This functioned as a handle. As the joint burned, there was no need to keep scrunching our fingers toward the last burning ember. Just hold the wire extension—an elegant invention. As soon as the weed set in, I knew I'd really be able to impress Todd with the depth of my artistic interpretations.

"Steve, will you take a look at these?" He pointed to half a dozen sheets of paper thumbtacked to the wall. "These are sketches of some future pieces—maybe, at least. It depends on what you think. Take your time, soak in them a bit, and I'll be right back."

Now my opinion mattered. I held the life or death of future pieces. Taking my responsibility seriously, I stood close, stepped back, walked around to view them from various angles. Pondered. Posed. Finally I turned, and there was Todd, two drinks in hand. "What are these?"

"Singapore Slings. I had them in the fridge."

The drinks were frothy pink, but like the joint with the wire, they were something new. I accepted one and felt myself becoming quite the sophisticate. The drink tasted sweeter than I liked, but it slid down smoothly while I offered my learned insights. Todd nodded patiently as I spoke.

After I'd critiqued two sketches the top of my head

began to feel numb and the sensation flowed toward my ears. "I need to sit down."

"Of course you do." But there were no seats.

I'd drunk some, smoked some, but this was like a brain bomb. My body felt like it was filled with mushy gel and I was dizzy. "What's going on, man?"

"Just a little benzo in your Sling." His face became a blurry swirl, and a hungry quaver entered his voice. "Oh, you're going to do marvelously."

"Wha…?"

He reached for my hand, and as he walked I trailed behind, an obedient pet. Fear wanted to fill me, but instead a distant vacancy kept me passive. We swayed down a dim hallway where the walls closed in from an undefined horizon. He shuttled me into the bedroom.

With a little push from him, I sat on the bed, arms falling limp. I understood where I was, but I made no effort to get up. Todd bent down and lifted my feet to swing them onto the bed. As my legs rose, my torso toppled and I stared at the ceiling.

"Don't worry." He pulled off my sandals. "These'll only get in the way."

A cotton-ball fuzz filled my vision, and waves of heat rolled across my balloon head, while my body seemed to have disappeared. I felt a sinking dread, knowing my ego had led me here, accepting his gratuitous compliments, blustering myself with self-importance. For the entire trip, I'd never forgotten that every ride, every person, and every place I slept could be dangerous. Many times I'd felt like I was standing next to a roulette table and just playing the odds.

Todd leaned over me to unclasp the straps of my overalls. Then he grabbed the frayed ends of my pant legs and gave several long tugs until I lay naked.

I could see Todd holding my overalls, and I wanted to fight, but I couldn't. Instead, I remembered a fight I'd had when I was in ninth grade. Some guy had made me angry—I was angry a lot then—so I started swinging. We were in a school hallway, and as I swung wildly, I noticed the hall had filled with kids and noise. Fists, faces, a torn collar, the rattle of a locker door—the details were all a blur, but from behind me, I heard a voice clearly say: "I hope Theme loses."

From the side of the bed, Todd placed one palm on my hip, then one along the small of my back, and rolled me over.

24

Out of the Blue

	MAY					
	1	2	3	4	5	6
7	8	9	10	11	12	13
14	15	16	17	18	19	20
21	22	23	24	25	26	27
28	29	30	31			

I awoke on a couch in a predawn hangover and walked out of Todd's house into the blank silence of morning. Streetlights hung in suspended animation as my bubble of reality floated through a meaningless painting. *Shake it off. Keep going. You'll be okay. I'm so stupid.*

I made it to the boardinghouse and curled into my sleeping bag.

Several hours later, after some coffee and a peanut butter sandwich, I asked John, one of the original roommates, if he wanted to go to the beach and swim. I didn't feel like thinking about the night before; I just wanted to get clean in the sea.

As soon as we reached the beach, John cupped his

hand next to his mouth, forming a megaphone. "Hey! You want to take us sailing?" He aimed his holler at a boat anchored offshore.

"Sure," the lone guy on deck hollered back. "If you can get some women."

I wasn't really into chatting up girls just then, but sailing sounded like an excellent way to get my mind focused on something else. This guy undoubtedly noticed the three young ladies sunning themselves down the beach and figured if John and I were worth taking sailing, then we could get them to come with us. They lay side-by-side face down on bright beach towels, sunning in bikinis. As we approached, they covertly elbowed each other.

"Hi there," John said. "I don't suppose you just heard that?"

Of course they had—the entire beach had.

"Well? What do you think? You want to go sailing?"

They sat up, looked at the forty-foot boat, its white hull resting on the turquoise water, and then looked at us. One shrugged her shoulders, as if to say, "What the hell, why not?" Then she asked, "How are we going to get out there?"

"Swim," I said.

While they walked to their car to store towels and beach stuff, I searched for a place to stash my wallet. It only held eighteen bucks, phone numbers of a few friends back home, and my driver's license, but they were the sum total of my valuables. I walked up the beach, looked around to see no one was watching, and buried my wallet in the sand, marking the spot with my flip-flops.

The sea cleansed my body and mind as I did a gentle

breast stroke until I reached the boat's ladder. Each stroke distanced me from the night before.

Our host decided we'd motor to a reef and go snorkeling, since there wasn't a stitch of wind. We all whooped like cowboys heading out on the trail as I pulled up the anchor and the skipper pushed on the throttle. I think it suddenly hit us guests that not only would we be getting a guided dive trip in the bluest, clearest waters in America, with plenty of food and drink, but it would all be free.

On the way to the reef, which was about two hours offshore, we introduced ourselves. Our female friends were on vacation from New York City and had never been on a boat before, except ferries. The skipper was a trim rogue in his mid-thirties who spent his time sailing throughout the Caribbean. I referred to myself as an adventurer on some sort of quest or something, and John said he was an electrician. Time passed easily while we talked and laughed, sunbathed, and ate sliced oranges and bananas.

Halfway out, I pulled a ginger ale from the galley icebox, walked to the bow, and drank it by myself. As I stood there, I couldn't stop myself from feeling shame: the shame that it took only petty flattery to breach my guard, the shame of not being able to protect myself, and the dread that I'd have to harbor this secret forever. How much less of a man was I now that I'd been raped?

Looking across the calm sea, I inhaled like never before and exhaled from the well of my being. Another deep breath, exhale, another breath... I gave up all hopes of changing the past and accepted what had happened. I'd made a mistake, learned a lesson, but I wasn't sure who to blame. I'd heard of women who'd been raped and somehow felt they were to blame, at least partially. I'd always thought that was crazy. How could people blame themselves for being a victim? But now that's how I felt, and it was real. I took some comfort that with this feeling I wasn't alone, but I was confused, and that made sense. I stopped the incessant thought of *How could I have let that happen?* My chest loosened, and all my thoughts slowed. I took time to notice the moment, live in the present. *Don't let the past ruin today.*

Ahead of me lay the blue surface of the world.

As we approached the reef and the sandy sea floor rose to meet us, the water became pale and transparent. The fathometer said forty feet deep, but as I leaned over the bow, it seemed I could touch the bottom. I lowered the anchor, and it bit into white sand between coral canyons. Our boat tugged like a hot air balloon on the end of a tether, and we gazed on the landscape below.

Hundreds of tiny fish swarmed, undulating with yellows, blues, and purples as the sun caught their glistening scales. I'd seen tourist brochures on glossy paper with bright inks showing pictures of reefs like this. But no ink is as brilliant as a tropical fish or as electric as a ripple of light through the water. We started sifting through a pile of snorkeling gear, making faces and crossing our eyes as we tried on the masks.

Unannounced, and unwanted, the gray fin of a shark cut through the water's smooth surface.

We couldn't see the shark, just the fin. I'd caught a lot of dogfish, small sharks, and at least the fin didn't seem too much larger than those. This fish swam about fifty yards behind us, heading away. In silence we watched the ripples it left and then glanced at each other; no more funny faces. I looked back into the water where the reef fish performed their pyrotechnics and said to the rest of our crew, "I'm still diving."

It took a couple minutes of swimming around to get comfortable with the gear. When the others saw nothing bad was happening to me, they all came in too. One of the women kept coughing and choking, spitting as she cleared her mouth. She tried but couldn't inhale through the snorkel with her face in the water. Eventually she climbed up the boat ladder, seemingly content to watch us, and called, "I'll look out for any sharks."

With outstretched arms, I tipped my torso upside-down, bringing my feet and fins up so they lifted out of the water. I envisioned myself as a humpback whale at the surface when its broad tail slowly arcs into the air before diving. Maybe when they do that, they're waving goodbye to the sky.

A myriad of corals surrounded me: lean tendrils as thin as a pianist's fingers intertwined and grew into a mass the size of a bus; broad fronds, like hand fans held by ladies in a humid church, were interspersed across the sands; short green spikes grew into forests on rocky black outcroppings; wispy-white kelp undulated in the current. My head jerked around trying to see everything. As my heart pounded louder I raced toward the sun, popped my head out of the water, and spit out my mouth piece. "Wow!"

I'd managed to stay under around ten seconds.

I needed to calm down or I wasn't going to spend much

time below the surface, so I rolled onto my back, floated limply, and closed my eyes. The sun's light drifted down on my weightless smile. It took a while to internalize that we would spend the rest of the day here and that I didn't need to rocket back down. My body felt like it was expanding as the pressure of time stopped pressing in.

On my next dive, with a much larger volume of air in my lungs, combined with moving in slow motion, I stayed under about half a minute.

"There's a million fish down there," one of the girls shouted to the group while we all caught our breath.

John, generally the strong, silent type, repeated throughout the day, "Come here! You gotta see this! You gotta see this!" Whenever we were on the surface, we'd shout to each other, but once I was underwater, supported in the planet's amniotic fluid, the world became silent.

Some fish swam in schools of hundreds, and some swam individually. They blazed as if each had swallowed neon lights, and every scale acted as a polished lens. The yellows stood out the most, followed by reds, oranges, silvers, and blues. Each species wore its own immaculate uniform. Every dive brought a new astonishment: crosshatched stripes, psychedelic checkerboards, raccoon eyes, flames, beaks, marshmallows, fighter jets, tangerines, peacocks—too many to name. I drifted, corkscrewed, and flew among them, free from the constraints of gravity.

Then there were the big daddies. Once, a goliath grouper stuck its football head out of a hole in the coral by my ear. Its maw slowly opened, and I found myself looking into a breathing cave. At one point I looked back, and close in there was a school of about twenty torpedoes with teeth.

Maybe they were wahoo; maybe barracuda. My thoughts raced as I tried to figure out if I was in danger. I pumped my fins to move away, not to escape—that would be impossible—but just trying not to annoy them.

Mahi-mahi with bulbous blue foreheads looked like underwater aliens.

The immersion of my senses quieted the circus that generally performed in my head. I didn't need to know everything about my surroundings. I just needed to be part of them. There was no past or future. The now commanded every ounce of my attention. I could feel the water flowing between my fingers, the hair on my legs sweeping back and forth with each kick, and in the soundless expanse my vision sharpened to see every fish scale. On many of my dives, I'd relax motionless once I got close to the bottom, just be.

We'd taken a few short breaks, but after several hours, we swam back to the boat for good. I handed my mask and fins to a person on deck, and that took all my effort. As soon as I climbed the ladder, I flopped down on a flotation cushion in the cockpit, exhausted to feel normal gravity. The woman who'd stayed aboard had prepared a large plate of crackers and fruit.

For part of the cruise back, I once again sequestered myself on the bow. I'd just experienced a blink in an endless panorama. *Where'd it all come from?* Wondering that seemed pointless, but that hasn't stopped people from every corner of history proclaiming answers. Each variety of fish, of coral, and us swimming with them, seemed connected. What sparked the force that has divided so many times? To stay true to myself, I couldn't continue accepting that random molecules were responsible for everything. Our chemistry can fuel us, but it can't explain why we seek our origins. I was forced to accept the unknown, the unknowable.

Despite my feelings of being at peace—at least temporary peace—with one of life's biggest questions, the closer we got to the beach, the more anxious I became. I hadn't thought of my wallet until now. Maybe someone had stolen my sandals and I'd have to dig up a swath of beach to find my wallet. Or maybe everything was gone. As we approached shore, I couldn't see my sandals.

After setting the anchor, I quickly dove off the boat and swam in. I jogged up the beach to spot my flip-flops resting where I'd left them, my wallet still buried beneath.

"You've got some good karma, buddy," John said, coming up behind me. "I'm surprised that stuff didn't get ripped off."

"Yeah, guess I'm the karma kid." I'd never given karma much credence, but maybe things were more connected than I'd thought.

"Karma my ass." His voice hardened. "You just got lucky, boy."

While John and I walked to the boardinghouse, we talked about the day and how it blew away our expectations. Once in the room, though, I scanned the scattered mattresses, clothes, garbage, and guys lying around; that place held nothing more for me. I closed my eyes and fantasized that each of the men transformed into a friend from home, their familiar faces smiling as we reconnected. That lasted only a second.

I gathered my shirts, overalls, socks, and harmonicas

and stuffed them into my backpack until it bulged again like a full sail. Soon the sun would be setting, so I walked out, not to Mallory Square, but to Highway 1, where I hoisted my thumb. Like the snap decision I'd made to leave home, I decided to head home.

25
Intersections

	MAY					
	1	2	3	4	5	6
7	8	9	10	11	12	13
14	15	16	17	18	19	20
21	22	23	24	25	26	27
28	29	30	31			

Loneliness powered me. Money didn't matter. Food didn't matter. Reaching my friends and family mattered, but they were on the other side of the country and I had only eighteen bucks.

As a hitchhiker, any detailed planning would be absurd. But I didn't want to backtrack over the same route that had brought me to the Keys, so I decided to travel north until I reached somewhere halfway up the nation and then hang a left. That felt like a plan even I could stick to.

The South Dixie Highway was my first path northward. Whenever I heard the word Dixie, I thought of the antebellum South, or maybe Pete Fountain blowing his clarinet in a jazz club. This highway was neither. Each side of the road was hemmed in by a dense wall of short trees, or maybe they were considered tall bushes, but when I looked into the snarled maze they created, it was impossible to tell what was dry land and what was black water. It was an endless landscape capable of hiding infinite mysteries. The thought of walking into it scared me.

One ride dropped me in Leisure City, Florida, a tidy place with street signs large enough for the blind to read. Most of the people dressed in white, from their coiffed heads to their patent-leather shoes, and I got a lot of wary stares. My ride pulled into a diner about a mile off the road, and the driver bought us burgers before saying goodbye. A kind act for sure, but after that I got lost walking back to the highway and ended up wandering through a residential area. I could hear the din of the highway in the distance but couldn't see it, and none of the streets I found led me all the way to the noise.

Frustrated, I decided to make a beeline for the sound. The direct route steered me calf deep into fetid water. I sloshed along until I reached a slight hill where the highway's rumble was louder, but my approach just opened up to another residential street with more tidiness.

A gentleman with a hunched back stood in his picture window and spotted me rising from the swamp. He opened his door. "Get the hell out of here you goddamn hippie!"

I never thought of myself as a hippie and felt like flipping him off, but I didn't. He was right. These people didn't want me. He'd probably moved here in part to escape people like me, and I was poking a hole in the cocoon of Leisure City. He'd lived a long life, and he probably had many stories, but I didn't know any of them, didn't know what to respect or despise.

If I walked down the street, I envisioned the old man coming after me with a pitchfork and his walker. Or I could head back into the water and slog toward freeway noise. The swamp won, and eventually the highway was just ahead. But before I padded up the last embankment, I paused in a thicket and took off my overalls and socks to wring them out. They reeked of rotting leaf litter and warm mud.

Subsequent rides were short. It seemed each time I stepped into a car, the driver would say, "I'm just going to the next exit." My stink wasn't helping any. Multiple times I stood at the entrance of an on-ramp for over an hour just to reach the following off-ramp. Creeping down this highway wasn't going to get me home. By now I was on Florida's Turnpike, a toll road, and NO HITCHHIKING signs were everywhere, but I decided to risk hitching on the shoulder since so much more traffic passed there. After each ride dropped me at the end of an off-ramp I'd walk back down to the highway.

At one point I'd been bent over fussing with my pack, and when I glanced up, I saw a Florida Highway Patrol cruiser driving my way. *Don't see me. Please, please, don't pull over. I don't want to go to jail again.* I might as well have been a red elephant.

He pulled over.

I walked up to his cruiser, my heart pounding louder with each step. At least I was wearing boots this time, even if they stank. But the smell meant the other inmates would immediately hate me. I walked slowly, knowing there'd be no bail a second time around. *Is this going to be for a month?* When I was only a few steps away the trooper leaned across the front seat and pushed the passenger door open. I guessed that meant he wanted me to get in. But why in the front seat? With my stomach in a knot, I stood at the open door and peered in.

"Hey, baby!"

"Hello," I responded, as if my greeting might break glass. I hoped he just wanted to have a friendly talk, so I kept standing outside.

"C'mon, get in."

Why isn't he asking for my ID? I lowered myself into the car as slowly as an eighty-year-old, and as I sat down I noticed his holster, with the gun in it, lying on the front seat.

"The captain's been after your ass all day. You're lucky I found you first."

I closed the door but still couldn't figure out what this guy was getting at, or why I was sitting in front, or why his gun was on the seat.

"I'm on my way home," the trooper said. "Got off duty about five minutes ago. Buddy, the radios have been buzzing with reports about you all day." He pulled back into traffic. "The Turnpike's a lousy place to hitchhike."

"No doubt."

What sort of protocol was he following?—pick up kid, greet him as baby, sit him in the front seat, don't ask for ID, leave gun loose on the seat. I tried to notice any weird vibe, but he seemed stable enough.

"Today hasn't been all peaches and cream," I said with half a smile, not knowing if my mild attempt at humor would go over.

"Peaches and cream? You smell like shit." He let out a laugh. "Where you headed?"

"Seattle." This was the first time I knew the answer to that question.

"Seattle! Jesus, why don't you just hitchhike to the moon?"

"Already have." I thought of Sam Andrews at NASA.

We started talking about the weather and why I smelled. This was just idle chitchat, but I didn't ask where we were going; no need to plant the idea that he should take me somewhere specific—like jail. After about fifteen minutes, this felt like any other ride—with the exception of the cop/gun thing—so I relaxed. "What's it like being a cop?"

"It's great. Wanted to be one since I was a kid. Every day is something different. Even this is a first for me…I mean, picking up a hitchhiker." He gave me a stare, making sure I understood how unique this was. "It can get to me, though, some of the stuff I see. Hell, even some of the stuff I do bothers me." His voice fell. "Lately the stress has really been piling up, you know."

I didn't know. "I'm sure you can get into some pretty stressful situations." I barely extended my left hand, pointing to the pistol, without making any motion like I would come near touching it. "Have you ever had to use your gun?"

"No, never. Guys can go a whole career without ever firing their weapon, and I'm still in line to be one of 'em."

Eventually he started talking about his wife. "She doesn't understand. Works as a receptionist at a dentist's office." Her job sounded boring to me, and apparently to him too. He popped his palm hard against the wheel in cadence with his words. "Eve-ry-thing-is-con-trolled-with-her." He took a breath. "People are scheduled. They check in, she smiles. They check out, she smiles." We sat for a few moments in silence. "She's got a pretty smile, though. I've always liked that about her."

The radio blurted some words and numbers and then snapped quiet. He stared ahead with blank eyes. I may have been sitting next to him, but he drifted far away.

"I've been…drinking more lately. She hates it, but it helps me relax." He clenched a fist. "I know cops have a high divorce rate, and I'm starting to see why." He rallied a splinter of a smile. "She says I should've married one of the guys on the force.

"We argue a lot more now. She'll ask about my day, and when I start telling her, she seems bored, like she just wants me to hurry up. Maybe it's because that's how I feel when she starts talking." The engine droned. "I don't know if we're going to make it."

Even though I heard Stud say the same thing two months before as we drove across Texas, I still had no idea what to say. I didn't want to sound trite. "Maybe going to a marriage counselor could help smooth things out."

"We've already tried that. After a half dozen sessions, neither of us noticed any changes, so we stopped. I don't know, maybe we didn't try hard enough, but no point in spending the money if there's no results." He sighed again. "I think maybe a cycle has begun that we can't stop."

Miles passed in silence.

"When I get home, I'm going to ask for a divorce."

"Today?"

"Yeah."

Maybe that's why he gave me the ride—he needed to hear himself say these few words with another person listening. Or maybe he needed to perform one purely altruistic act before killing his marriage.

I'd always thought my parents would get divorced. When I was a child, hearing them fight, their yells of "Go to hell," "Fuck you," and "Now what the hell are you doing?" left me filled with fear. I'd lie in bed wondering if we didn't love each other enough. *If they split, where'll we end up? When'll I get to see them? Why don't they love each other? Do they hate each other? Are we kids the only reason they're staying together?* I wanted us to stay together. We were a family and all I had.

Even so, I'd intentionally leave to escape the fighting. I'd say I was going to a friend's house but just find a tree in the woods and sit and cry.

By the time I reached my teens, the fighting had worn me down enough that I half hoped they would divorce. We were still a unit, the kids and parents, so breaking us apart would have been tough, but so was staying together. I believe the stigma of divorce kept my parents together. Admitting that magnitude of failure for an upper-middle-class family, for them specifically, wasn't an option. I suspected that intense frustration fed the anger that propelled my father to beat me. I stayed away as much as I could: working late at school, spending nights at friends' homes, sleeping on the side of a green at a golf course. We all had to live double lives. But we looked damn good.

My mother's drunken behavior was a major reason

they fought. None of their arguments brought up her drinking directly, though; that would have pierced into the truth. But her actions, lack of actions, and attitude kept them constantly dissatisfied with each other.

At one point, when my sister Corrine was ten years old, she and I were in the basement. She was sitting on a couch, hunched forward with her elbows on her knees and her head bent toward the floor. "Steve?"

"Yeah." I sat down next to her.

"Mom's drunk again."

"I know. She just can't stop."

Corrine stared into my eyes. "We should talk to Dad."

I winced. Maybe it would just be easier to put up with our mother's drinking for decades than raise the issue with our father. I was eighteen, and the beatings had stopped about two years earlier, so I wasn't too worried about that, but once I approached him, I couldn't take back the accusation that his wife was a drunk. This was the woman *he* picked. But I knew Corrine was right and that I had to be the one to approach him. "I don't know what to say to him."

"There are treatment places," she said, "like hospitals, where people learn to stop."

I knew about treatment centers, but having my mother go to one would be admitting our sham. How could we look at each other after having lived in denial for years? Were we all to blame? What if anyone outside of the family found out because of me? I felt sick.

"He's not going to go for it." Now I was the one staring at the floor. "He'll get furious."

"I know. But we've got to do something. We *have* to do something."

Chris and Corrine still had years to live in that house. I lifted my head. "Okay."

Corrine smiled. She had hope that I'd make things right. Even I felt some of her hope.

My father was in his den, which was at the top of the basement stairs—stairs I'd been thrown down more than once, and my head felt numb as Corrine and I walked up them. When we reached the doorway, I just stood there. He was sitting at his desk and glanced at me and then went back to his work. Corrine stood behind me. I couldn't think of any way to ease into this. There was no way to let the topic naturally evolve. "Mom needs help to stop drinking."

His head snapped up.

"Corre and I were thinking maybe she should go to a treatment center. That might help her."

He was frozen, and I thought he was in shock. How dare I? But within moments his eyes hardened to a glare.

"We really think this is getting bad. We need to help her." I could hear the words, and they were the right words, but I couldn't believe I was saying them.

Dad stood up. His lips pressed thin as his face reddened. "No. That's not an option."

"But what else are we going to do? This'll just keep going on and on and—"

"No! That's the end of this."

"But—"

"NO!"

I sank and couldn't look at Corrine.

The clicking turn signal broke me from my thoughts. "Is this your exit?"

"No, but it's a good place for you to get a ride. There's a lot of traffic and a wide shoulder." Once the cruiser stopped, he sat still. "This has been one of the strangest days of my life. Sometimes I've got practically no idea what I'm doing."

"You and me both."

Then, in his police voice, "Make sure you stay off the highway. You know, stick to the ramps. You're less likely to get caught on those."

We left our intersection.

26

Windshield Reflections

	MAY					
	1	2	3	4	5	6
7	8	9	10	11	12	13
14	15	16	17	18	19	20
21	22	23	24	25	26	27
28	29	30	31			

Traffic didn't amount to much in the early morning on a road outside of Dade City, a town about fifty miles north of Tampa. Two young black boys in dusty T-shirts and jeans walked toward me on the side of the road. A car approached from behind them, and two young white boys hung their heads out of the windows, cupping their hands to their mouths. When they were next to the boys walking, they shouted "Niggers!" The adult driver didn't flinch, but neither did the black kids.

After standing an hour, I started to dig in the gravel shoulder with the tip of my boot until I noticed I'd cleared a circle the diameter of a tennis ball. I took a few steps back and started spitting at it. Target practice. Modifying the position of my lips and the force I blew with allowed me a variety of ways to keep missing. As a pastime spitting didn't offer much, so I pulled out my knife and practiced my quick flip, snapping the blade open and trying to speed up getting my grip around the handle. Flip, grip. Flip, grip... This wasn't something I generally did standing on the road—people just weren't that keen about picking up a hitchhiker playing with a knife: *Oh, let's stop for this chap*—but no one was around.

I heard an engine roaring toward me. The car approached so quickly, I still had my knife out when the driver skidded to a stop. Two young men sat in front and an old man in back, so I put away my knife and got in the back. I barely had the door closed when the driver hit the gas, tossing me back in the seat.

"What's in this?" I instantly asked. I'd never accelerated like that before.

"Got's a four-forty," the driver drawled. "Thaz more than three hundred fifty ponies unda the hood."

"Shit house."

"Used to be a po'leese intercepta," the passenger said in the same drowsy cadence. "Plymouth Fury. Full three hundred seventy-five horsepower."

The old man next to me sat motionless, his eyes drooping half closed. The guys up front slouched low, and I could see only the crowns of their heads above the seat back. They didn't seem to be moving, except their mouths.

This isn't right. Who would pick up a guy playing with a knife?

We barreled down the road to a stoplight and then came to a grinding halt. Ahead, every block had a stoplight. Before I could think, our light turned green. The driver floored it, tires peeling. The back of the car sank as power cranked on the wheels. *What the hell is he doing?* We could go only one block before the next red light.

Leaning against the old man's dirty pant leg was a gallon bottle full of white pills.

"What's in the bottle." I didn't sound curious—the question came out like an order.

"Quaaludes," said the driver. This was the same drug that had left Luke splayed at the bottom of the stairs in Key West. At the next light, we came to another skidding stop, cocked at an angle and halfway into the crosswalk. "I guess there's 'bout five hundred. You wanna buy some?"

Staring at the bony man next to me, patches of crusty skin splotching his gray face, felt like reading a book of suicide notes.

"I'll get out here. Thanks."

The driver grinned at me through the rearview mirror. The light turned green and he jammed on the gas.

"Let me out at this next stoplight, man."

Ahead of us, a lady stepped into the crosswalk pushing a baby stroller. She jerked her head toward us and yanked the stroller back onto the sidewalk. We came to another skidding stop.

I reached for the door handle and pulled, pulled again, and again. Nothing.

None of them paid attention to me. I shuddered, realizing this had been a police car—the driver controls the back door locks.

"Let me out now, man." I leaned forward. "I want out now!"

Green light. Wheels squealed.

"Stop the goddamn car! I want out!"

My knife—I reached for it. *Am I going to stab the driver? Why, so we can crash? What about the other two? Do they have guns?* I held the leather sheath tightly but didn't draw. Didn't know what to do.

None of them budged. Taking the brass butt of my knife and breaking the window might get their attention, but the door would still be locked. I couldn't climb out through the broken glass while the car was moving.

"Stop the fucking car!"

The old man croaked, "Samuel."

"Yes Uncle."

"Let the boy out."

"Yes Uncle."

A slap of relief hit, but I wasn't out yet. At the next red light, I heard the locks click, and I slammed open the door, yanking my pack out with me. As the light turned green, the engine raced again.

I was standing in the middle of five lanes heading into an intersection, blocking cars. I ran for the street corner as cars honked. People glared at me. Once on the sidewalk, I paced in a slow circle, taking deep breaths until my heart slowed.

I wanted to reach friends and family even faster now, but I wasn't ready to get in another car. Walking would calm me down—if only I could walk to Seattle.

After a mile of secure footsteps, my nerves settled enough for me to hang out my thumb, but I was getting more spooked with every ride. By early afternoon a beat-up green Ford Pinto pulled over. Once again, I had to dance with chance.

"I'm Vern," the driver said, which, as it turned out, would be quite chatty for Vern. Bushy hair covered his bowling-ball head, and a mop of brown beard hung to his chest. His gut pressed against the steering wheel, and the green driver's seat molded around him like an avocado surrounds its seed.

The green vinyl dash was curled and cracked, with pale yellow flakes of foam scattered across it. A plastic Smokey the Bear proudly holding his shovel was glued on the dash. Drilled down through Smokey's ranger hat was a hole stuffed with a handful of joints.

"Where are you headed?" I asked.

"Dayton." He scratched at his beard. "That's the Dayton in Ohio. How about you?"

Bingo! Jackpot! Relief flushed over me, knowing I'd be covering a solid chunk of country at last. "Yeah, Dayton is on my way." I checked to make sure I controlled the door lock.

I figured we'd be spending at least the next fourteen hours in Vern's tin can, and it took about twenty minutes for him to ask me to drive. Almost immediately his deep snoring let me know that I was in for some solitary windshield time. We stopped at two gas stations to pee and fill the tank, and each time he'd get back into the car and fall asleep. I drove through nine hundred miles of silence.

Smokey and Vern's thermos of coffee were my companions as I abandoned myself to thought, especially about why I chose to leave. A vague satisfaction hinted that I'd made the right choice to wander. Maybe that's all the affirmation I'd get: no graded paper, no wink or nod, no one to bear witness. But I accepted that sometimes that's how life must work. I'd just have to trust that my judgment—as flawed, questionable, and dead-ass wrong as it sometimes was—would be the final arbiter deciding if I'd done the right thing.

That was the first time I'd convinced myself that I'd made the right decision to leave. Maybe I was trying to justify the whole trip, but it didn't feel like that. I pictured what I might have been like if I hadn't left, spiraling deeper into a pit of self-loathing. I felt good about myself for taking action, but I still didn't know if I was running toward something, or away. In only a few days, that answer would be given to me, and as with everything else on this journey, it would be nothing like what I expected.

My maturing had occurred in fits and starts, not just on this trip, but throughout my teen years too. While growing up I'd thought change would be more measured, like the flow of an hourglass. I finally realized that simply being older no longer equated automatically with being wiser or even being experienced. I'd come across many people only to realize that with each flip of the hourglass their years repeated the year before. A lack of curiosity kept some of these people from growing, but that stunting could hide within the camouflage of age.

Early in this adventure, I'd romanticized about adapting to survive in different situations, swashbuckling my way across the continent, but I learned the reality was stark and hard. Still, the need to experience the new and unknown, to discover, overrode the privation, loneliness, and danger. It seemed humans had always been that way. Exploration must be hardwired into us. Evolution has stamped into its survivors the compulsion to seek.

No one encouraged me to set out, let alone by hitchhiking. Maybe our desire to investigate is a way of helping us to touch the intangible. If a god existed, did it ingrain in us the hunger to look for him or her, it or them?

As I drove that green shit wagon, success and bewilderment filled me. Like Ben Franklin, I just kept standing in a storm waiting for lightning to strike. Then once a bolt hit, I was left holding questions.

As night fell it began to rain, and the world closed in. Windshield wipers squeaked a steady beat over the murr of the heater, but they didn't mark time—they erased it. On the bottom of the windshield, I could see the reflection of my transparent hands resting on the steering wheel; as the road rolled toward me, through my hands, I became a highway ghost.

The radio didn't work, and when nothing distracted me, I'd developed the habit of turning my thoughts toward Katie.

In the middle of our senior year, I'd entered her into a contest sponsored by the *Seattle Times* for Humanitarian of the Year. Entering her seemed to matter. I wrote a submission of several paragraphs, mailed it in, and then a week later I left for Alaska, keeping her entry a secret. She won the award. After asking everyone she thought might have nominated her, she finally had to call the newspaper to ask who had done it.

She never told me how that made her feel, either receiving the award or knowing that I'd submitted her. I was so focused on getting her recognition that I didn't foresee my reaction if she won. Her winning left me with a hole—she was good enough to win something I never could.

Katie had always wanted to see Alaska, so I found a log cabin for rent in Ninilchik, a village on the Kenai Peninsula. The cabin faced across Cook Inlet to the earth-shattering crags of Mount Iliamna. Blazing crimson fireweed and wildflowers surrounded the hills, and I was sure we could work out the details to live there for a few months. The cabin had just a main room, a big woodstove, some furniture, a sleeping loft, and an outhouse. At a nearby cannery, I knew of a maintenance job that could support us, so I wrote her asking if she wanted to spend the summer there before heading to college. In my fantasy, the summer held some work and a lot of love. The whole thing felt like a long shot, but longing compelled me. She wrote back and declined: too busy, had a job, didn't have enough money, and although she didn't say it, I took too many risks for her to chance getting close. Her rejection didn't surprise me, but as I read her letter each word drained away more of my energy, leaving me slumped.

After I returned from Alaska, Katie held herself within a mist of hesitancy. I understood she didn't share the same love I felt for her. But still, sometimes when we talked she brought up the possibility of intertwined futures. I planned to stop by Pullman, in Eastern Washington, to see her at WSU before reaching Seattle. I needed her shelter.

Hours passed, and I drove by cities large enough to make it onto my one-page map of the United States. I could've stopped anywhere and spent time exploring the towns, but I didn't. My desire didn't let me. In Georgia I watched Macon, Atlanta, and Marietta whiz by the windows. Tennessee brought Chattanooga and Knoxville. In Kentucky there was Lexington, and well after nightfall I drove into Ohio and past Cincinnati, where I thought about Mary Ann and Cindy waiting tables somewhere amid the horizon of lights. Finally, Dayton.

"Vern," I said, giving his shoulder a push. "We're here." We were pulled off at the exit he'd mentioned while gassing up three hundred miles before.

He lifted his head from against the window and used a hand to knead his face so it shifted around like a rubber mask. "What time is it?"

"About one-thirty."

"Right on. We made good time. Hey, thanks for driving."

As I peeled myself out of the driver's seat, I recalled the temperature on a sign we'd passed earlier, forty-three degrees, which would have been cold but not too bad for sleeping outside, except for the rain. After fifteen hours behind the wheel, my joints had solidified into concrete, while the coffee and weed had worn off long ago. My back had been warm, propped against the seat, but it now felt clammy and cold. As drops streaked my face, I realized if I got soaked it wouldn't take but a few hours for hypothermia to begin.

With low clouds and only one light that appeared to be a motel far down the road, I couldn't get a sense of my surroundings. Thick woods lined both sides of the highway, and the only recognizable feature was the dark outline of the freeway overpass where Vern and I had parted ways. Unless it was raining, I avoided standing under overpasses—they trapped noise and echoed. Even when traffic was light, each car blasted by in a gray mist. Heavy traffic pounded my ears and left me standing in a grimy fog, but that beat standing in pelting rain.

That night, though, the overpass didn't help. The rain slanted in, powered by wind, and nowhere was dry. In my fatigue, I'd sat on a concrete barrier for an hour and the cold had burrowed in deep.

A year earlier I'd contracted hypothermia in Canada's Yukon Territory. Somehow I'd heard, and naïvely believed, that the best way to stay warm in a down sleeping bag was to strip so the bag would catch the most heat. Wrong! By morning I could barely move or think. I didn't even know where I was. Luckily a companion helped me out of that one. I had no companion this time.

Looking down the road to the motel, I weighed my options: tough it out until sunrise, knowing that in the morning I'd still be wet and cold with no way to get dry, or walk to the motel and attempt to get a room. The memory of my Yukon experience decided for me.

I had about nine dollars but knew that wouldn't be enough for a room; not even close. All I could do was try.

"May I help you?" The clerk wasn't much older than I was.

"Yeah, I hope so." Now I needed to appear confident, like I had enough money. Maybe that would help. I had no idea what else to do. "How much is your cheapest room?"

"Queen or king bed?"

"Oh, I don't know, maybe three or four kings? I like jumping on them." A little humor might help. He smiled at this soggy straggler.

"We have one room for thirty dollars." He slowly looked up from the counter and seemed almost afraid to ask. "Will that be for one night?"

"Yeah...well, more like a few hours."

He gave me the I-expected-this face.

"I've got eight bucks and some change. That's it." I glanced out the glass doors to the raining murk.

"Okay, you've got it."

"Thank you very much." I wasn't funny anymore. "You saved a stranger tonight."

I plunked the money on the counter. He picked up the bills but seemed pained as he slid the change over the back edge of the counter into his cupped hand.

I'd now exchanged the problem of contracting hypothermia for the problem of having no money or food.

27

Mojo Rising

	MAY					
	1	2	3	4	5	6
7	8	9	10	11	12	13
14	15	16	17	18	19	20
21	22	23	24	25	26	27
28	29	30	31			

Breakfast was several hearty cups of water, but I felt rested and ready to bound into another day. The lonely desperation that had filled me in Key West subsided and I took a more holistic look at the trip and my life. Free and adventuring, I'd be young only once, and I was taking advantage of that. No money—no big deal. Something's bound to happen.

The first ride that morning lasted little more than an hour, but we crossed Southeast Asia, Africa, and Brazil. Derek had flown back from Brazil two days before to visit his ailing grandmother in Dayton and was now driving home to Chicago. He was deeply tanned, probably in his mid-thirties. A short man, he cropped his beard low on the sides and wore a button-down shirt colored with alternating green and yellow leaves in a tessellated pattern. On his right wrist was a red cord bracelet. His eyes chimed with a warm blue.

"Once I spent about three months in Southeast Asia." He glanced up as if trying to recall a phone number. "New Guinea, Indonesia, the Philippines, and Thailand," he said. "Just traveling with my girlfriend."

Envy crept in, but it left when I realized I couldn't fault him for having had what I wanted: a traveling companion, especially a woman. Not that this trip would have been the one to bring her on.

"Last year we stayed in Bangkok for a few days but then decided to head inland, into the mountains." He told me how they'd trekked on a guided tour through Thai villages, walking through steamy jungles. "We'd get into the villages, really tired, with our boots soaking wet, and these old women would come out and offer to rub our feet. They'd take off our boots, dry our feet, and start massaging them." His head tipped back, and for a moment his eyes closed halfway. "Man, it felt great."

I imagined a green valley with silent mist drifting over the jungle canopy and trails snaking between the trees. Brown thatched huts dotted the distant hills.

"Then these women would pull out pipes full of opium." He half shouted, "Now that's service!" as if the world's hospitality industry should take note. "But about a day after leaving Thailand, I started throwing up. Couldn't figure out what was wrong. By the time we landed in the States, I was craving the opium and was in damn withdrawals.

Sick as a pig. We were only on the trek *three weeks*!" His words slowed. "That stuff is wicked. Watch out."

I told him about my trip and how I'd covered about five thousand miles so far.

"Sounds like you've probably had a few scrapes with excitement," he said. "I spent some time hitchhiking."

Now I figured my adventure would be comparable to one of his.

"It was through Kenya."

Nope, not comparable. "Why'd you choose Kenya? Are there even many cars there?" I naïvely pictured the country as little more than people living in stick huts and herding cattle. "How'd you get rides?"

"There were plenty of rides. It's all about the people. They're the best, just so friendly. I think it's because they don't sit around glued to all the sensational news reporting that we have here. They don't think every stranger's out to kill them."

We talked with an ease and openness that reminded me of being with my friends. I even imagined us as mentor/mentee as I listened to his stories.

"My most outrageous trip ended the day before yesterday. I just flew in from São Paulo, Brazil." Any animation left his voice. "That's where things got weird." He scrutinized the dashboard gauges, as if measuring his sanity. "Really weird."

"I can imagine." But as it turned out, I couldn't.

"I was in the mountains in the northeastern part of the country, and I got to know some of the local villagers, people I bought food from each day. After about a month, they invited me to a ceremony." He used his left hand to roll a section of the twine bracelet between his forefinger and thumb. "A voodoo ceremony."

I knew almost nothing about voodoo.

"I haven't told this to anyone yet. It happened just last week. People'll think I'm nuts." He sat for a moment in silence and appeared to be judging whether he should tell me—if I deserved the first telling. "I still don't know if they used the good type, but I think it was black magic."

So far his storytelling had been great, but his driving was a bit erratic. He didn't seem to trust rearview mirrors, so changing lanes involved cranking his head practically all the way around to look behind him. Then, while in this twisted position, he'd yank the wheel. I wanted to say something but had learned that no one likes a backseat driver, especially when it's some hitchhiker kid. We lurched into another lane and he continued.

"It was late afternoon, and the villagers had just killed a big pig. There was a pool of blood in the grass surrounding a pile of shiny guts with flies all over it. We walked into a field, and in the middle was a short building with a tin roof. It didn't have any walls, just some framing poles and a roof. I could see a group of people, maybe forty, and I could hear drums. Lots of drums."

In my mind I heard the drums' hollow thumping, getting louder as I approached.

"As we got closer, and I could see through the crowd, there were these guys beating some long, tall drums that rested on stands. Kind of like congas, but fatter and rickety, all beat up." His eyes grew wide. "It's the first time I'd heard drumming with no coordinated rhythm, just random pounding, some of them going fast, some just beating every once in a while."

"Nothing you could hum a little tune to?"

He furrowed his brow, and it was time for me to shut up. After adjusting the rearview mirror for what seemed an incredibly long time, he spoke again. "Pretty soon everyone was dancing as crazy as the drum beats, nothing in unison, and in the middle of everything, a fire was burning, not some huge blaze, more of a campfire." He began to speak faster, as if he'd stopped worrying about what I'd think. "My fruit-stand friends told me it would be a healing ceremony, and there were six men who looked like some sort of officials. These guys were jet black, shirtless, and all muscle, but they wore bright red skirts that reached down to the dirt. And they stomped in place, kind of a mad dancing." Derek's eyes widened. "Behind them ten women wore hooded white robes. The hoods were so big and hung forward so much that their faces barely showed, and they stood rock still, as if no one was even in the robes, just stiff ghosts."

Stomping, drumming, red skirts, white robes with black holes where faces should be, pig guts, and a fire. Maybe he was full of crap—maybe his name wasn't even Derek—but he didn't seem like the type who would lie just to boost his image in front of a stranger he'd never see again.

"The shaman—shaman my ass—he was a fucking witch doctor. He walked to the fire holding a long rattle covered with feathers and a cross with Jesus on it. It was dripping blood, and from a cup at the end of the rattle, he poured a bunch of the blood onto the fire. It sizzled and stank. Up to then, the smoke smelled nice, like a beach fire, but after that it smelled metallic and felt like it scraped my throat."

Derek made several attempts at starting his next sentence. Each time a couple quick words came out, but then he'd stop. He finally took a deliberate breath. "Then the witch doctor started shaking the rattle over the head of a skinny old man standing in rags. Everyone else was dressed nice, almost like they were going to church. They all wore bright clothes, most of the women in full dresses and the men in pressed shirts and shorts, slacks, hats, you name it—all except the old guy. He just had on a dirty T-shirt and shorts, no shoes, and stood still next to the fire. As the witch doctor shook the rattle, the people nearest the fire began dancing more crazy. Some were jumping up and down; others were spinning, flailing their arms, stomping back and forth. I didn't know what to do. To be honest, I was starting to get scared." His voice pitched up. "No one was in control. I had to watch out I didn't catch an elbow and get my teeth knocked out."

I pictured spirits shaking rag dolls.

"Then a bunch of them started yelling and howling. They didn't sound like a pack of wolves; more like people trying to escape a burning building, screaming in fear and pain. The old man under the rattle dropped to the ground and started convulsing, basically having a seizure. I thought he was going to roll right into the fire."

Derek glanced over to me, making sure he had my full attention. He did.

"This kept going for almost an hour until the sun set, and down there it gets dark in a hurry. Then all of a sudden, the old man stopped twitching. He just lay there on his back with his legs straight and arms at his side, like someone in a coffin." Derek started licking his lips with quick flashes of his tongue. "By now everyone was dancing and screaming, really screaming; sweat was flying, rancid smoke was everywhere, and drums pounded so loud I couldn't hear myself think. I swear I could feel…they like…something was there…I could feel them being possessed…it was everywhere." His forearms quavered, and if his hands hadn't been gripped on the steering wheel, they would have been shaking. "I worked my way to the front, close to the fire. I was getting banged around pretty good. They were freakin' me out. But I don't think they even noticed me.

"I thought the excitement had been too much for the old man. I didn't even see him breathing. I could swear to God he was dead. But that was nothing."

Derek stopped telling the story and pulled himself back into the present. "My exit's up here in just a mile." Flipping on the turn signal, he craned his head until he twisted enough to look out of the back window, and we swerved into the right lane. We'd part ways at the exit.

"Then I practically crapped my pants." He ran his hand quickly through his hair. "The old man started to rise off the ground. Levitating. Really fucking levitating. I mean lying back flat as a board and floating off the damn ground!" His eyes grew wide in utter disbelief. He clearly understood how farfetched this sounded. "Really! I couldn't believe it! The old man got about three feet in the air when he started to float sideways, *over the fire.*"

By now Derek was half shouting. "He just floated

there, about a foot over the flames. But he didn't flinch, nothing! After maybe ten seconds or so, he floated sideways to the other side of the fire and just drifted back to the ground." Derek stared at me hard. "He wasn't even burned, not at all, and I was looking for burns."

He had talked his lungs empty and needed to take a big breath. "He just lay there still as a dead person." Derek's shoulders had been clenched up but now slacked back down. "Then my friends found me and grabbed me from behind and told me to leave."

"Whew," I let out, somewhat skeptical. "You're not bullshitting me, are you?" I didn't think he was, but if I didn't ask I'd feel like a fool.

His eyes cast down.

My next words came as deliberate as I could make them. "I believe you."

I later learned that voodoo is anything it wants to be. It's been practiced for thousands of years but still has no rules and no central leader, only ceremonies cascading down the generations through individual villages. Catholic missionaries unintentionally poured Christianity into the voodoo soup several hundred years ago. If there's an overriding belief, it's that there are spirits all around us all the time. Disrespected spirits hurt or possess people, causing disease and bad luck. Respected spirits help the believers. These spirits aren't exclusively large entities that power the cosmos but are average people, especially the recently dead. Voodoo says that it's not just people that have spirits—trees, rocks, lizards, virtually everything retains its own spirit.

I again remembered that morning early in the trip

when I'd woken up in the Mojave Desert. Bright flowers sprang from parched ground, willing themselves to life. I'd felt surrounded even though there wasn't a soul in sight. Was I feeling the spirits of the flowers, rocks, something more—or nothing but imagination? Was Derek's experience tangible proof of a force beyond the tangible? Did the faith of the people around the fire create a physical power?

I stood on the side of the road with more thoughts and feelings about unseen forces than I'd ever had, but with no idea what to believe, if anything.

28
Arabian Night

	MAY					
	1	2	3	4	5	6
7	8	9	10	11	12	13
14	15	16	17	18	19	20
21	22	23	24	25	26	27
28	29	30	31			

The couple was trim, tall, and buoyant with energy. In their convertible VW Bug, we headed west out of Indianapolis toward a sunset. The last eight hours had been frustrating, since I'd covered little distance, and I decided this would be my final ride of the day. The loose canvas top slapped the frame as we sped up, becoming a cracking whip.

"Right now," Jonathan shouted over the slapping canvas, "I'm writing a play." He wore his brown hair over his ears, but not shaggy. "And Liz is an interior decorator."

Liz's hair was shorter than any woman's I'd ever seen—shorter than Jonathan's—and colored a light burgundy. In the dusk her mohair sweater with loose fibers blurring her outline made her look as if she were wearing a soft mist. When she looked back at me her neck muscles ran long and smooth.

"So did you read that a Korean minister married over a hundred couples in London today?" she asked.

It seemed obvious that I didn't receive daily newspapers, but I appreciated her question to start the conversation. "Really?" I hollered back. "Sounds intimate." We laughed.

They continued to shout about current affairs, filling me in on recent national and international news.

It didn't take long before we had reached Danville, Illinois, where they were turning south on Highway 1. "I'll get out here. Thanks for the ride."

Since my food and money had run out the day before I planned on another meal of water. Throughout the trip, being hungry hadn't bothered me much, but I'd understood I'd be able to eat when I wanted to. Now, though, with no idea when I'd eat next, the hunger was more oppressive. There was nothing to stop my body from feeding off my muscle and what little fat I had left.

Liz turned casually. "Why don't you come and have dinner with us? You can stay the night if you want. We have plenty of room."

Trying not to pump my fist in the air and shout, "Score!" I graciously accepted her offer.

We drove for a short while and came to the town of Paris, which seemed a fitting home for a writer and an interior decorator. Paris was a small town in a huge part of America, the part where politicians wave their hands over a map to identify the heartland. Paris was old but had well-kept architecture, tall white church steeples, stone arches, and columns that lent a feeling of continuity with the past. Jonathan said the population hadn't grown since World War II but hadn't declined either.

We pulled into a gravel parking lot that surrounded a square brick building four stories tall. Each level had rows of tall narrow windows recessed into the walls, some broken, others boarded; some with curtains, others bare. In the dim light, the windows looked like sunken eyes that stared with worn disinterest. When Jonathan shut off the engine, we were in front of huge double doors below an arched iron frame that looked like it used to hold a sign.

Jonathan and Liz's VW wasn't that great, but they didn't seem like the kind of people who'd live in a flophouse. Yet Jonathan beamed as he gazed at the dark façade. "What do you think?"

"It's big," I said, looking up, but not beaming. "Do you guys live here?" I tentatively slung one strap of my pack over a shoulder.

"We bought it about a year ago," Liz said while pulling grocery bags out of the trunk. She handed a few bags to me. "It was cheap, and we fell in love with it." She shared Jonathan's beam. "It was built in 1926, and we think it's got a lot of potential."

They didn't live in a flophouse; they owned one. *They're slumlords. Heck of a business.* I envisioned a bunch of crusty alcoholics inside, each renting a stale room. Trying not to sound as if I wanted to run off and sleep in the woods, I asked, "So, is business pretty good?"

Jonathan produced a Frisbee-sized key ring that must

have weighed ten pounds and then, as he walked up the front stairs, said, "Oh, it's not a business—it's our home."

The keys jangled as he twisted one in the massive front door lock. Once inside, I could see why they loved it. The lobby centered around an eight-pointed onyx star inlaid on the white marble floor. Concentric rings of additional white marble spread to the walls, and light came from a gold chandelier centered in a dome above the black star.

"Wow," I said. Now I was beaming. I scanned the room and could see several different wallpaper patterns where various layers had peeled off, each layer reflecting the decorating sensibilities of previous owners.

Liz pointed to a metal accordion cage covering a dark doorway. "That's the elevator," she said, exasperated. "But we're going to have to walk. We're on the fourth floor."

I set down my bags and pulled on my other shoulder strap. One strap wasn't going to keep my pack on with bags in my arms and four flights of stairs to climb. The leading edge of each wooden stair curved back, worn from thousands of footsteps. Large dark balusters marked landings at each floor, and vague silhouettes on the wallpaper marked where pictures had once hung. The higher we climbed, the darker it became, since the lobby chandelier was our only light.

We reached the top of the stairs and headed down a narrow hallway where there was just one plain door. Jonathan pulled out his huge key ring again, opened the door, and disappeared into the darkness. Liz followed him. I stood there by myself in the dark but took another step trying to follow them.

Bam! Light detonated.

I suddenly found myself looking into a festive ballroom. They had knocked out the interior walls across the entire footprint of the building. Aside from a few support columns, the space opened as an unobstructed single expanse. From a dingy hall carpet, I stepped onto a polished oak floor.

"What do you think?" Jonathan shouted as he headed for a refrigerator against the far wall. His footsteps echoed like a lone basketball player crossing a court.

"It's huge!"

"See?" Liz said, with more than a little vindication. "I told you it has potential."

The only door, other than the one we entered, looked distant and small. "Is that the bathroom?" I asked, putting my bags of groceries on a counter next to the fridge. It was, and as I swung open the door, I stepped onto salt-and-pepper granite tiles that supported a white porcelain clawfoot tub. The walls were a rich maroon, and there was a sitting area with red velvet chairs. The room evoked a quiet historic grandeur, but when I finished peeing and flushed the ancient toilet it sounded like a hippopotamus sucking down an alligator.

Back in the main room, I watched Liz turn a slow pirouette, extending her arms to point in all directions, as she said, "I got to work with a huge blank canvas." She arched her head back. "I felt like Michelangelo."

Each wall invited investigation. Different fabrics covered the vertical acreage. Even though there were hundreds of patterns, they all blended like a thick forest: branches, flowers, grass, stumps, leaves, bushes, berries, vines, birds, mud, and saplings; the elements were all different, but none was out of place.

"Texture is key," Liz said, recognizing my astonishment—a look she probably saw every time someone new walked into this gallery. Drapes undulated across vast walls, flowing to the floor, where they piled in luxurious excess. In addition to covering rough brick, the drapes' thick beauty kept out the cold.

Hovering in the midst of its own splendor, the fabric-covered ceiling conjured images of a sheikh's tent, with tapestry radiating from each of the support pillars. I envisioned the Arabian Desert waiting outside. The walls and ceiling billowed, giving a sense that the room surged with life. Adding to the sense of an Arabian camp, large floor pillows lay scattered like distant dunes.

Their kitchen was a long counter interspersed with a sink and appliances. Jonathan was leaning against the counter when he asked, "How's lamb sound?"

"Sounds like music to my stomach."

"Then you're in luck. A friend of ours butchered one of his this morning and gave us a hindquarter."

"That's fantastic. But what are you guys going to eat?" I was only half joking. I hadn't eaten since morning the day before near Dade City, and that wasn't much—half a peanut butter sandwich. After a while, with the smell of the haunch roasting and a glass of red wine in my hand, I stopped worrying about food.

For the next ninety minutes, the three of us prepared a Middle Eastern feast with roasted lamb as the centerpiece. I chopped vegetables and cooked rice. Jonathan created a sauce with dried fruit, and Liz made tahini to spread on bread. When it was time to eat, we sat on pillows around a low table.

"We're pretty short on money now," Jonathan said, after eating a large amount of sautéed vegetables. "It took about all we had to buy the place and make this floor livable."

"But we'll make it," Liz said. "We've got a five-year plan."

"Yeah, but only enough money for another three months." Jonathan said.

Enough money for three months sounded like a fortune. A five-year plan sounded like an eternity. *Will I ever have money, or even a plan?*

Jonathan tipped back his wine glass and, after draining the final contents, said, "The people in town think we're just romantics without a hope of pulling this off."

"The grand plan is to transform the first floor into a theater and use the second and third floors as a bed-and-breakfast, " Liz said. "Some of the rooms'll be reserved for people going through tough patches. But we can only take it one step at a time." She gazed at Jonathan with quiet confidence.

He stared back to her, but his words were for me. "We've got everything wrapped up in this place." His voice rose with pride. "But I tell you what, it's not romance that tore out the walls, installed a kitchen and bathroom, refinished the hardwood, and fabricated custom brackets for all these wall hangings."

"You got that right," I added with tipsy emphasis.

Liz rolled back onto her pillow and fixated on the ceiling. "Of course we'll keep this floor for ourselves. It's too much *us* to let go of."

Jonathan stood to carry his plate to the counter. "I don't know what we're going to do if this doesn't work out."

"Don't think that way," Liz said. "You're too negative sometimes."

"I'm realistic sometimes." His voice became brittle. "We both know there're no guarantees."

She reached out and petted his calf with slow strokes.

After dinner the three of us washed dishes. The long counter lent itself to an assembly line for washing, drying, and putting away.

"What's that in your hair?" Liz asked me.

"Where?"

"In the back. There's a clump." She ran her fingers through the curly hair on the back of my head. "It's matted like dog's fur."

I felt embarrassed but knew what she was talking about. Months of wind, rain, road grime, saltwater, and sleeping outside had taken their toll on my hair, which now almost reached my shoulders. The knots had gotten bad enough that I couldn't brush my hair, let alone drag a comb through it. As the knots intertwined, they'd formed mats. "Oh, those," I said.

"You can't be able to brush this, can you?"

"Not really." *What brush?*

"Why don't you let me cut it?"

If I were her I would've been afraid to touch it. "You sure? I mean, you don't have to bother."

"I cut Jon's hair all the time and cut my brother's when we were growing up. I kind of like it."

Dinner and a haircut. How did these people become

so giving? Were they raised in families that practiced charity, or maybe received it?

While I was growing up, charity was a painting in a museum—something to be admired from a distance. My father would make a running joke at Christmas: "I wonder what the poor people are eating tonight."

"Oh, Keith, that's terrible," my mother would say. "Don't be like your father, children."

He'd laugh, understanding the hyperbole of his Scrooginess. But we never did anything to find out what the poor were eating or how we could help them or anyone else.

As Liz's fingers roamed across my head, I could feel her breath on my ears and smell her perfume. Her palms slid along my neck as she brushed my hair. I let her tip and rock my head however she wished to get any angle she needed, and I could hear the scissors slicing away. With her fingertips, she brushed bits of cut hair from my cheeks.

"There you go. No more mats." She smiled and wrapped her arms around my shoulders, pulling me near. I lingered. Releasing me, she gave my nose a gentle poke. "You've got enough hair, I don't think you'll miss much."

The floor lay covered in dirty curls that I offered to sweep.

It didn't take long before we all started getting sleepy. I had been eyeing a long purple couch, unlike any I'd ever seen. When I sat on it, the cushions extended deep enough to support my legs all the way out to my calves, and it stretched long enough to sleep an NBA player. This must have been in the hotel lobby. It was upholstered in a velvet lullaby.

Before drifting off, I thought about how Jonathan and Liz were putting everything they had—money, emotions, hopes, energy, imagination, their futures—into making this building the foundation of their ambitions. In them, I saw the stout resilience needed to build dreams, along with the doubts that the dreams might never come true.

For some reason they had been so kind to me, and in the morning, all I'd do is leave. I couldn't offer them anything as a thank-you, and I felt small. From under my breath, I was compelled to say, "Hey, God. This isn't much, but if you're there, maybe you can help them out some. I don't know how. You're probably not going to rain money down, but that'd be okay." I pictured Jonathan and Liz scampering as they picked up bills from the ground. "They're good people. Maybe there's some way you can pay them back for what I can't."

29

Connected

	MAY					
	1	2	3	4	5	6
7	8	9	10	11	12	13
14	15	16	17	18	19	20
21	22	23	24	25	26	27
28	29	30	31			

Mark Twain wrote this land,
the green pastures of Missoura.
May holds summer in its womb as
birds sweep brushstrokes
with wings of magenta, yellow and black.
Lounging beneath a gnarled oak
the wayfarer whistles for no reason.

A young farmer drove down the narrow road hanging his elbow out the window of a '64 Dodge truck. The rig didn't qualify as a classic but had stout lines and permanent dirt. He saw me sitting under an oak as I wrote a poem and pulled onto the soft shoulder to shout, "You need a ride?"

I jumped up, stuffed my journal into my pack and tossed that into the rusted bed already hauling dirty shovels and a spare tire. "How'd you know I needed a ride?"

He was staring below the steering wheel. "Oh crap." Resting on the floor lay an empty Styrofoam cup in a coffee-brown puddle. "Oh well, after fourteen years of cow manure that floor's seen worse." Using his foot he slid the cup under the seat before he turned to me. "Nobody just sits out here in the middle of nowhere, so I figured you needed a ride." He extended his calloused hand. "I'm Tom."

As we accelerated I felt a calm sense of accomplishment, knowing my persistence was keeping me moving west. My faded overalls—Farmer Johns as a lot of people called them, even though I'd never been a farmer—coordinated nicely with the countryside and the truck. I noticed the torn seat and the heavily scratched shift lever sticking up from the floor. "This truck's seen a few miles?"

"Yep, nothin' fancy. It gets me by, though." Tom wore clean blue jeans and a white button-down shirt. He held his head high, eyes up. I could tell he was only a few years older than I was.

We drove by fields lush with deep grass, tawny outbuildings, and dairy cows. Between farms the air smelled light with wildflowers and spring grasses. As we passed each milking barn, the scent of pungent ammonia filled the cab.

"I drove out this road at four this morning," he said. "But I missed today's milking." Then, as if on autopilot, he added, "We got 246 head, and they need to be milked every morning."

"So you're a dairy farmer?" I wasn't above asking obvious questions to help move conversations along.

"Have been all my life," he said, pointing to the right. "There's the Crestons' dairy. Looks like they built a new silage bunker."

I wanted to say that it was a solid one, but I didn't have any idea which building he meant.

"I work with my folks. It's their farm, but I'm their only son, so I'm figuring on workin' it when they can't anymore."

"Seems like you've got a long-term plan." *Jonathan and Liz have a five-year plan, This guy's got a plan. Am I the only person on the planet who doesn't know what the hell he's doing?*

"Yeah, I guess so. But when you like doing somethin', why stop? That's what my pop says."

"He sounds like a smart guy."

When I was growing up, I'd known many boys who admired their fathers, and I always envied them. Their dads weren't perfect—they got mad and yelled, but at reasonable things, and at least on the outside, those boys seemed comfortable in their lives. The last thing I wanted to do was follow in my father's footsteps. But now I was making my own footsteps: meandering, uncertain, but mine.

It appeared neither Tom nor I felt like saying much, so we didn't. Each farm we passed marked our silence.

As we looked out the windows, watching the green world stream by, I thought about plans. Since I didn't have a plan, that left me able to pursue any path that looked promising. But that also left me with nothing today and no prospects for tomorrow. If I were to work within the framework of some plan, I might have the optimism that shone in Tom's eyes. Although I had a loose plan of reaching home in several days, it didn't impress me as much of a life plan. But I knew that I'd have some sort of a plan eventually; I was too driven not to. Even though I was good at berating myself, I didn't want to do that just because I didn't have a grand plan. For now I just needed to sit in that cab and enjoy the view.

"Whew." Tom ran a hand through his hair. "Lord, today." He rocked his head to stretch his neck. "I've never had one like it." He'd been sitting still as if this were a humdrum day, no different from any other. Before I could ask him what had made the day so different he said, "My first was born this morning." His eyes were swimming. "A son. My wife had a feeling it'd be a boy."

"That doesn't happen every day." My understatement bounced off him.

"I can't believe it. She stayed pregnant forever." He chuckled. "The doctor didn't need to give him a swat on the butt. That boy just went at it. I got to watch him take his first breath." Tom held his breath. "It was like time stood still." Fields grazed past our windows. "You know what? Besides my wife, and the hospital people, you're the first person who knows."

I gave a nod. "I'm honored." Even though I hadn't earned any honor, I somehow felt it.

Tom shook his head like he'd been startled. I imagined he realized that no matter what would happen across the span of his life, talking about his son would be something he'd do countless times.

"I thought about calling my folks around eight o'clock when he was born, but I knew they'd both be working anyway and nowhere near a phone. I've called a few times since then but no answer." His smile showed no fatigue. "Heck, when I held my boy for the first time, the nurse said she couldn't tell who was crying more, baby or dad." He reflected a moment. "I get that from my pop. He's gonna bawl."

"You've got plenty goin' on. Why'd you bother to pick me up?"

"As I was being raised I was taught that we're called to love each other, and that makes the world better. But now there's a real reason it needs to be better." He looked surprised at his words, and he grabbed the shift lever but had nowhere to shift—we were already in third. "So I just stopped and asked if you needed a ride, you know, to help someone, make things a little better."

How could giving me a lift help his infant son? Does he think we're connected? Maybe he was raised around hippies who get all flappy about karma. But Tom seemed as far from being a hippie as a person can get, and he didn't actually say karma. He said love.

Love isn't a word to be used lightly. I felt it should be reserved for the deepest and most intense emotion I could feel—that anyone could feel. Love should be protected and kept in a pristine place where few are allowed to enter, let alone some anonymous tramp. Maybe Tom's love was bigger than he could hold and he had to let some spill on the side of the road. Could love be precious but not rare?

Somehow, Tom's action made vague sense. I felt certain that one day his son would benefit from the same kindness Tom offered me, that the boy would probably receive many kindnesses from many strangers and would return them to others. Had I been receiving love from all the people who'd picked me up and I couldn't even see it? Not burning romantic love, of course, but a type that might be everywhere. If it was everywhere, then I'd be part of it. I could return those favors, that love, to people I hadn't met yet. Maybe I too could give it away.

"So much just changed," Tom said, the unknown echoing in his voice. "Have you ever smelled a new baby, right off the top of their head?" He didn't wait for an answer. "I can't describe it, really. Haven't smelled anything like it before, but it's peaceful. Made me feel things are going to be okay."

Even with Tom's exhausted excitement, I could tell he felt peace, quietly looking forward to spending the rest of his life helping and leading his son, as his father continued to do for him. Lifelong commitment had occupied less than a speck on my horizon, but now I sat next to it.

"You know, when I was younger, I thought as I grew up I'd figure things out, that so much wouldn't seem so unknown."

"Me too," I interrupted.

"But, man, this one's got me." He raised his voice. "I don't know squat. It seems things just keep changing faster instead of slowing down. Seems irresponsible for the hospital people to even let us leave with a baby. I hope he comes with a manual, because knowing me, I'll just stick his feet in the ground and hope he grows." Tom giggled like a toddler on Christmas morning. "My wife had a baby shower and now we've got more doo-dads than I can count. How do parents do it? You know, keep up with the changes?"

"I guess older folks are more practiced."

"I guess so. This morning I felt like saying to my wife how things are changing so fast, but she was bushed, and she's knows it anyway. She also knows I've never been happier." He thought for a moment. "I mean in my entire damn life."

Since I'd stepped into the truck, it seemed Tom had matured several years but also become younger. New responsibilities wrapped around him; yet the world held more wonder.

I tried to place myself in his shoes. When I reached his age, maybe I'd be in his position—or maybe I'd still be standing on some roadside. How could I ever be a parent? I didn't have a cracker to my name. Would I ever walk out of a hospital with a baby?

"What's his name?" Naming a child seemed one of the least important aspects of raising one, but I was wrong.

"John August Ruddy." Tom stared out across the pastures. "Named him after my pop." He gave a sly smile. "It's a surprise."

30

All She Has

	MAY					
	1	2	3	4	5	6
7	8	9	10	11	12	13
14	**15**	16	17	18	19	20
21	22	23	24	25	26	27
28	29	30	31			

I'd arrived at the middle of the middle of America. Towns that I thought existed only in corny movies became real—in one hamlet, white picket fences fronted deep green lawns, a white gazebo with lattice sides rested on a grassy plot in the town square, and Roman columns rose from white marble stairs that led to the courthouse. Next to the courthouse City Hall, a simple square building built of stone that reflected a solid people. Next to it the church, with a white spire that rose above all else. I half expected a silver-haired woman wearing a white apron and a floral dress to pull over holding a plate of warm cookies.

"Jesus Christ, I hate this," a young woman snapped

once I stepped into her black VW bug. She brushed black stringy hair from her eyes, took a look at me, and said, "I'm Lulu."

"Hate what?"

"All this Pollyanna." She swept her arm through the air, grating her black fingernails across the town. "You know, a lot of sick things go on in these pretty white boxes."

Her eyes looked like white planets surrounded by the empty space of mascara, and her black overcoat blurred into frayed ends at the cuffs and around the collar. A black leather skirt led down to black nylons showing oyster-white legs through round tears. She stomped her black tennis shoes on the clutch pedal and accelerator.

When I tossed in my pack, I could see that the back seat held the sediment of her life. On the bottom were cardboard boxes printed with booze brands that she probably got free from a liquor store; piled loosely on those was a toaster, stereo speakers, and a guitar amp. Topping the pile were clothes still on the hangers, as if they'd been bear-hugged out of a closet and tossed there. They filled the car with a musk of wet fabric that had soured.

She railed against the manicured world as we kept driving through her Pollyanna. The gardens, sidewalks, well-dressed people—all received her glare and criticisms. Eventually she ran out of caustic steam and began to talk about herself. "I'm an actress in Manhattan. Been there about two years, but it's tough."

Picket fences kept guiding us down the streets.

"I grew up around here," she said quietly.

"Looks like an okay place." I knew she'd come back with a different opinion.

"Yeah, it's okay if you like taking everything in your fuckin' life and hiding it."

Hiding I knew about; so many layers. One of them was unveiled six months earlier when my father's mother had died of cirrhosis of the liver: she drank herself to death. No one had ever said anything about her drinking. We tried to hide it even from ourselves. For her last years, whenever I saw her, she just sat and complained that her throat hurt and a "good stiff drink" would help—that meant straight whiskey. After a few drinks, she'd pee herself. Then we'd carry her to a bedroom in silence and hide her. Several days after her death, my uncle and father were talking with their father, and my uncle asked if he was sleeping okay. My dad scowled at his brother, as if that was the dumbest question anyone could ask. Of course he was sleeping fine, maybe better. I don't recall any funeral.

I told Lulu that my family had lived in New Jersey when I was in fifth grade and we'd taken day trips into Manhattan to see the museums. "Manhattan is pretty much the definition of a great place to visit, but I wouldn't want to live there." I sounded like a hick.

"No, it's not really that great." Her energy seemed to drop as she pulled a cigarette from her coat pocket. "I've got a place on the Lower East Side. It's small, but I share it with two guys." The cigarette hung from her black lips. "They're actors too. We've got a radiator."

We passed a quiet side street where a group of boys rode their bikes. "All kinds of people in that city, every type there." She coughed hard. "It kinda surprised me. There's lots of competition." Envy and disdain mixed in her voice. "Most of those girls have been to acting classes. I've been thinking about it some." As we sat at a red light, she stared at her hands and then blankly evaluated her clothes. "I can sing too."

I kept quiet.

"My parents wanted me to be a straight stick." She turned to me and bobbed her head in exaggerated glee. "It'll be peachy when I get married: kiddies, doggies, a white fence." Her head stopped bobbing. "They thought that would make me happy."

Drizzle began falling, but she waited before turning on the wipers. "What made me happy was my mom's cooking. God, that woman could cook."

Lulu didn't strike me as the type who cooked much.

"I can't believe it," she said slowly. "Mom would actually put hot pies next to an open window to cool."

This was the first time I'd seen a hint of a smile. Not a light smirk or quick lip lift, but a lasting hint. She turned and gazed at me, as if to say, "See? I can smile."

"That reminds me of the old Sunday comics," I said, thinking of the Katzenjammer Kids. I sounded hokey but kept going. "The kids always snuck up to the window and would steal the pie."

"Yeah, I tried that once." She almost laughed. "Burnt my fingers." She fixed her gaze on many of the homes and shops we now passed. Then she suddenly pulled to the side of the road. "This is it. I'm not going any farther."

We sat at a nondescript cross street. Lulu leaned forward to get a better view out of the passenger window. "My mom lives down this block."

I nodded, but her statement surprised me. Until

now she hadn't mentioned anything about seeing family. Before getting out, I had to ask, "So if this place is so crappy, why are you here?"

She clamped down for a while. "My cousin called a couple days ago. Mom's sick." A car drove past as the passengers stared at us. "Really sick." She blinked but couldn't stop the mascara from streaking her cheeks. "Mom needs someone to take care of her." Lulu glanced down the street where she grew up and then said with a slow, deliberate cadence, "I'm going to stay." Her voice fell to a whisper. "I'm all she has." Lulu seemed to understand that worked both ways.

31
Scars

Whenever I thought of morticians I envisioned them as ghouls hiding secret desires to wrap themselves in cold sex. So when the driver of my ride into Kansas City said he was a mortician, my stomach dropped, picturing stainless steel tables holding gray bodies—imagining myself as one of those bodies.

His name was Bill. Up to then I'd never thought of morticians as having names. Bill was middle-aged and wore a wedding ring; odd for a necrophiliac. He wasn't wearing a black suit that contrasted against ghostly skin, either. Instead, he was tan and wore jeans and a blue T-shirt. How could he be an undertaker without the suit and pallor?

"Looks like you might have a few miles under you." He spoke with steady pace. "Where you headed?"

"Seattle." My answer seemed too simple, even shorter than polite conversation could tolerate. I don't know if I wanted to talk or if his apparent willingness to listen pulled out the words. "It's longer than the miles, though. Mostly it's the time. How long it'll take."

"Sounds like you're weary."

"A bit." I minimized.

"What pushed you onto this trip?"

Pushed? Why'd he say that? "Resentment, mostly" came out more quickly than I expected. "I resented everything, especially all the candy-ass-kissing kids in school." An anger welled up in me. "They just partied, pissing away their parents' money, and I thought I was better than them. But as it turned out, I mostly just spent time smoking pot by myself while thinking about what screwups they were." I tried to reclaim some dignity. "At least I was just pissing away my own money." I couldn't believe I was saying these things: private thoughts, shameful acts. "I hated myself. It wasn't always like that, so I knew I could change, but I had to get away to do it. I couldn't figure out any other way."

Embarrassed and ashamed, I was revealing myself as a pompous baby, but I kept talking anyway. "Resentment isn't the only thing, though." For no reason I ran my right hand across my knife sheath. "There's only so much school can teach, and I wanted to learn more. I mean, the world's pretty damn big."

"You've got a lot of motivations there." He glanced at my pack on the backseat. "Enough of them to push you out before you could even grab a tent." He drew a wrapped sandwich from a small paper bag resting between us and handed me the food without a word.

"Thanks, this'll help." I took a bite and swallowed fast. "Hell, I don't know if I'm coming or going, and sometimes don't even know what I'm doing." I pointed to my head, twirled my index finger and crossed my eyes. Crazy. "But of course that doesn't stop me from doing it."

"Pretty intense feelings," Bill said. "But these'll pass. Don't worry about it. Trust in yourself that you'll figure it out."

"Sounds nice, but today I don't know if I'm a hero or a coward." I looked out the window, staring at nothing. "I was even in jail."

"What for?"

"Being stupid." We laughed.

"So did you learn anything?"

"Yeah, when I'm thinking of doing something and that little voice in the back of my head tells me I shouldn't do it—it's right. In fact, it's always right."

"You know what I think?" He paused. "I think the smallest voice we hear is God's."

"Why do you think that? Don't you think God would flex a little more muscle?" I didn't want to sound contrary, but I had to say it. "I think that's just my voice. I mean, it's always there."

"Have you ever been wrong, Steve?"

"Only about a million times."

"Well, you said it yourself—that voice is never wrong. So how could it be yours?"

I always knew when I was making a conscious

decision to go against that voice in the back of my head. It was easy to disregard but impossible not to hear.

Bill listened. I opened up. I gave him some childhood details; told him how I'd felt propelled forward, even without a destination; shared my feelings of almost nonstop loneliness; spoke of how I helped some people; said how every place was little more than a speed bump before my next destination, which put me nowhere all the time; that I'd even lost my sanity at least once. And I promised not to yodel for him.

Finally, I said, "I've blabbed a ton. How'd you do that, Bill? How'd you get all that out of me?"

"Listening is more than just waiting for your turn to talk. People talk when they're ready." He looked over at me. "You're ready now."

If there's a Morticians Hall of Fame, Bill should be in it. He was a journeyman listener, especially when it came to loss. Maybe our conversation seemed natural for him, since I'd lost myself.

"I can't say what you're doing is normal, but I think it's necessary. We all find our paths. I mean, look at me—I'm a mortician. If I want someone to stop bugging me at a social gathering, I just tell them that." He laughed. "But I love it."

Maybe I wasn't lost, just finding my path. I was being true to myself, even if I wasn't sure of what the truth was.

"My oldest is seventeen," he said. "With her, when she's hurting, I can see the same emotions I'll see in an elderly widow. In some respects, we don't change that much as we go through our lives. We just get better at recognizing where we are."

"What's it like always working with people who are grieving?"

"It's easy, when you listen. The whole experience of talking about the details that a funeral requires makes the death become more real for them, and when they hear their own words, they understand they're still moving forward, that life will go on. That helps them work back into their lives."

Soon I'd be working back into my life. I'd been afraid that when I returned, everything would be the same, but now I felt confident there'd be a difference—me. My puzzle had new pieces.

I thought about how I'd handle it when my parents and friends died, maybe even a wife or a child. It scared me. But I knew other people got through things like that. "Luckily, time heals all wounds."

"No...no it doesn't." Bill the mortician took a tone of professorial care. "All those events we go through, all those things that pass, they aren't left completely behind. They become part of who we are, like scars."

Looking back, I now know Bill was right. Maybe the scars are less visible as time passes, but even when you're lying on a stainless steel table, stripped of everything, they're still there.

32

Never What You Expect

	MAY					
	1	2	3	4	5	6
7	8	9	10	11	12	13
14	15	16	17	18	19	20
21	22	23	24	25	26	27
28	29	30	31			

Cornstalks as tall as men extended beyond the Kansas horizons, like an alien army standing in formation waiting for their orders. I was surrounded.

Rides came quickly but were short: grandparents, a single mom, students, a barber, a guy who smelled like diesel, and others. They were all close to home, maybe driving to the store, heading to a friend's house, going to work. For most of them, the small towns defined their sense of place. Faces and places were familiar to them, and venturing into the unknown seemed unknown. I fluctuated between feeling superior and feeling envious:

superior for venturing but envious of their comfortable familiarity.

Much of that day I had crept across Eastern Kansas in a disproportionately large percentage of muscle cars. "It's a long ways between anything, so runnin' fast helps," one driver said. The creases in his hands were lined with the remnants of black grease, and a Marlboro hung from his lips. He drove a yellow Olds Cutlass with dual air scoops on the hood that looked like black-barreled nostrils. "Yeah, I've got a Turbo 350 tranny, Cragar SS mags on the 60s in back, and a 442 with an Edelbrock four-barrel under the hood." His right hand held the pistol-grip shift lever. That ride was short, but fast.

My total progress for the day was around sixty miles, landing me just west of Topeka. Knowing the moon would soon rise out of the corn, I decided to keep trying for rides into the night. Cars approached, blinding me with their headlights, and after each passed, darkness rushed back in so that the moon and I stood as mute partners. With every breath I took, the night deepened. Finally, it got late, around eleven, and I'd been standing in the same spot for over two hours. *No one picks up a stranger in the dark. Guess I'll sleep in the corn.*

Just then a yellow turn signal blinked. I couldn't see the vehicle behind the headlights, but I could tell it was big. Rows of golden lights and red reflectors appeared like an electrified lifeboat in the night as it passed before me and pulled to the shoulder. It was an 18-wheeler.

As I reached up to the handhold, the driver let out a big "Howdy!" that I could hear through the open passenger window. Pulling myself to the door, I said howdy back.

STEVE THEME

Marv was an older man wearing a Mack Trucks hat. As he started shifting through the sixteen gears, he said, "I'm goin' to Denver. Got to be there by sunrise. Where you goin'?"

"Denver."

"Well that's a happy coincidence." He patted the steering wheel. "This here's my baby. She's new, not yet ten thousand miles."

Even in the dark, I could see a clean sheen across the cab's interior. This tractor had everything: air suspension seats, stereo, CB and VHF radios, a sleeper cab with a TV, a padded leather ceiling, climate control, and a chrome bulldog on the front of the hood. I felt myself transforming from a powerless kid to king of the road.

"Where've you been today?" I asked. Because it was night, this ride could be more risky than most, and I wanted to gauge as quickly as possible if Marv sounded deranged or seemed like he wanted to harm me. I'd already looked through the curtain into the sleeper cab to check if anyone was lurking there.

"It's been a long day," he said. The dash lights cast deep shadows on his sallow face, reflecting miles of weariness. "I started in Cincinnati. That was ten hours ago." Here was a driver who needed someone to help keep him awake.

Marv talked about how he'd been working in a factory in Detroit until he was fifty. "I had to get out. Be out. That's all there was to it." I could tell he'd said those words many times. The road was now his home, even though he and his wife owned a house on the Lake of the Ozarks, in Missouri. Marv squared his jaw. "The money's good, and I get to see the country. I love this job. Been doin' it ten years. I'm goin' to keep takin' care of this rig," he said. "Wouldn't let anyone else drive it, that's for sure."

It was good thing Marv enjoyed driving, because we had over five hundred night miles between us and Denver. Under that moon, we sailed through a calm sea of fields. Waves of corn, just the tops flickering with the wind, no longer seemed alien but smooth and distant.

"I miss the lake, miss it a lot," he said. "And my wife wants me there more." He sighed. "It's not just the lake I miss."

"I know what you mean," I said, and shielded by the dark, I felt more free to speak. "In fact, I've been really lonely for about the last two months. I've hardly seen the same person for more than a couple hours."

He nodded, seeming to understand the shattered continuity created by nonstop travel.

"My sons are grown, older than you." He told me about their interests growing up. "Once, for my oldest, I built a model Conestoga wagon for a school history project. I don't know if that boy touched anything on it until he carried it into the class."

"Yeah, in grade school science fairs, I competed against fathers like you." We both laughed.

"They're gone now, each still in the Detroit area." He squinted down at the gauges. "I guess that's not true. I'm the one who's gone, not them. Anyway, my wife has more time on her hands these days. Says she's finished doing all those house improvements she wanted to do. So I told her to find some more." He grinned and inhaled enough so that his shoulders rose. "Yeeeep—" He exhaled his entire breath on one word. "We were even thinking she could ride with me. But she's getting older, and climbing in and out of the cab, nights in the sleeper, nothin' but diner food, and you know, showering at truck stops. It wouldn't take long and she'd have a meltdown." This time when he exhaled, no words came out. He stared into the night.

"I wish that part could have worked." He looked at me. "When I was your age, I didn't have a damn idea about what type of work I wanted to do. I guess that's why I landed on a Chrysler factory floor." He flipped some switch. "Guess I'm lucky—I'm finally doin' what I want to."

I also felt like I was doing what I wanted to, even if it was only for a few more days.

Around two in the morning Marv pulled over for gas. "Time to stretch the ol' legs and drain the lizard."

Lizard draining sounded good to me too; one thing I never imposed on drivers was to ask them to pull over so I could pee. I left it to them to recommend stops. After I came out of the restroom, I could see Marv topping off the fuel tank on the driver's side. "How much does she hold?"

"Oh, plenty." His voice slowed. "Say..." He gave me a long stare now that he could see me under the station lights. "Do you know how to drive a stick?"

"Yeah. Why?"

When we climbed back into the cab, I found myself sitting behind the leather-wrapped steering wheel. I vacillated between thinking this was an incredibly bad decision—by both of us—and thinking that driving the big rig would be super cool. As I sat in the driver's seat, arms spread to reach across the breadth of the steering wheel, I replayed Marv's words. *This here' my baby. Wouldn't let anyone else drive it, that's for sure.* I tried to understand what could change a man's mind so quickly. He was sleep-deprived for sure, and that could impact his judgment, but once I buckled in, Marv trusted me and that seemed enough. I depressed the clutch, hit the starter button, and gave the hulking diesel a rev to get a feel for the accelerator.

"Just let the clutch out easy," Marv said.

"Yep." I was already concentrating on easy, real easy. The truck glided forward. No lurching; just a gentle flow. The slow momentum, combined with the huge weight, was relaxing. I looked in the driver's side mirror and saw the long trailer pulling out as if I weren't driving it, but I understood that I controlled the mass. With some relief, I eased into the cushioned leather seat and shifted to second gear.

"Not bad," Marv said. But we weren't out of the parking lot yet.

"This is pretty cool." I hadn't been scared but definitely anxious, and now my confidence increased with each shift of the gears.

"You know," Marv said, followed by a long pause. "I normally wouldn't do this."

"Have you ever let anyone drive your rig before?"

"No. Never." He stared at the moon.

I could almost see him aging as he spoke, watching his reflection come and go in the window. Once we reached the highway, he pointed out the gauges, and I drove a while with the cab lights on to get my bearings.

"I'm okay now. I'm going to flip off the lights." Once the cab darkened, the dash gauges lit up with yellow, red, and green, and each one pointed with its own orange arrow. Our reflections in the windows disappeared, and night poured in.

"You look pretty tired," I said loudly as Marv's head started bobbing into sleep.

"It's been a long, long, day. Going since six."

I didn't see any point in telling him I'd been going since sunrise. "I'll wake you before we get to Denver." That formed our unstated contract—I'd get a long ride, he'd get sleep.

He lay curled against the seat's side wing. "Okay, but I normally wouldn't do this," he said one last time. It seemed he was trying to convince himself he could still take being a long-haul trucker.

We passed under clouds and the moon no longer lit the fields. The road was wide and clear, with no scenery. My hands lay light on the wheel; the truck could practically steer itself. All the gauges held steady in their silent glow. I'd never driven a tractor-trailer combination. Hours of night awaited me.

Just keep it between the lines, big boy. I wonder what we're hauling. How many tons are back there? What if I have to swerve? What if I have to slam on the brakes? What if we get pulled over? What the fuck is going on!... Okay, okay, don't freak out. Don't fall asleep.

A cup of coffee from Marv's thermos helped, but not much. After an hour my head filled with the same old questions that just wouldn't leave: *How did I work myself into an emotional corner that caused me to leave on this incredibly reckless journey? Why couldn't I rise above my scorn and live happily? Is this the best way to get what I need? What do I need? What am I losing? How the hell did I end up here—driving this semi across Kansas in the middle of the night?*

Under my breath, quietly enough as to not wake Marv, I said, "Sometimes this just seems like a giant insane asylum you've got here." I didn't have anyone else to talk to, and I was tired of asking myself questions. "Hey, God, what's going on? I'm just one of the inmates, no one special, but...I don't suppose you know why I'm doing this?" In the void of night, maybe I had someone's attention. "There are times it seems like this is the only right thing I could be doing. Sometimes it just seems ape-shit crazy and makes me feel lost, even meaningless."

It seemed like the truck wasn't moving but that instead the road was racing toward me out of the dark, only to disappear under the bulldog on the hood.

"That's okay. Thought I'd ask anyway." I held out a distant hope for some clarity. Without that, the entire trip would be pointless.

Dawn rose up behind us from the prairie, and ahead of us the sun lit the white peaks of the Rocky Mountains as they pointed into a blue sky. The mountains reminded me of the previous winter when a group of friends and I had created the Eternal Fraternity of Snow Pirates. We rafted, hiked, camped, skied, got cold, and then drank rum. By the end of the winter, our ranks grew when we added two honorary Mud Maidens, one of which was my sister Janelle. I had good friends and I'd never been a loner, at least not until the months before leaving on this trip.

The frozen summits appeared to rise straight out of the switchgrass, since the base of the Rockies was still beyond the horizon, blocked by the curve of the earth. I kept expecting to see the mountains' lower elevations revealed as I neared. Apparently I wasn't as near as I'd thought. As I kept driving, and driving—sitting on an air-suspension seat, whisking along at sixty miles per hour with the heater on and a cup of coffee next to me in its custom holder—I couldn't stop thinking about the westward-bound pioneers who'd crossed this ground on foot. None of them had ever seen mountains so enormous, and they had no reference to grasp their scale. Each day the Rockies must have mocked them from a distance. According to historical accounts, after these hopeful people spotted the first peaks, it took weeks before they arrived at the mountains. For many it was during this time that their morale plummeted as their food dwindled and it didn't seem like they were making any progress.

I later read the diary entry of a Mormon pioneer girl dating from October of 1856. She was thirteen years old and had pulled a cart by hand with her younger sister from St. Louis to a crossing at the North Platte River, Nebraska:

> The water was deep and very cold and we drifted out of the regular crossing and we came near being drowned and the water came to our arm pits poor Mother was standing on the bank screaming as we got near the bank I heard her say for God Sake some of you men help my poor girls. Several of the brethren came down to the bank of the river and pulled our cart up for us. Mother was there to meet us her clothing was dry but ours was wet and cold and very soon frozen. Mother took off one of her

under skirts and put it on one of us and her apron for another to keep the wet cloth from us for we had to travel several miles before we could camp.

It doesn't take looking back many generations, if any, to see we're all stock of hardwood.

Even though the sun was up, the cab was still silent. Everything outside was clear, but I still didn't have an answer to the question I'd asked in the dark and so many other times throughout the trip: Am I brave or a coward for leaving? But now, somehow, the smothering weight of needing to know exactly how I felt about myself was gone. When I stopped my self-obsession, that's when I got my answer—the question didn't matter.

I REACHED THE EXIT MARV wanted, downshifted through the gears, eased onto the shoulder, and brought the truck to a smooth stop. Through a tired smile, I let out a long sigh as my hands flopped into my lap. Sitting there, I couldn't believe what I'd just done—couldn't believe someone would ask me to do it, couldn't believe that I'd said yes, couldn't believe the ride didn't end in disaster. After convincing myself everything was really okay, I reached over to Marv and gave his shoulder a shake. "Marv, we're here."

He pulled his head up from the chair wing. The bags under his eyes were darker than when he'd fallen asleep.

"I hate to say it, buddy, but it's time for you to go back to work."

Marv shook his head and looked around. "You did a hell of a job there, partner."

We got out, and I stood with my pack over my shoulder as Marv walked around the front of the truck to me. "I'm heading up to Boulder," he said as cars passed—my potential rides. "You want to come and be my unloader? I'll pay ya."

I hadn't eaten dinner the night before or breakfast that morning and had no money, so I gave his offer quick but serious thought and then declined. In Key West I'd known I would run out of money and food before I reached home. But faced with the reality of hunger, friends and family still mattered more.

33

Blind and Tired

	MAY					
	1	2	3	4	5	6
7	8	9	10	11	12	13
14	15	**16**	17	18	19	20
21	22	23	24	25	26	27
28	29	30	31			

The snow and crisp air pushed away the fatigue of driving through the night. Around noon I found myself standing at the summit of Vail Pass. I could see the elevation marker—10,662 feet. Everything was dry and bright. Crystalline hills drew a sharp line to create a jagged horizon, and the glimmering hard white contrasted against the soft blue of the sky. I felt taut and alive.

The place was so beautiful and peaceful, I decided to enjoy the wilderness by bushwhacking away from the road.

Climbing up and over a small slope, I quickly escaped sight of the highway. The snow had a top layer of icy crust that I kept breaking through, sinking thigh deep. To lighten up some, I took off my pack. Even so, one awkward movement and I'd break through again before I could take another step. As I walked, the crunch of my boots on the fragile crust drowned out all other sounds.

At the base of a stump where snow had melted, there were delicate flowers breaking ground in the few areas where the dirt was exposed to the sun. Short stalks supported petals that looked like fireworks detonating only inches off the ground.

I sat silently on the stump, not moving a muscle, and the rough country enveloped me. First I noticed the trickling sound of millions of droplets melting beneath the snow as they began their journey to the Pacific. On the stump's base, beetles wove their way around its soft darkened fibers. The brisk wind smelled of clarity. A woodpecker in the distance resumed its tak tak tak—tak tak tak, and high above, a hawk circled.

I thought of the many times Katie and I had sat quietly in nature. Sometimes we'd go cross-country skiing, and each trip included times of silence. Nature felt even bigger when she was with me, maybe because I felt bigger. We'd go on walks and lie in the grass, sometimes roll in it. I knew she still cared. I didn't know how much, but that didn't matter. Any level of caring was good enough. Ever since I'd left Key West, she'd been becoming more real because I knew I'd see her on my way back—in a few days I'd be looking into her eyes.

It took only fifteen minutes for the cold to soak in, and I needed to move. After walking about a mile, I decided to head back to the highway. It would have been easy to keep going deeper, but I wasn't carrying any survival gear and no one knew I was there. Just a broken ankle or a twisted knee could turn me into an obituary.

Once I was back at the highway, I hung out my thumb, and in short order found myself standing next to a state patrol cruiser.

The trooper rolled down his window. "What are you doing?"

"Heading home." I avoided directly incriminating myself. Once again, posted along the highway intermittently, but ever so clearly, there were NO HITCHHIKING signs.

He casually brushed crumbs from his chest. Then, without bothering to look up, said, "You can't hitchhike from here."

"It's kind of the only place," I said, half pleading. There were no off-ramps on this two-lane highway. I lifted my hands, palms to the sky, showing I was pretty much out of options. He helped me with another option.

"See that parking lot?" He pointed to a flat patch of snow about fifty feet off the road. "You can wait there until a car pulls in, and when they leave, you can ask for a ride."

"Uhh…right." I didn't try to hide my disbelief. This parking lot was still blocked by a two-foot berm of snow that was created from the plows clearing the road.

He waited while I trudged over, crossed the berm, and stood alone calf deep in snow. The trooper then gave a satisfied wave and cruised off. I began to shiver and felt ridiculous standing in this no-car zone. Once the trooper was out of sight, I walked back to the highway. In a moment a large orange snowplow was headed my way.

"Looks like you could use a ride," the driver said as I opened the heavy orange door.

"Yeah, it's pretty chilly out here." Pointing behind us to the arctic parking lot, I added, "A cop wanted me to wait in that lot until someone pulled in and then hope that they wanted to give me a ride."

"Hells bells." The driver let out a bellowing laugh. "Nobody's even going to be able to get into that lot for another couple weeks."

The heater motor purred, and I felt safe sitting in the stout machine. We hadn't gone far when the driver dropped me outside a CDOT maintenance station. The wide entrance to the facility made a nice place for a car to pull over.

A small white Toyota pickup with two guys in the front stopped. I hopped in the truck bed, trying to focus on the spectacular scenery instead of the cold. The two up front were in their early twenties and carrying on a conversation, waving their arms, laughing, and constantly adjusting the radio as stations faded and then blared. The window on the back of the cab didn't open, and they had rolled up the side windows, leaving me no way to easily communicate with them.

My hair was whipping into my face, so I pulled out a blue bandana and tied it around my head. The truck bed was covered in remnants from past loads of sand, and the grains now scattered in the wind and worked their way around my glacier goggles to sting my eyes. The glacier goggles had been my sunglasses throughout the trip. These are thick, black-rimmed glasses with sturdy arms that wrap entirely around the back of the wearer's ears. They came with leather blinders to block all light from the sides, which would have been great now, but I'd tossed those out because they blocked my peripheral vision. Best of all, the glasses were indestructible and inexpensive. I had sat, slept, and stepped on them, buried them under luggage, and worn them almost every day. Even without the blinders, the glasses kept most of the sand out of my eyes. I leaned against the back of the cab, intermittently playing a harmonica.

I tried to grasp the magnitude of the Rockies—mountains that divide a continent. They're wider than some ranges are long. There was so much more to see than what I was experiencing that I swore to myself I'd return. Across the valley, dark granite slopes speckled with firs and aspens rose to the sky.

There was little room for error driving on that pass. The shoulders were narrow to nonexistent, and the corners were blind. On one side, cliffs shot uncontrollably up, and on the other side was a river.

We slowed suddenly, and I turned to look ahead. A line of cars was stacked bumper-to-bumper behind a lumbering semi that struggled with the twisting road. No big deal. This would just give me more time to enjoy the scenery.

After several minutes, though, our truck jerked and veered left into the oncoming lane. I figured there was a straight stretch of road and we would pass, but when I turned to look ahead, I didn't see any straight stretch. I saw a long line of cars leading to the truck as it disappeared behind a blind turn at a sharp right bend.

If there was an oncoming car rounding the corner, we'd have no time to avoid a head-on.

For a second I froze. *Are these guys out of their minds?* I had suspected they were high by the way they were so animated, but this shot to insanely high. I glanced to see if the passenger was getting the driver to turn back to the right. No, he just sat and smiled.

I lapsed into momentary helplessness, a victim anticipating an impact. The blaze of vulnerability took me back to a night with my mother and father. I stood hunched, looking at my feet and the brownish linoleum floor, forearms pressed against each side of my head, like a boxer. As I jolted with pain, all I heard was my hysterical mother. "Notinthehead!" Eventually I dropped.

As we raced forward, the people in slower cars turned their disbelieving eyes on us.

I stood and placed my hands on top of the cab. I spread my legs for balance, raised to the balls of my feet, and got ready to jump. Then I rocked back and forth slightly, like a tennis player awaiting a powerful serve.

I flash-analyzed which way to leap. To the right was the line of cars. If I choose that direction, I'd roll under their tires instantly. To the left was the river where large boulders were strewn next to the highway, remnants from the road's construction.

I decided left. At least there could be a chance to live, however slim. Even though I hadn't slept in about thirty hours, adrenalin kicked in full force. It helped cement my decision.

I stood ready.

Gasps came fast, short, and cold.

The wind caused tears, blurring my vision.

We accelerated.

The inner assurance I'd felt when the mafia hit man had held his gun to my head was nonexistent. I was terrified.

As the corner neared, my muscles tightened. *If a car appears right now, I might not even have time to jump.* The landing didn't matter now, only the decision.

We quickly rounded the corner, and I could see the road ahead. There were still several cars to pass before we would reach the plodding truck, but the empty road ran straight enough that I knew we'd pass before the next oncoming car could hit us. I froze in my stance, not breathing. Jackhammer heart.

As I finally lowered myself, my cold joints felt stiff. They stung. We pulled ahead of the semi, and I could see the truck driver shaking his head.

Once we were back in the correct lane and the immediate danger had passed, I pounded on the back window. They looked at me as if nothing had happened. I shouted and motioned for them to pull over. They seemed surprised but indicated they'd stop once there was a place wide enough.

As soon as they stopped, I jumped out.

My hands trembled, and the pack fell to the ground. I followed, sitting on my pack, head in hands, trying not to relive what had just happened. I ground a boot heel into the gravel to reassure myself that I was safe on the side of the road. The adrenaline drained away and I could barely move. I couldn't help but think about my family and how devastated they would have been; how they would have had to deal with the pieces of me that were scooped up and sent to them.

"What am I doing?" I asked aloud. Then I yelled it, my voice ringing off the rock hills. Then I screamed it so loud pressure pushed on the backs of my eyes. "WHAT THE HELL AM I DOING!"

No response. No one to hear me.

If I had been able to stay in that one spot for eternity, I would have. Instead, I stared down the twisting road and accepted that the only way out was to rise again and extend my thumb, while trying to hope for the best. Under my breath, I said, "God, I'm tired."

34
Wide Nights

The day rode on through Colorado, past the towns of Eagle, Gypsum, Antlers, and Rifle. The scenery was still majestic, but after I'd screamed to no one asking what I was doing, I spent most of the rides that day staring into my lap. A dozen miles west of Grand Junction, I decided to stop hitching for the day. The sun had set hours ago.

About a quarter mile off I-70 I saw the silhouette of a derelict cabin. It was a good bet that no one lived in the shack and I could settle in there for a safe night. The moon provided just enough light to see across the sparse terrain. Sagebrush and gullies hid in shadows of shadows, and I stumbled over uneven ground but made it past old coils of barbwire, now just black lines in the night.

STEVE THEME

Once I reached what had been the distant silhouette, it became a real cabin with a bent trike, some bedding, and a folded aluminum lawn chair strewn by the front door. These were the only remnants of a family that had called this plot home.

Inside, a corner of the floor sagged away from the wall, creating a gap where a field mouse of light crept in. The rest of the floor was covered with thick dust blown in from the surrounding scrub. I didn't have a flashlight, only a small lighter, and in its flicker I could see creosote stains running along the cracking lumber. Thin gaps between the planking of the walls let in more flecks of light. It felt like I was checking into a motel made of old match sticks.

From a hole in the wall where glass had once filled the front window, I looked out to a dark expanse where black hills rose from a distant southwestern plain. Again, I became a dot amid the immense, but this expanse of the planet seemed to be mine. There may have been people somewhere out there, but it felt like I alone had that view. During the trip I'd come to learn how little space I needed to sleep, and there were always crevasses and hidden spots to work with. Every night I hid amid the world's empty spaces.

After unrolling my sleeping bag I lay there and thought about some of the places I'd slept.

One night in Tennessee a ride had dropped me next to a big box store in the early stages of construction, just a concrete slab the size of a football field ringed by four bare concrete walls. I decided to sleep there, knowing I'd be gone before the workers arrived the next morning.

Lying on the hard slab, nudged against the base of a wall, I'd felt exposed even though no one could see me.

Several hours later, while I lay curled up facing a wall, I heard a loud whooping noise coming at me, fast. Before I could even open my eyes, I registered bright light through my lids. I popped my eyes open, and the wall I'd snuggled up to loomed blistering bright. A blast of wind started swirling construction dust, and while I was trying to make sense of the wind and dust, I envisioned a truck racing across the floor toward me shining its high beams. When I rolled over, the light blinded me and there were sirens.

What in the hell is going on? A drumming thawp, thawp, thawp, thawp pounded in my ears. This is way too loud and bright if it's just someone who wants me to leave. And the fury of wind made no sense. After several seconds a bizarre clarity emerged.

Craning my head to the sky, squinting past the spotlight, I could see a police helicopter hovering directly over me. I kept looking up, staying in my bag—no running. The chopper continued slowly descending, to maybe a hundred feet; the roar of the engine, the slap of the blades drowned out the sirens. Powdery concrete dust whipped into a choking cloud. The light moved off me to scan the rest of the building and then bolted back to me. I kicked my feet apart to spread the sleeping bag and make it more visible, to show I'm just some guy sleeping. That didn't change things. They were clearly looking for someone, and I was at the top of their list. Slowly rotating, the copter swept its light across the tops of the surrounding trees and then again snapped it back down on me. I felt like a cornered rat and sat blinking.

They scanned me one more time, and then the machine and its light shot away. I looked like someone had just poured a bag of gray flour over me.

On the floor of that small shack in the scablands, and still trying to fall asleep, I thought about one warm night east of Sacramento when I'd climbed up a steep hill with nicely spaced pines where I could disappear within them before walking too far. At about a hundred feet elevation above the road, I started walking across the hill searching for a place to lie down. An outcropping ahead looked perfect, with a nice pocket that even slanted back into the hill so I didn't need to worry about rolling off.

As I approached I began hearing music, then people's voices. This didn't make sense, since there were no homes or roads on the hillside. I approached the outcropping slowly but still didn't see anything. Then, at the point where I could look over the edge, I peered down. About a hundred feet below me was a country club. My perch was directly above the clubhouse.

An expansive cedar terrace spread out, leading to a large blue swimming pool with the club's red crest inlaid on the bottom. As a cherry on top, a wedding reception in full swing filled the estate. A tall wood fence enclosed the area with NO TRESPASSING signs. They meant me.

Men and women circled the clear pool: pillars of black jackets and long glistening gowns, everyone holding drinks. Some people disappeared through the clubhouse's sliding glass doors into what I imagined was an extravagant spread, complete with colorful bouquets and a centerpiece ice sculpture. From inside a band played songs that drifted up to me.

No one knew, but I'd crashed the party.

As a benign observer, I couldn't comprehend the lives behind the people I saw. They all looked like movie stars, but of course they weren't—at least, I assumed, not all of them. Silver platters floated on waiters' hands as the servants wove easily between the stars. To envision myself down there, mingling and chatting away, was beyond my imagination. I felt it would take longer than a lifetime for me to gain any position to belong in a crowd like that, even as a waiter.

I hunkered on my outcrop where dried grasses formed the perfect blanket to set my hoagie rolls. I pulled some sharp cheddar from my pack, sliced it with my Buck, and made a sandwich. Lying back and looking uphill, I listened to the music while eating, washing my meal down with water that had a plastic aftertaste.

The band started playing the pop song "Sign" by the Five Man Electrical Band. They sang about an interloper being told he's not welcome, with signs posted everywhere making that clear—my private irony.

I smiled. They deserved their fun. A big day for the bride and groom offered me a chance to lie on my back, stare at the clouds, and enjoy live music.

Later in my journey, on the Gulf Coast around Pensacola, Florida, I'd found a small strip mall backing to an elementary school parking lot. A row of crimson-leafed bushes lined the far corner of the mall property, creating an opaque blind to sleep behind. A few feet from the base of the bushes, a Cyclone fence ringed the end of the school's parking lot.

I slipped between the fence and hedge. My long thin, slot seemed quiet, and the school was a strong baseball toss away. The school day had long since ended, and I slept well until slightly before I wanted to wake up.

While still dozing I heard an engine, opened my eyes, and then saw a car pull up on the other side of the fence. It backed into the parking space nearest me, with its taillights about a foot from my head and the exhaust pushing hot and dense into my face. When the engine stopped, I lay completely still, thinking maybe it was just chance that the car had parked next to my head. The driver's door creaked open, and a guy in a sport coat and slacks stepped out. He didn't look at me, even though we were practically close enough to shake hands. I rose up shortly after that and could see more cars arriving, but they all parked in another section of the lot. The car by me was alone.

Then it dawned on me. He'd parked there to block the children from seeing a vagrant bum sleeping next to their school. I couldn't fault him—I probably would've done the same if I were in his position. My place in society hit me in the face like the exhaust I'd woken to.

As I rolled up my bag, I had to remind myself not to base my worth upon the reactions of others. With the ten thousand disdainful looks I'd received from people who drove by me, I was well practiced at reminding myself of that. Some days, though, my armor wore down and I felt those looks were justified. I left before the children could look at me.

One place that had been dry and private was a large concrete drainage pipe that hadn't yet been buried. Its curving walls kept me lying long and strait. Wide highway medians with tree cover were convenient but loud. Some nights I could hear the rustlings of raccoons, coyotes, deer; maybe some dogs. I usually couldn't see them.

Many dawns brought a glistening cover of dew. But I'd simply lie there—morning air is the best—and before long the dew would evaporate, unless it was raining.

Rain brought challenges, and at night it seemed to fall with malice. When it rained, or if the sky even hinted at rain, I kept my eyes open for a more protected place to hole up. Without a tent, I needed to improvise. On nights it rained, I usually found awnings or some form of covered shelter. Lying wet on cold ground is a surefire way to contract what I called cold sickness, something I'd experienced twice before this trip, and I'd had hints of it during the night I spent in the Mojave. I didn't want any repeats.

Cold sickness is the precursor to and last line of defense from hypothermia. It feels like the instant pressure of diarrhea, the urge to vomit, and a sudden fever. It takes only a minute or two to fully manifest, but each time I'd had it, it warmed my body quickly. In each case I'd been able to find some source of warmth, but on this trip, that'd be unlikely. If I couldn't find a dry spot to sleep, then I'd find a large tree and sit with my back to the trunk. Maybe I'd get only a bit of sleep, but at least I'd stay reasonably dry under the tree's canopy and in the morning I wouldn't be gripped by dream-state hallucinations and immobility.

STEVE THEME

But that night, in that cabin, all I needed to do was reminisce. Coyotes crooned long, slow notes, and their ease with the dark comforted me. I extended my arms above my head for a long stretch. Then I took a second to appreciate that here, behind a door, with private walls and a ceiling, I felt at peace, invisible to the world.

35

Temple Love

	MAY					
	1	2	3	4	5	6
7	8	9	10	11	12	13
14	15	16	17	18	19	20
21	22	23	24	25	26	27
28	29	30	31			

The morning rose empty—empty cabin, empty stomach, and not even a breeze to tumble across the valley. As I looked west, the blank road struck out to nowhere.

This expanse needed a tune. Each time I blew on a harp, I played a unique song. The rhythms, styles, keys, and moods—combined with my inability to read music—made every tune an original composition. I wasn't afraid to let my rhythms reach over the hills, announcing my presence as I stood next to the cabin. As the coyotes bedded down in those early hours, they heard me howling. The strains echoed me, and in turn, as I heard them, assured me I still existed.

Raw terrain rules the two hundred fifty miles between

STEVE THEME

Grand Junction, Colorado, and Provo, Utah. I hung a right off I-70 for Highway 6, a less-used but more direct route to Provo and subsequently to Salt Lake City. The highway followed an immense dry valley that once again left me feeling microscopic. My driver and I passed the Starvation Wildlife Management Area. A scrap of dirt road accessed the area's mountains of baked rock. I imagined myself standing in the surrounding wilderness, high on a peak, and wondered what the landscape would look like. Mars came to mind.

JOHAN PICKED ME UP IN a rental car outside of Salt Lake City. He wore his black hair slicked to one side, sported sturdy black prescription glasses, and was slightly built. His rental car smelled like cologne. He'd recently received a master's degree in political science from BYU. I'd always thought that that major didn't prepare anyone for anything, and by *anything* I meant making money. My stomach knotted as I realized how embedded my thinking was and how that attitude echoed my father's. Money's easy pull could drag me away from making a happy living to making just a lucrative one. Maybe not even that.

I asked Johan what it was like going to college in Salt Lake City.

"It wasn't just while I attended school; I was raised there my whole life. We were brought up spotless, in the church all the way." The whiteness of his cotton shirt reinforced his words. "As a kid, my family worshiped in Temple Square mostly." His voice didn't carry the tone of happy nostalgia but maintained the indifference of a biographer.

He explained how Mormon mandates encompassed all aspects of life: laws, architecture, education, gatherings, diet, dating, marriage. "There was no escape. I couldn't even kiss my wife until our wedding night." His words were curt. "It's our way, called courting. It's all supervised."

"That's a lot of rules," I said, to let him know we were of the same mindset. "It sounds pretty crazy, not even kissing until after you're married." I'd never heard of that. "You're not BSing me, are you?"

"You're right." He let out a slow breath. "It's crazy."

"How's that get you closer to God? I mean, what's the point?" I wasn't trying to start a debate—since he was driving and I didn't want to get kicked out—but I didn't understand.

"It doesn't get us closer to God necessarily, but courting is designed to make sure we pick the right mate and stay married for life, and then into eternity." He tipped his head down and rubbed his forehead slowly, repeating, "Into eternity."

He appeared older than someone who took a straight shot through college, so I asked what he'd done before getting his degree.

"I was a missionary. You know, one of those guys riding a bicycle and wearing a suit that always looks out of place." He grinned. "Actually, I spent two years in Ecuador and to tell you the truth, they've been the best two years of my life. I couldn't talk to anyone back home for the first year, except on Christmas—those are the rules, but I liked that." Now he sounded more relaxed. "I got a real look at how fortunate we are." He paused. "Americans take a lot for granted."

"Like good food." I wasn't taking food for granted, having not eaten for two days. Sometimes I became a bit unsteady as a loose sensation would roll over me. Most of the time, though, I felt solid and just made sure to drink plenty of water.

"Funny you should mention food," Johan said. "I worked at a nutrition center where we fed kids. I was on a humanitarian mission, not a proselytizing one. I specifically requested that. Converting people is fine, but feeding them is better. Once their bodies are fed, then the hunger of the soul can be addressed."

"Sounds like you really helped the kids." Although it wasn't on the scale he'd done, I'd helped some kids when I worked at a YMCA. I even saved a few from drowning. But one boy, a third-grader, stood out. He had recently moved to Seattle from Compton, California. His mother wanted to escape the gang violence and save her son from that life. The boy and I were in a gym one afternoon while all the other kids were on a field trip. He was in a sort of detention for being disruptive earlier in the day and had to stay with me. Not that I was feared, but after a few years of working there, I oversaw other counselors, which meant I didn't have my own group of kids, leaving me at the Y for the afternoon. The boy and I had shot some hoops at a low basket for small kids. I'd hoist him above my head, and he'd do an eight-year-old's version of a slam dunk.

When his mother picked him up that afternoon, he told her he wanted to be like me. Her eyes got watery, and she took me aside to say thank you. She then wanted to explain why he might have behavior problems. She told me, in a halting voice, that just before they left Compton four older boys had beaten up her son on a street corner. She started crying, and I put an arm around her. She then said they circled him tightly so no one could see in.

"Suffer little children, and forbid them not, to come unto me: for such is the kingdom of heaven." Johan's voice cut through my memory. "Jesus said that. It's from Matthew, 19:14. I didn't convert anyone, but I fed thousands of meals to children." He beamed. "Best days of my life."

In time he segued to discussing his life after the mission work. "My wife and I met in college and started courting." He squinted, almost painfully. "So, do you have a girlfriend?"

"Not really, but sort of."

"Well that sounds definitive," he said through a slightly sarcastic smile.

"I don't know what's going on." I gazed out the window, deep into the mountains. "We started dating our junior year in high school. That was three years ago. We haven't been dating the entire time, but that's when it started." Katie and I had spent much of the previous year apart, but when we were both in Seattle, we'd seen each other almost every day. "I really like being with her and want to be with her more, but I don't know how much she wants to be with me."

"I still don't know if you have a girlfriend."

"You and me both." My thoughts started to haze. "But in the next few days, I plan on seeing her at school, at WSU." I'd been thinking about her plenty, but not talking to anyone about her. My mind jumbled, and I could hear her laugh, could picture the cupid's bow of her lips, her long hair.

Johan began tapping his fingers quickly on the steering wheel, pinky first and rolling to his index finger, and then repeating. "That can get frustrating, I know," he said. "I've been in a number of situations where I couldn't love the person I wanted."

That didn't seem quite the same as my situation, but it appeared we shared some frustration and longing. He turned, gazing at me as if watching a sunset. Then, in a hushed tone, he said, "There have been times..." He bit his lip hard. "—I've been attracted to men."

"Oh." Now his gaze made sense. "That's got to be tough. I mean, you know, being Mormon and all." I imagined Johan, like the man I'd met in Mississippi who wanted to "feel of" me, had spent most of his life at war with his feelings, questioning why they'd betrayed him.

Johan waited for me to say more, maybe reciprocate, but when he could tell I wasn't going to he said, "I've just divorced. I lost everything. The church took it." Now he looked at me, without shame. He seemed to indicate that receiving his punishment had freed him.

"What do you mean the church took it?" I thought divorce fell under civil law, not something the church decided. I figured the church couldn't just walk in and take things, let alone everything.

"I stayed married for three years, and then, last month...last month I got caught. By my wife." He looked out his side window, averting my eyes. "Having sex with a man—in my marriage bed."

Once again, I didn't know how to respond. For the

church to take everything from someone in the name of a loving god seemed hypocritical, but I'd heard most religions absolutely, positively, no exceptions, didn't tolerate homosexuality. The man in Mississippi lived in fear that he would be imprisoned. I didn't know much about law, or sex, but I'd decided that what other adults did behind closed doors was none of my business.

"We had a temple marriage and a temple divorce." Johan's words slowed. "The First Presidency got involved." He shook his head and concentrated again on the road. Then, in a whisper, on the edge of sounding grateful, he added, "They let me keep my clothes."

"Are you still a Mormon?"

"It's all I know." His eyes took on a watery glaze. "I still love God, but they say he doesn't love me."

36

Eternally Yours

	MAY					
	1	2	3	4	5	6
7	8	9	10	11	12	13
14	15	16	17	**18**	19	20
21	22	23	24	25	26	27
28	29	30	31			

Throughout the trip I'd considered writing letters to friends and family, but I didn't. Underneath what I thought might be simple laziness swirled my desire to feel that I'd washed myself clean of the self-loathing and resentment that I'd left with. I wanted to make contact only once I'd become new. Now I felt ready.

I'd made my way to Boise, Idaho, and had plans to reach Pullman, Washington. That's where WSU was, and not much else—except Katie.

So far I'd only made two phone calls—a medicinal call to Mark when I experienced my psychotic episode, and one for bail. With my third call, I reached out to Katie. At a phone booth in the corner of a gas station parking lot, I leaned my blue pack against the outside of the booth. It now had a gray nylon cord replacing the shoulder strap that had broken during my shortest-ever wait for a ride. I stepped out of one car, and just after setting down my pack another pulled up, with a married couple in their mid-seventies. I couldn't believe one car had pulled over before the other had even left, and in my haste I jerked up too fast on my pack and tore the strap loose.

As I held the black receiver to my ear, it was silent. Not having the dime needed to get a dial tone, I pressed zero to reach the operator and asked to place a collect call. I caught myself not breathing during the rings, worried that no one would pick up but also because if she did, I wanted to make sure I'd hear her. Throughout the trip I had no baseline to measure how much I'd changed. She'd be my first measuring stick.

"Hello?"

"Will you accept a collect call from Steve Theme?" the operator asked. I wasn't supposed to speak until Katie accepted the charge.

"Yeah!"

Hearing her voice caused a surge of excitement that surprised me—I'd thought my emotions were already on overdrive.

"Hi!" *Now what?* "It's me." *Dumb opening.* The operator had already told her that.

"You're safe! Where are you?"

My chest tingled; she cared. "I'm just outside of Boise." My thoughts crisscrossed, tying up my words. So much had happened. My head began feeling numb. Through a weak exhale, I said, "It's just good to hear you."

"That's great you're near. What are your plans?"

"I'm thinking of stopping by in a day or two. Yeah, in a day or two, that's all, maybe three. I'm not sure, but three at most. I'm pretty positive of that." All I could manage was shallow breathing. I still wasn't sure she'd feel comfortable seeing me. "How's that sound?"

"Sounds great!"

My thoughts spun like helicopter blades rising to the sun.

"Studying for finals hasn't started yet, so this should work out perfect. Really perfect."

"I've got a ton to tell you, but I'll just save it until we're together." *Together* was the only word in the world that mattered to me.

"Wish I could say I've got a ton to tell you," she said. "Things have been pretty boring here."

"I've got enough stories for both of us, unless you've got some really awesome boring stories," I kidded. *She's not laughing. Did I just sound stupid? Am I making any sense?*

"Don't worry. You'll be the only one with stories worth telling." She gave me the name of her dorm, and that was all I needed.

After I hung up, it seemed like feathers were flitting around in my lungs: light, but also itchy and foreign. With a few big exhales, some of the feathers drifted away, enough that I could breathe easily, and I wanted to think about the call.

I walked behind the gas station and sat on a concrete block. Wildflowers and grasses bursting with spring yellows and greens covered a pasture that led to some hills.

In the garage behind me, an air compressor clanked as it ran, and I could hear the mechanic shouting to the pump jockey that it was time to lock up.

Even though I hadn't eaten for three days, except when a guy shared Twinkies with me, the grinding in my stomach subsided. Katie wanted to see me. She sounded excited, and not just polite excited. Understanding that someone wanted to see me gave me substance. I stared at my hands as if they weren't mine and watched them clasp each other. Their firm grip, the solid feel of bones under skin, confirmed I was part of this world. I belonged.

I closed my eyes and thought of nothing, but I wallowed in love, or something like love, and felt its enduring energy. Stories throughout history—troops returning home, teenage couples staying married for life, siblings reconnecting after decades, an old friend traveling thousands of miles to attend a funeral—showed me examples that love commands the power to lay waste the constraints of time.

Eternity reflects no light and tips no scale, but when I sat in silence, I could sense eternity. Not infinite time, like a road that runs forever, but a void of time, an eternal instant. Timelessness made perfect sense, the only sense, and felt like an expansive home. All things became now, but nothing was crowded and there was endless room for more. Our perception of time mutated into a cruel illusion, where days become years and then decades; we age, experience longing, and endure. In that infinite moment, I gained a new compassion for all of us caught in this temporary trap.

My eyes bolted open and I stared straight ahead.

What? Where did that come from? Did that really happen?

I sought my inner scientist and remembered the law of conservation of energy, one of the cornerstones of physics: energy can be neither created nor destroyed but has the ability to change form; energy is eternal. Time is relative—that had been proven through countless experiments. In fact, time stops under the right conditions.

With my mind reeling, but now back in this world, I was feeling time and the energy of love. When I listened to time whisper its secrets, it seemed that love might endure as our only remnant, the indestructible and eternal energy. I've never returned to that timeless place but have thought about it for years.

Eternity showed itself as a state without time. Everything here became backward.

37

Hillbilly Heaven

	MAY					
	1	2	3	4	5	6
7	8	9	10	11	12	13
14	15	16	17	18	19	20
21	22	23	24	25	26	27
28	29	30	31			

I walked through a green valley surrounded by the snowcapped cathedrals of the Rockies north of Boise. Once again, the world became mine as every horizon filled with solitude.

I honked on my harmonica loud enough so that if there was a heaven, it could hear. I played for all those who'd come before me, and I realized I'd never considered that before. I'd only played for myself. Alone in the valley, I unleashed my tune.

I played as a minstrel in a royal court surrounded by the majesty of the peaks. At first I felt small amid this expanse, and then I became vast. Rustling leaves, a brook, birds; any of nature's sounds embellished the tune. Long, wide notes wailed between the chasms. Sharp, pointed notes ricocheted off the hills. Gentle melodies ended the recital, making the world small again.

All that effort of blowing, combined with my hunger, left me lightheaded as I walked back to State Route 55. I surveyed up and down the naked road. Wearing ratty clothes, carrying a backpack that held more ratty clothes but not a crumb of food, it struck that I'd become a roadside beggar. What surprised me was that I didn't mind. I'd grown to have faith that the intrinsic human desire to help others would roll down the road and carry me one step closer to home.

Slow. I wanted to walk slow and absorb the moment. Strolling along the shoulder, I felt as if I were breathing the universe. Space swirled in my lungs. Inhaling, I drew air that had crested the mountain tops; exhaling, I mingled with wind that blew across the valley. Peace filled me once again.

I heard heavy crackling in the brush. Something was running toward the road—fast—from behind me. I turned but couldn't see into the bushes. This wasn't some skunk. Maybe I'd spooked a deer. But a deer would run away.

After deer, I thought bear. This was grizzly country. Grizzlies kill people—not a lot of people—but there was nothing stopping me from becoming one of them.

Branches along the tops of bushes started shaking. I still couldn't see anything.

Thirty yards down the road, a big dog came bolting from the brush, barking like mad and running straight for me.

In an moment he'd cut the distance in half.

I jolted into the ready position. That's what all my coaches had called it: baseball, basketball, football, soccer—it's the same stance in all sports—knees slightly bent, torso leaning forward, feet spread shoulder wide, arms in front. In a second he'd be on me.

I jacked my knife from its sheath, flicking my wrist to open the blade and jumping the handle into my palm. The stainless point aimed up. If he lunged, front legs leaving the ground, I could get a good uppercut—sink into his neck, or better yet his chest, penetrate his heart and lungs.

Barking cracked against my ears.

As I flinched my arm back an inch or two, ready to swing forward and deliver a death blow, he cut to the right, just missing me. I spun to face him. He spun to face me.

His barking became more frantic, canines snapping. He thrust both front paws forward, bringing his chest down. I took my eyes off his lowered chest and noticed his butt up high and his tail—wagging—dog speak for play time.

I let out a long breath but still gripped my knife until he jumped side to side, paws outstretched, which convinced me to put away my weapon. "Boy, you scared the shit out of me!"

He wagged hard enough that his entire body wiggled.

I extended my hand. "Well come here, you doofus." I guessed he was a black Lab and German shepherd mix—two of my favorite breeds. Judging by his behavior, paws, and coat, he was around a year old and every bit of seventy-five pounds.

As he wagged his way to me, he plowed into a leg

and slid along my thigh from his head to his haunches. I gave him a rough pat as he passed by. Whirling, he made another pass, this time rubbing his other side against me and setting me off balance.

"What were you thinkin', huh? Runnin' at me like some whacko." Talking calmed me. "You're just a pup, not a griz. Just a goofy wad of energy." He pushed his head between my knees, and I grabbed it with both hands, giving his squared skull a hearty rub. "So now what?"

He bounded, plowing repeatedly into my legs.

Dog attacks had played through my mind many times during the trip. Plenty of dogs had charged me. When that happened I'd raise my arms, take a few quick steps straight at them and let out a roar. Not some pretend lion roar, but a loud human roar—violent and angry. I envisioned that if I had to defend myself using only my hands, I'd gouge out their eyes. With this dog everything happened so quickly that without my knife I'd have charged him and gone straight for his eyes. With the knife I felt secure standing my ground and waiting until that last moment to see what he'd do. My payoff for all the time I'd practiced drawing my knife had lasted only one second, but it was worth it—he still had his eyes, and I wasn't mauled.

We were the same: young, energetic, throwing ourselves at others without any idea of their intentions, not always that bright, but willing to reach out. He wouldn't stay that way, and I knew I wouldn't either, but we were exactly where we should be. Living our lives at the stages where we were, no airs or posturing, just two boys running at recess.

We kept zigging and zagging and after a half hour he took to the bushes, once again a joyful gust. A couple minutes later, a car pulled up.

Shaggy brown hair escaped from under the driver's yellow CAT cap. With vigor and boom, he blurted "Hey!" As we bolted back onto the road, he said, "I stuck a 350 V-8 in this here puppy." His puppy looked an awful lot like a 1976 Chevy Vega, a car slightly larger than a breadbox. "The increased torque bent the frame some, so it drifts to the right. But other than that," he slapped the dash, "she drives fine."

Thus began my time with Jack.

His forearms bulged from flannel sleeves torn off at the elbows, and his jeans had dark grease stains ringing the pockets. A thick stubble covered his face, and I figured he was a bachelor in his prime. I felt comfortable right off. We were driving toward McCall and passed a sign that read Warm Lake Road.

"So is that real?" I had to ask, since the idea of a warm lake seemed ridiculous in the Northwest. "Like, is the lake actually warm?"

Jack looked at me, eyebrows raised. "Well, duh, Einstein. We've got a ton o' hot springs."

"That's pretty cool," I said. "I don't think I've ever been in a real hot spring."

"You gotta be kidding." His eyebrows were still raised. "There's one near here that most people don't know about." His speech quickened. "It's right up thataway," and he pointed into the hills. "You wanna go?"

By now I'd developed a fine sense for detecting when men wanted to give me more than just a ride, and that sense flipped into high alert when they suggested visiting isolated places. But Jack seemed like a straight-up—and straight—guy: not well groomed, not leering, not tongue flicking, not casually reaching out to stroke my arm, not asking about my favorite position. Besides, basking in a hot spring beat spending the afternoon in a hot car. "Hell yes, let's go!"

Once we left the highway and hit a dirt road, the back end of the car broke loose, causing dust to billow and gravel to shoot like a rooster tail from a speedboat. Over the hysterical engine, Jack shouted, "This is my hillbilly hotrod!" His huge grin showed specks of Copenhagen chew stuck between his lower teeth.

We drifted around rutted corners, careened through dips and hills, rumbled across—and into—potholes. As we sped over washboard roadway, I could feel my eyes rattling in their sockets, and more than once I pushed my foot on the floor attempting to brake. Finally we came skidding to a dusty stop at a wide patch in the road. Jack hopped out and stretched his arms high above his head. I stepped out a little wobbly.

A slight wind passed along the treetops, but other than that, the world now floated in quiet space. The gentle scent of evergreen needles drifted on the warm air, and we were surrounded by tall conifers under a blue sky.

"This way," he said, half jogging to a thin trail, where he disappeared into a maze of undergrowth.

Once I caught up with him and matched his brisk pace, I asked, "How long have you lived around here?"

"My whole life," he said between slightly labored breaths. "It's been a good twenty-six years. No complaints from me."

His pace slowed a bit. "Been doin' some loggin', been a ranch hand, done some mechanic's work. Mostly, though, I love these mountains, the fishin', huntin', the whole shitaree." He held out his hands so his fingers brushed the tops of pine saplings as he passed. "Where you from?"

"Seattle."

"So you're a city boy. You don't know what you're missin'."

"I might."

"City folks have all their hoo-ha, but a lot of 'em don't know shit from apple butter."

"At least not until they take a bite." We laughed at city folks and took an upward spur on the trail.

"So why are you hitchhiking? Why don't you just drive?"

"Money, I guess." Even if I'd had a car, I probably wouldn't have used it. The trip was about gaining exposure to more types of people. But money was the simple answer.

"Well, why don't you get a job?"

"I've had a buttload of jobs." I wanted to get irritated at Jack, but he didn't know anything about why I left. "I spent most of my money on school." I didn't want to sound like a total dork, so I added, "and the rest on pussy," which was a lie.

"Good God, man, quit pissin' it away on school." Even from the back of his head, I could tell he was smiling. The trail stopped at the base of a small granite cliff next to three pristine pools. "You ever have a classroom like this?"

"Not until today."

"The pool nearest the cliff is the hottest, and they cool off from there," he said while taking off his shirt and pants.

Lying in the hottest pool, I let my cooked-noodle legs

drift from under me so that I half floated, allowing me to gaze up the cliff face. Rocks jutted and cragged, while a few gnarled trees latched on with tenacious roots. Lichen grew in shades of yellow, green, and reddish to almost black. We lay surrounded by towering pines, making the Grecian statuary of exclusive spas look puny.

"All your pussy money can't buy this, my friend," Jack said. "This is God's country."

"So you think God made this?"

"Shit-o-dear, I don't know. The only thing I know for certain is that it wasn't me."

We lowered into the second pool, where the heat didn't take itself so seriously. Relaxing there felt like floating in a healing pond that only wizards from a secluded shire could know about. I lay silent, listening to chipmunk banter. The final lukewarm pool eased our transition back into the air, preparing us to walk once again among mortals.

"I don't know how anybody couldn't live here," Jack said as he got dressed. "If I had a choice of anywhere to live, this would be the place."

As I tied my boot laces, I envied Jack, not for where he lived, but for how he felt about it.

"I'm not rich. In fact, if truth be told, I'm kinda poor." His face reflected the calm of the pools. "But I've got to be the luckiest man in the world. I didn't even have to die, and I still get to live in heaven."

38

Death and Porn

	MAY					
	1	2	3	4	5	6
7	8	9	10	11	12	13
14	15	16	17	18	19	**20**
21	22	23	24	25	26	27
28	29	30	31			

Death Alley—that's what people called the ten-mile stretch of Highway 8 separating the University of Idaho and Washington State University. The road was the same on both sides of the state line, but not the drinking age. Until 1987 the drinking age in Idaho stayed steady at nineteen, but in Washington it was twenty-one. That difference created a vacuum, pulling students across the border each night to the town of Moscow. Getting to Idaho was no problem; the road earned its nickname for what happened when they tried to return.

At the midpoint of that blurry road, the low rolling hills of an expanse known as the Palouse surrounded me. This land is covered by endless fields of wheat, most of which is exported to Japan and made into noodles. If the Midwest is the breadbasket of the United States, the Palouse is the ramen bowl of Japan.

By now I hadn't eaten in four days. My last real meal had been the lamb shank with Jonathan and Liz at their home/hotel in Indiana. Since then I'd passed plenty of grocery stores but wasn't too keen on shoplifting, not even a pack of gum—I could still remember the reek of the Monroe County jail.

During these days I determined there are two types of people in the world: those who get grumpy when they're hungry, and those who get grumpy when they're tired. Luckily, hunger—at least when it lasts only a few days—doesn't bother me much. But at this point, I wouldn't turn down a quick odd job to earn a meal, unless it was too odd.

I walked off the gravel shoulder and waded into a hip-high field of wheat. Each spike-topped stalk held plump grains, each of which was covered with a fibrous sheath. Chances were, they'd been sprayed with pesticides, but I figured the seeds were protected, and if not, how much damage could one handful do? I peeled back sheaths until I had enough of the greenish seeds to cover my palm. While chewing the grain and wondering how the tiny seeds surrounding me could feed a nation on the other side of the world, I heard an engine in the distance and trotted back to the road.

A long black car pulled over. As I walked up from behind, I passed a long chrome feather on the side of the sedan. Forward of the chrome, a window was covered with pleated curtains. Then I passed an unusually long door with a large chrome handle. Finally, I reached the passenger door.

"How ya doing?" the driver asked.

"Is this a hearse?" The interior was as black as the exterior, with plush leather seats and a leather dash.

"It's a Caddy," he said proudly. "Bought it from a funeral home about a year ago." He seemed in his mid-thirties, and his slicked black hair made his head look like a greasy bowling ball. His belly bulged out, and black jeans covered the speed bumps of his thighs.

"I don't suppose you're a mortician?"

"Nope. I just liked the ride." A grin crossed his pudgy lips. "Bought it on a lark." He wore gold-framed sunglasses, and gold necklaces hung over his hairy chest in the unbuttoned gap of his polyester shirt. A gold Rolex constricted his wrist. If he so desperately wanted people to know he had money, maybe he should've just worn a hat made of hundred-dollar bills.

As we pulled onto the highway, the only noise that came from the car was the air-conditioner.

"I grew up around here, but I hate farming." He sounded both apologetic and defiant. "Instead, I sell planes to those hayseeds. Mostly Cessnas and Beechcrafts, and once for a company in Pullman, a used Lear. That turned a nice buck." He licked his lips. "A lot of these farmers are richer than God. And cheap!"

"I hear Abe Lincoln howls each time a farmer pinches a penny." I had nothing against farmers, but I again became a chameleon to make the driver reveal more of himself.

He explained how many of the large farms have their

own airstrips and hangars. "I was a natural to sell planes to these guys. Always been a promoter and always liked flying." We passed a small airstrip next to the road. He pointed to a Cessna with a For Sale sign. "That's one of mine."

"I probably won't be buying today." We laughed. I tried to imagine ever having enough money to buy a plane, not that I'd want one.

He turned and took a longer look at me. Now that I could see him square on, his lips shimmered as if he were wearing lipstick or had just sucked on a cherry lollipop. "I also make movies. That's mostly a hobby though." He seemed to be waiting for my response.

"What type of movies?" They probably had something to do with flying.

"Mostly hot ones. You know…" His grin thickened. "Porn."

"That's a unique hobby." My less-than-enthusiastic response deflated him some.

"I've been doing it for a few years now. Luckily, there's a lot of college girls,"—he cackled—"who want to be in movies." He kept laughing as he ran his tongue around his lips again. Once he'd finished cracking himself up, he said, "You're a good-looking guy."

I should've seen this coming.

"Think you'd like to star in one?"

The car hummed with a deathly silence. He followed quickly with "I'll pay you a hundred bucks, and we can do it this afternoon."

This wasn't adding up. "Seems like it'd be pretty easy to find guys around here that would want to do that."

"No, finding the girls is easy," he said. "Getting guys is tough. At least the ones I want in *my* films."

Before I set out on this trip, had a friend presented me with this type of fantasy scenario, I probably would've said that my answer would be "Yes indeed, sir, I'll help you. It's the least I can do." Presented with the reality, though, I remembered reading a story in the *Seattle Post-Intelligencer* about a hitchhiker in Texas picked up by a couple. They told him they were going to an orgy and invited the hitchhiker. Once they were at the house, the three had a drink; the hitchhiker's was spiked. After he passed out, the couple left and the owner came home. In the basement, he had installed an autopsy table with restraints.

Eventually police found bones of three victims buried in the backyard. They had been dissected and were never identified. I didn't want to play those odds.

But the money pulled. With an empty knot in my stomach, I fantasized about sitting in a restaurant buying a steak—cross-hatched grill marks charring the surface, its red meat full of juices—caramelized onions, hot mashed potatoes draped in gravy, and Black Forest cake for dessert.

Then I had a vision of dirty bones. "No, I've got to get to WSU today to see a friend."

"I can get two girls, no problem." Pleading tinged his salesman's voice. "And I've got some pot. Have a few drinks."

"Definitely no."

Maybe he had no intention to harm me; maybe the whole thing would've been getting high, sex with two girls, good money, and a big meal. As I watched the stranger's hearse drive away, some fantasies lingered, and my stomach hurt, proving I was still alive.

39

Yes

	MAY					
	1	2	3	4	5	6
7	8	9	10	11	12	13
14	15	16	17	18	19	20
21	22	23	24	25	26	27
28	29	30	31			

Waiting slows time. When I reached the WSU campus, I called Katie again, but there was no answer. So I walked to her dorm, entered the lobby, sat in a yellow plastic chair and wait...ed...not...know...ing when she'd show up.

Eventually I heard her voice and she appeared across the foyer. With one exhale my nervous energy drained. Her warm brunette hair softened my field of vision. We were half running by the time we wrapped around each other. I buried my face in that thick hair, and her smell triggered a rich, permeating peace. She nuzzled into my chest, the side of her face rocking in the curve of my embrace.

She moved her head up. "I missed you," she whispered, her breath caressing my ear.

Almost inaudibly, I answered, "You can say that again."

We loosened to see each other's faces. Ten thousand times, I'd seen drivers intentionally look away as they drove past. Katie poured her gaze into me.

"You made it," she said.

"I made it." The realization startled me.

Our embrace loosened and we parted—without a kiss. No matter. I didn't need to think about anything; the universe was perfect.

She glanced at her watch and grasped my shoulders, holding me at arm's length. "I'm late for a study group. You probably shouldn't come. It's just going to be boring."

"O-okay," stammered out. I wanted to give her some hint of what I'd been through, maybe get her to blow off the study group, but there'd be time. As she walked away, I watched her sway, mostly with grateful affection, but also more. We'd made out when first dating a year and a half earlier, but that ended with the clown. Still, that sway.

I spent the afternoon walking.

The campus floated under the sun like a raft on the gentle swells of the Palouse. Students were everywhere; most were wearing clean clothes, many of them fashionable. These were like the classmates I'd disdained as pampered pets before I'd left. *Am I going to feel even more out of place around my peers now? Did this trip do the exact opposite of what I was hoping for? Was this whole thing a huge mistake?*

I needed to quiet the monkeys in my mind or I was

about to slide into hopelessness, so I sat on a bench and closed my eyes. I felt my feet touching the ground, the bench pressing against my butt, and all I could hear were some birds. *Settle down. Things are okay. I don't need to focus on myself; maybe answering all these questions right now doesn't matter.* As my jabber quieted, I felt fine. My intellectualizing had blinded me to my feelings. There was no disdain; I wasn't feeling superior or resentful. I was just sitting on a bench, and people were just walking around.

Like the many people I'd come across, every one of these students had valid stories. I didn't need to inventory differences to justify distancing myself from them. Their fashionable clothes didn't strike me as reflecting snobbish entitlement. They'd just received some help. For the past two months, I'd been receiving help every day with every ride.

When Katie and I met again, she said with a glint, "I've got a plan."

"Lay it on me."

"My roommate is gone tonight, so you can sleep in my room with me."

Good plan.

"I thought guys aren't allowed in the women's dorms."

"Oh, so you want to bother me with details?" She brushed the hair from her face. "A couple friends'll distract the RA while you walk by her room." The RA was a senior assigned to keep an eye on the underclass residents so that they wouldn't sneak in men or commit other heinous crimes.

Up to this point, Katie and I had spent only a couple

of minutes together. "Hey, Katie?" I glanced away and then looked directly at her. "I'm pretty hungry. Think we can get some dinner? On you?"

"No problem." She seemed relieved that I'd brought up the subject rather than leaving her the task of asking if I had any money. "How hungry?"

"Screamin' hungry. I could eat a horse and its barn."

"Thought so. How long's it been since you ate something?"

"Little over a day." I didn't want to tell her the truth.

She took my hand. "Let's walk to some pizza."

Once our hands met, I felt more like talking than eating. I have no memory of what we talked about during dinner or where we ate. The connection is all I recall, feeling extended beyond myself and enveloped. Our energies swirled.

I could feel my full substance returning as we walked back to her dorm. With some food in me, my mental acuity and balance improved. She brought up things we'd done in the past; I had a past someone knew about. We talked of mutual friends; I had friends. Every sentence placed another dollop of affirming clay on the sculpture that was me.

As we stood in the dormitory lobby waiting for the elevator that would take us to her third-floor room I asked, "Now what happens?"

The red light above the door flicked on as a bell dinged. She stepped in and turned to me. "Now it's time for you wait here."

As the doors slid together, I blurted, "So your plan is to leave me standing in the lobby?" The last thing I saw was the middle of her smile.

STEVE THEME

As a young man in a university building for women only, looking inconspicuous is a challenge, especially while wearing dirty clothes and a worn backpack with a dusty red sleeping bag. I strategically placed the backpack next to a large potted plant and stepped away. Co-eds walked by with scrubbed faces and shining smiles. I smiled back, but I felt like a cow on ice skates. *How long is she going to be gone? What if I'm caught? What if the RA calls the campus police? Maybe this isn't such a good plan. What plan?*

Ding!

"So here's what's going to happen," Katie said as we rose on the elevator. "When the door opens you take just one step out."

"Why?"

"Because the RA's door is only a few feet from the elevator."

"Perfect." I wondered if my blue backpack would match the campus police uniforms. "Then what?"

"Wait for the signal, and when I wave you in, don't waste any time. Just walk by her door and keep going."

"What if she...?"

Ding!

The door opened, and two girls stood waiting. They were giggling, like—well, like giggling girls. This wasn't the polished CIA operation I had envisioned. I gave them my best cow-on-ice-skates smile, and they sprang into action, disappearing into the RA's room. Katie took her position standing in the RA's doorway.

Oh, the drama! The screeching voice of a grief-stricken woman helplessly wailing that her favorite pillow was gone; maybe it was even stolen. She'd slept on that since childhood. Katie rolled her eyes at the girl's frantic overacting. With hummingbird speed Katie's hand started flapping. My signal, I assumed, triggering me to stride down the hallway.

The hall stretched on forever, and I just kept going, breaking into a trot. From behind I heard footsteps running toward me. Here it comes, oh crap. I'm busted; another bony grip on my elbow, this time a mad RA.

"Slow down, will ya?" The voice was Katie's. "My room's back here."

I turned and trotted in the other direction. She opened her door and I slinked in. Katie fell onto her bed laughing. I dropped my pack, sat on the other bed, and let out a sigh.

She composed herself. "It worked!"

"So far." I glanced around her dorm room, which was little more than a glorified closet. "So this is your room?"

"My palace, you mean."

"Yes, m'lady. Your palace."

Rising from her bed, she came to me. "Buddy." She placed a hand on my shoulder. "You need a shower."

"You noticed?"

She left the room for a while and when she returned, said, "I've got you covered."

"For what?"

"A shower." She marched me to the one bathroom on the floor with showers. As I walked into the bathroom, she said, "I'll keep watch out here while you shower."

I leaned in close. "Feel free to sell tickets."

"Hurry up!"

I wanted to linger under the shower's amazing warm flow but had to save that for another day. Soap is good.

That night a dozen or so girls came by the dorm room to look at me. I became the evening's oddity and achieved some level of celebrity. It appeared everyone except the RA knew I was there. Late that night, after the girls left, we closed the door.

I slipped off my overalls, leaving me wearing boxers and a T-shirt. Katie walked to the restroom to change into a nightgown. When she came back, I couldn't help but notice her nipples pushing against the thin pink fabric, her smooth calves extending from the gown. We hugged again, but she'd made it clear we wouldn't be sleeping together, so I spread my bag on her roommate's bed. We both lay in the dark.

"Why'd you take this trip? And don't tell me it was just for adventure."

"Just for adventure."

She was silent.

"Not funny, huh?" I paused, deciding whether to tell her the truth. "Basically, I couldn't stand what I was becoming. I pretty much hated everything and everyone, especially myself. I felt like some bitter old man and never talked to anyone. I was stealing malt liquor and smoking pot all the time. Just trying to escape, and I knew exactly what I was doing, knew it was unhealthy in every way." I raised myself onto an elbow to face her side of the room and ran a hand through my hair. "The shame and guilt were killing me. I didn't know what else to do."

"For not knowing what to do, you sure did something.

You should've called me and maybe I could have helped you deal with that stuff."

"No, I was way beyond asking for help. I could barely talk to myself."

"How do you feel now?"

"Better than I thought I would. Today on campus I was just hanging out and everything felt fine. I was kind of surprised." I rolled onto my back, smelling the familiar must of my sleeping bag. "People are just trying to get by. Seems a lot of them don't know what to do. They might look like they've got it together, but they're just hoping not to fall off this wagon ride." I felt less out of place than I had for a long time. "I've even been thinking about the whole God thing."

"What God thing?"

"You know, like the big God thing."

"Oh, right. You're the last person I thought I'd hear say that." Katie had always shared my view of organized religion and the folly of a magical man in the sky. "So you've given up on evolution?"

"Hardly. Adam and Eve are still a fairy tale, but that might not matter."

She lay on her back staring at the ceiling, leaving me to look at her silhouette. "Are you still Mr. Concrete? Scientific proof mandatory to believe anything?"

"Yeah." My experiences hit like concrete; the proof lived in me. "There's still got to be solid evidence, but my definition of evidence has changed. I guess it's gotten bigger."

"Did you have some spiritual experience?"

"Maybe. Maybe more than one." I wanted to give her

an example. Cil came to mind—when I'd walked for days and we sat on her church's steps and I told her about Pell Grants as the choir sang "Guide My Feet"; or when I'd felt a calm presence even with a gun to my head; or when I'd been poisoned and knew some force kept me straining toward life; or when I'd said my half-hearted prayer outside of Denver that seemed to have removed my anxiety about being a coward or brave; or that energy is love and they are both eternal—but I was tired. "Maybe some God has been with me longer than I think. Maybe with you too. But it's damn hazy."

She rolled her head to face me. "I suppose you might as well thank something for surviving this whole thing."

"This place is weird."

"My room?"

"The world."

"We're on the same page there, buddy," Katie said. "So, are you ready to go back to Seattle?"

"Yeah, mostly. It'll be good to see people." Light filtered through the thin drapes, painting the walls in a hushed blue. "I've decided to go to Seattle Central Community College and get into a program for marine engineering. It's about hydraulic systems, working in engine rooms, stuff like that. I was looking at it before I left." I hadn't told anyone this, but the plan had solidified over the past several weeks. "With any luck, that degree'll help me work on king crab boats in Alaska so I can make enough money to pay for the UW." *Can I really do this? Why do I always take the long way to get somewhere?*

"Way better fit. And you know some of it already."

The wall heater clicked on and rustled the curtains.

"Do you believe in love?"

"Steve…I don't know what to say…I—"

"No. Not about us, but for anyone? There are all those people out there spinning around, and every single one of them is impacted by love, especially if they have none. I've been thinking maybe love is the concrete part of God." This was foreign ground. "Maybe it's so much a part of us, we can't even separate far enough to notice it."

Katie extended her hand so it crossed half the chasm between our beds. She let it hang there, waiting for mine. "I think we'll be together someday," she said, as if talking in her sleep.

"I thought you didn't want to talk about us." I held out my hand so our fingertips touched.

"Yes."

"Yes what?"

"Yes, I believe in love."

40

From Ashes

	MAY					
	1	2	3	4	5	6
7	8	9	10	11	12	13
14	15	16	17	18	19	20
21	22	23	24	25	26	27
28	29	30	31			

The car looked like fire.

"My dad gave it to me for my birthday," a friend of Katie's said, standing in front of the inferno red 1973 Pontiac Trans Am. A black phoenix spreading its wings in tall, flaming arcs was painted on the red hood. Each black feather was outlined with yellow pin stripes, each flicker giving off heat.

Word had spread to one of the men's dorms that I was going to Seattle, and the owner of the birthday present was driving there with a friend, leaving room for me in the back seat. The back seat was perfect for a person without legs, but by facing sideways I could unfold and get somewhat comfortable. After I squeezed into the car, it struck me—this was my last ride.

They were decent guys, and I appreciated that the driver had offered to help me home. His path was as far from mine as I could imagine: sports car, pressed clothes, hard-sided Samsonite luggage in the trunk, living in a college dorm with all his needs taken care of. But he didn't obsess on his trappings; different from me, but not indifferent to me.

As we accelerated down the on-ramp to I-90, he asked, "So what was it like? I bet the water in Key West felt like a bathtub."

"Yeah, and it was super clear. But there were jellyfish."

The driver glanced at me in the rearview mirror. "Meet many chicks?"

"Oh, you know." My tone inferred that gentlemen don't kiss and tell. But I didn't want to tell him that for much of the trip I'd been near broke and covered in road grime, not a real chick magnet.

We talked more about hitchhiking. Then, he said, "Man, I'd love to do that! Just get out and be free. No bullshit. No classes. No problems."

"Yeah."

When the driver turned up the stereo, we couldn't talk easily, so I stared out the window. Seattle was just four hours away.

The guys in the car were going to Seattle for some purpose; they were going to school, getting degrees. Maybe my trip hadn't amounted to a tinker's damn. I couldn't produce a certificate of achievement, couldn't point to anything I'd built. I hadn't established any lasting relationships. At most I was a brief memory among hundreds of people, none of them connected. I had left no wake.

A familiar whisper told me my journey had been nothing more than a sham, that life is a lonely series of meaningless events. That voice brought a diseased comfort, a familiarity: it was the old me. I told it to go fuck itself. I didn't need it anymore.

While the stereo blared, I thought about the cost of lost opportunity, an amount that I'd never be able to measure. What else could I have done with the two months? I could've been in school, could've been making money, could've been increasing my stature in society, could've been hanging out with friends: coulda, coulda, coulda. In each scenario I looked better, but only on the outside. I'd done an inside job, so I focused instead on what did take place.

That disgust for those people who looked like they'd had easy lives, mostly other college students, was gone. Spending time on the WSU campus felt fine. I didn't need to judge them or assume I knew where they'd come from—there were too many places to come from. Even if they had a lot of help and came from nurturing backgrounds, so what? Isn't that what I wanted? Isn't that the right and good environment? How could I look down on that? I could even aspire to help cultivate that type of family setting in the future—something to look forward to, assuming anyone would ever want to start a family with me.

Having gained some perspective on how I was raised, especially while in Gulf Shores with Bud, who was looking forward to whooping his yet-unborn son, I consciously wanted to separate from that sickness. I didn't need to look down on others who never experienced that, that somehow they weren't as tough as me. It wasn't even looking down on them. It was envy in disguise.

I'd grown to accept that science no longer could explain everything, but more importantly, it didn't need to. I'd experienced events I couldn't believe but couldn't deny: that man who said a prayer of protection for me on the first day that seemed to work, especially during the tropical storm when the only light on the horizon was shelter; feeling connected while surrounded by the desert's empty expanse; Andrew crediting a God of his understanding that helped him to recover from his alcoholism; Stud's gentle direction; voodoo and the floating man, even though I wasn't a witness to that; understanding that the little voice in my head was always right, and Bill the mortician calling that voice God's; love.

Science wasn't love. Maybe eternal love was for everyone; maybe there was no escaping it. Maybe there was even more. I didn't know, but I was willing to search.

I didn't hate myself anymore. Yes, mistakes were made—I sounded like a politician campaigning to myself—but that core malice was gone. Maybe just taking the journey, proving that I'd hold myself responsible when I needed to change, earned back my self-respect. Maybe it wouldn't last, but I wanted it to, and knew it was within my power to sustain that self-esteem. A glimmer of confidence lit what was once dark.

I had trekked seven thousand miles but couldn't have gone one inch without the charity of strangers, and that cemented a new fact for me: the vast majority of people are kind and generous. We are hardwired to help each other. We must be connected beyond simply occupying the same geography. How could so many people, such different people, share that universal core?

Thousands of people had driven past me. I may not have encountered them, but I saw the results of their efforts gracing their communities and the entire country.

In that Firebird as we crossed Washington's golden wheat fields, barren scablands, and wet-green mountains, I was stirred to picture an endless tapestry. I yearned to become a strand in that fabric, and I knew that any underlying scorn or resentment that lived in me would limit my ability to be woven. As the miles rolled by, I came to understand that I'd need to forgive, for my own sake. Waves of emotion engulfed me as I searched through myself and found new ground.

Knowing the trip would be over soon felt like losing an old friend, or maybe not a friend, but an era. I was watching a mini-history in my life come to a close. It was a good thing the music in the car was loud. I didn't feel like talking.

I wanted to take a mental break and just sit, but my thoughts wouldn't stop. Now some sort of God didn't seem absurd and I was willing to explore the existence of that possibility, but I wasn't basking in any divine light. Instead, I saw a distant sun that shines on everyone, but only if we inch out of the shadow of contempt.

For years I'd seen fear, superstition, and hypocrisy as the foundation of organized religions, along with heavy doses of intolerance. I'd closed myself to any traditional view of God because of what other people proclaimed. I'd been confusing God with religion.

....

As we approached North Seattle I piped up, "You can just drop me at the Lake City Way off-ramp." That felt safe. "I'll walk from there." Walking would force me outside of my head. After hours of thinking, I needed a walk to ready myself for home.

"Oh, that's okay," the driver said. "I'll give you a ride to your house."

"Um...all right. Thanks." The kindness I'd experienced on the road continued to the last possible moment, to the point where I'd be dropped at my doorstep.

In minutes, we'd reach my parents' driveway. A quick panic shook me. *How'll I be received? What'll I say? Was all this worth it? I'm not ready.*

Everything looked familiar: the sage-green split-level house, the orange cat figurine in the garden, the twisted pine we'd transplanted from a mountainside, even the cracks in the walkway.

As I approached the front door, the sun burned with an intensity that washed away colors. I looked at my denim overalls, and they appeared as hazy as white smoke. So did the house, the yard, the plants. I felt weightless, reduced to fragile ashes. Is this how I'd return? Weakened to the point that a breath could scatter me? Everything was without substance. But in the shimmering haze, I didn't need to squint. *Am I about to black out?*

No. With a few more steps, I stood solid on my center. I watched the Firebird drive away up the hill.

Colors returned, the bleached lawn going back to its

mottled green. I took a full breath with flared nostrils and felt the muscles across my chest expand. Clenching my fists brought a quiet strength. As I twisted the door handle, I whispered, "Please be with me."

"I'm home!" I sounded like a man returning from a day's work.

"Oh God!" Corrine screamed. "Steve's back!"

"What! Where?" My mother startled from her game of solitaire at the kitchen table. Looking bewildered, my brother, Chris, clomped down the stairs, followed by Janelle.

I dropped my backpack as they rushed toward me. Their arms wrapped around me and as each new member entered the embrace my arms spread wider to try to hold them all. Mom started tearing up.

My father came in from his workshop and stared at me, shirtless, worn overalls and boots with split seams. "Oh look," he said, "it's Little Jesus."

A burst of anger filled me. But that passed as quickly as it surfaced. When I didn't respond, he looked to the floor.

I told them I'd be heading back to school. They weren't interested in that—they wanted to know what had happened. "Too much to say."

"Well, then maybe you should write a book about it," my mother said.

I reached out and held my mother's hand, letting her know her boy was safe.

My sister Corrine and I, minutes after I'd arrived home.

The Route

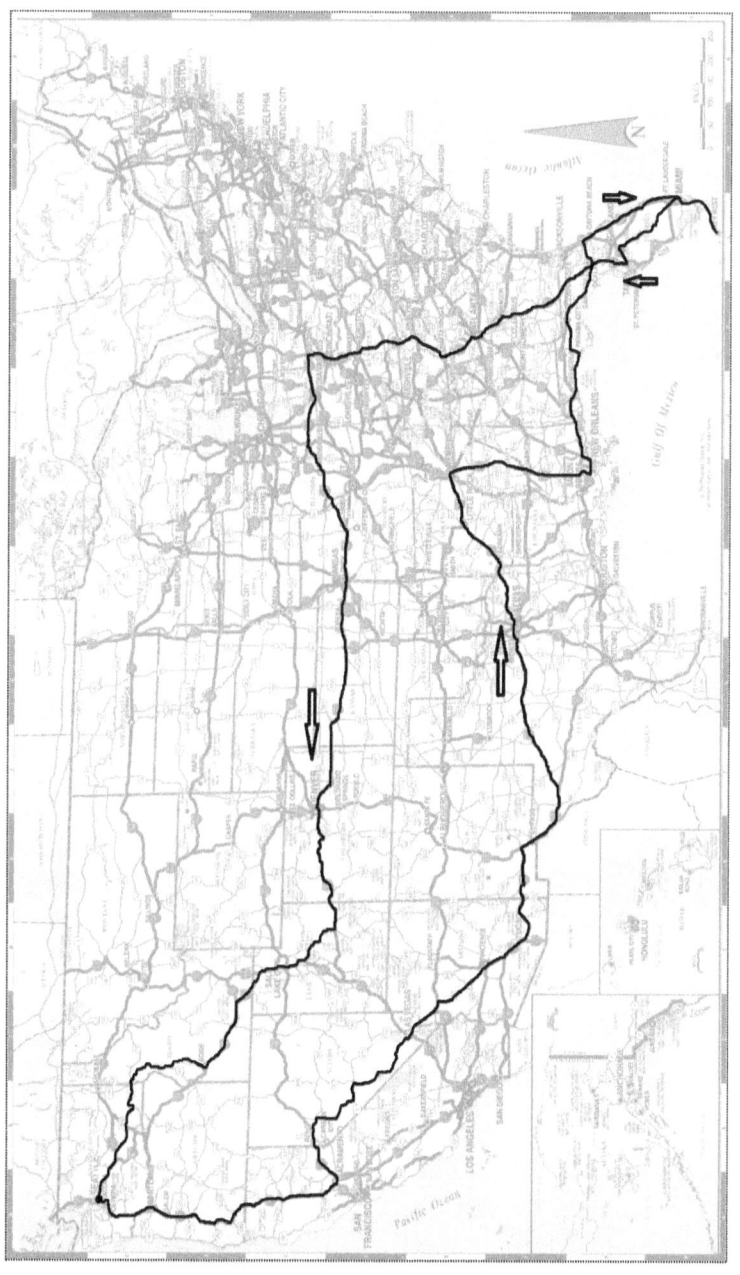

Epilogue

We understand ourselves flowing,
to surge, crest and wane
on the torrents
that carry us.
　　　　—Journal entry, Saturday evening, February 21, 2015

Acknowledgments

Grateful thanks for those who reviewed, critiqued, and cajoled. Without these people, and many others, this book would still be stuck in my head: Rosemary Lombard, Karen Greco, Sharon Appleman, Dora Raymaker, Margaret Donsbach, Cheryl Adamscheck (wherever you are), Seshadri Balaji, Lori Cronwell, Paul Navarro, Amber Cook, Anna Young, and my editor at Indigo Editing, Ali McCart, as well as the good folks at Inkwater Press.

About the Author

A ward-winning author and journalist Steve Theme has made a living by writing a bit of everything. His work has appeared in *Alaska* magazine, *WORK Literary Magazine, The Timberline Review,* various trade publications, and metro daily newspapers. He's been a speech writer, ad copywriter, ghost writer, and started his career by writing software manuals. Theme won the Oregon Writers Colony Short Story Award and has worked with countless authors to help promote their books.

Steve is a native of the Pacific Northwest and currently lives with his wife and three children in Portland, Oregon, where you can't swing a dead dog without hitting a writer.

stevetheme.com
facebook.com/pages/Steve-Theme-Author

If you enjoyed this story you may want to consider writing a review on Amazon or on other sites.

www.ingramcontent.com/pod-product-compliance
Lightning Source LLC
Chambersburg PA
CBHW030431300426
44112CB00009B/955